Ohio Volunteer

John Calvin Hartzell

OHIO VOLUNTEER

The Childhood &

Civil War Memoirs of

Captain John Calvin Hartzell, OVI

EDITED BY
CHARLES I. SWITZER

Ohio University Press • Athens

Ohio University Press, Athens, Ohio 45701
www.ohio.edu/oupress
© 2005 by Ohio University Press

12 11 10 09 08 07 06 05   5 4 3 2 1

Frontispiece: John Calvin Hartzell (date unknown). From Albion W.
Tourgée, *The Story of a Thousand* (Buffalo, NY: S. McGerald, 1896), p.
236.

Library of Congress Cataloging-in-Publication Data

Hartzell, John Calvin, 1837–1918.
  Ohio volunteer : the childhood and Civil War memoirs of captain John
Calvin Hartzell, OVI / edited by Charles I. Switzer.
    p. cm.
  Includes bibliographical references and index.
  ISBN 0-8214-1606-5 (cloth : alk. paper)
  1. Hartzell, John Calvin, 1837–1918. 2. United States. Army. Ohio Infantry Regiment, 105th (1862–1865) 3. Ohio—History—Civil War,
1861–1865—Personal narratives. 4. Ohio—History—Civil War,
1861–1865—Regimental histories. 5. United States—History—Civil War,
1861–1865—Personal narratives. 6. United States—History—Civil War,
1861–1865—Regimental histories. 7. Soldiers—Ohio—Biography. 8.
Portage County (Ohio)—Biography. I. Switzer, Charles I. II. Title.
  E525.5105th .H37 2005
  973.7'471'092—dc22

                                                        2005001381

To my wife,
Marilyn Bennett Switzer

Acknowledgments

I wish to thank Dr. C. B. Johnson for his help in reproducing pictures and typing the manuscript, my granddaughter Karen Yarcho for her assistance in word processing, Susan McMahan for providing copies of chapter 1 and maps, Loren W. Collins for providing a copy of the typescript of John Calvin Hartzell's memoirs and for contacting Hartzell descendants, and Fred Walz for valuable help in making the final mailing.

Contents

Illustrations

Introduction

John Calvin Hartzell, the third son of Frederick and Mary Ickes Hartzell (fig. 1), was born in Deerfield Township, Portage County, Ohio, on November 27, 1837, "the year in which Queen Victoria began her reign," as he points out at the opening of his memoirs. He spent his boyhood years on a farm in a colony of Hartzells and McGowans (the family name is spelled both McGowan and MacGowan). Hartzell's Civil War military service in the Union army is recorded by Judge Albion W. Tourgée in *The Story of a Thousand: Being a History of the Service of the 105th Ohio Volunteer Infantry*[1] and in Hartzell's own memoirs, preserved as "Some Autobiographical Writing by John Calvin Hartzell, Captain of Company H., One Hundred and Fifth O.V.I.," which he wrote between 1896 and 1898 at the request of his extended family.[2]

Hartzell enlisted in Company H of the 105th Ohio Volunteer Infantry (OVI) on August 5, 1862, mustered in August 21 at Camp Taylor near Cleveland, and was elected second lieutenant by soldiers in the unit. As he observes in his memoirs, "A Second Lieutenant with the other company officers present . . . is a sort of useless appendage" (chap. 9). Hartzell went into battle with Company H at Perryville in October and became company commander on the death of Captain Robert Wilson.

In his own estimation, Hartzell was totally unprepared for assuming command of Company H, 105th OVI: "So here I was less than sixty days from the plow tail, destitute of any kind of a proper education or fitness, chucked, as it were, a square peg into a round hole" (chap. 9). After the Battle of Perryville (October 8, 1862), Company H was engaged in the Battle of Chickamauga, the siege of Chattanooga, and the Battle of Missionary Ridge (which Hartzell calls Mission Ridge), plus several smaller skirmishes. (For maps of Civil War sites significant in Hartzell's memoirs, see figs. 2 and 3.) At Chickamauga, where he was in charge of the division wagon train of supplies, he disobeyed Major General Jeff C. Davis's

Figure 1. Frederick and Mary Hartzell, the author's parents. This photograph accompanied the typescript copy of John Calvin Hartzell's memoirs.

orders by securing the train before deploying his men to attempt to stop a rout. Hartzell participated in the famous charge up Missionary Ridge that took place without orders from either General Thomas or General Grant. "We were never expected to take the hill," Hartzell recalls, "and they never expected us to make the attempt, but here we were." He remarks laconically, "There were two of the greatest surprises ever known, one for us and one for our enemy." Apparently the advance was ordered only to the foot of the ridge. When Grant saw the men continue up the ridge, he sternly asked who gave the order for the advance; since the success of the event seemed in grave doubt, no one claimed the honor. Characteristically, Hartzell accounts for the charge with an ironic understatement: "The best explanation . . . is that the men were working for Thirteen Dollars ($13.00) a month and wanted to get in a full day on this occasion."

Hartzell was eventually promoted to first lieutenant and, on September 8, 1864, received his captain's commission. In the spring of 1864, Hartzell was assigned by special order of Secretary of War Edwin Stanton to forward recruits to the various theaters of the war, carrying with him large sums of money, from $10,000 to $65,000 a trip—bounties to be paid recruits upon delivery. He continued this special assignment until the close of the war and was able to boast that he lost none of the money—and very few of the recruits—entrusted to his care. Captain Hartzell traveled more than forty thousand miles by rail and made numerous trips down the Atlantic coast and the Mississippi River, surviving a number of life-threatening experiences along the way. This assignment allowed Hartzell opportunities to view the war from a longer, philosophical perspective, tempered as always by humor. "Among the curious incidents he mentions," reports Albion Tourgée, is Hartzell's discovery of "one of the Captains of the Thousand . . . among a company of recruits, who having resigned because of ill-health had re-enlisted as a private soldier for a handsome bounty."[3]

One of the more harrowing experiences Hartzell describes in the autobiography was a train wreck caused by Confederate bushwhackers (chap. 14). Initially Hartzell thought he was mortally wounded—"entirely killed"—by a head injury. It turned out that the source of the blood dripping in his face was the soldier above him in the pileup. They were subsequently rescued by Northern troops. In John Calvin's evaluation, although it was of course "unpleasant to be cheated out of a good smoke and the stub of a ten cent cigar," the incident was nevertheless "only one of the little jokes of war, and something similar was happening every day of every year, but they counted for next to nothing in the great result [victory for the North], except to the victims." To die in "some notable battle, of which history should make some record" would be much more desirable, in his estimation, than "to be snuffed out in some . . . trifling byplay." After the train wreck, Hartzell divided up his own money among his men so they could buy supplies along the way, giving his name and home address to each soldier. "All seemed full of gratitude," he recounts, "and would certainly pay me back the first payday." With supreme irony, the author notes: "I kept no record of their names and never heard [from any] of them again, so I think they all must be dead."

Figure 2. Map of the western theater, showing sites significant in John Calvin Hartzell's Civil War memoirs. With Company H, 105th OVI, Hartzell was engaged at Perryville, Kentucky (October 8, 1862), Milton, Tennessee (March 20, 1863), Chickamauga (September 19–20, 1863), the siege of Chattanooga (September 23–November 25, 1863), and Missionary Ridge (November 25, 1863), as well as in several smaller skirmishes. In the spring of 1864 he was detailed to the duty of forwarding recruits from Columbus, Ohio, to the armies of the west. He remained in this special service until the end of the war, surviving a train wreck and Confederate ambush near Cave City, Kentucky, and making several trips down the Mississippi, with stops in Cairo, Memphis, Vicksburg, Natchez, and New Orleans. He delivered troops to Savannah, Georgia, and was with Sherman's forces at Atlanta.

Figure 3. Map of the eastern theater, showing sites significant in John Calvin Hartzell's Civil War memoirs. From spring 1864 until the end of the war, he was assigned to troop delivery and made numerous trips along the Atlantic coast, "always going by way of New York," delivering troops to camps and battlefields including Richmond, Petersburg, Fredericksburg, and Alexandria, Virginia, as well as Savannah, Georgia, and other points south.

John Calvin Hartzell's entire period of service from the date of muster on August 21, 1862, to discharge at Cleveland on June 8, 1865, was two years, nine months, and eighteen days. He was able to join his regiment for the Grand Review in Washington on May 24, 1865.

JOHN CALVIN HARTZELL's memoirs came to my attention through my longstanding research interest in the writing of the MacGowan sisters—Grace MacGowan Cooke and Alice MacGowan—who enjoyed popular success in the early twentieth century, publishing more than thirty novels, a hundred short stories, and poetry.[4] Alice MacGowan dedicated her Civil War novel, *The Sword in the Mountains* (published in 1910), with this inscription:

TO

CAPTAIN JOHN CALVIN HARTZELL

(LATE OF THE ARMY OF THE CUMBERLAND)

UPON WHOSE WRITTEN PAGES THESE PRINTED ONES OF MINE DREW

SO HEAVILY FOR BOTH VERITY AND GRACE[5]

Alice MacGowan's father, John Calvin Hartzell's first cousin John Encil MacGowan, served in the Union army (1861–65) and was editor of the *Chattanooga Times* from 1872 until his death in 1903. Colonel MacGowan gathered a wealth of material about the war. Unfortunately, in 1907 that collection was lost in the fire that destroyed Upton Sinclair's Helicon Hall community in Englewood, New Jersey, where Alice and Grace were living. Alice was aware that John Calvin had written memoirs of his Civil War experiences that would be especially useful to her in writing *The Sword in the Mountains*, since he had participated in the Battle of Chickamauga, the Siege of Chattanooga, and the Battle of Missionary Ridge, all central incidents in her novel.

For me, the question remained: Did Hartzell's account, the "written pages" that her novel drew upon "so heavily for both verity and grace," still exist? Turning to the Internet for answers, I contacted a Hartzell/McGowan genealogist, Susan K. McMahan, who identified Loren W. Collins of Yucca Valley, California, as a possible source for the manuscript. Subsequently, he was able to supply me with a copy of the two-volume typewritten document.

Examination of the autobiography revealed Hartzell's influence on Alice MacGowan's novel, not only in tone and style, but also in a number of incidents from the memoirs that she incorporated in the novel. For example, the novelist borrows from Calvin's experiences (chap. 13) the scene in which Vespasian Seacrest, awakening at night when the campfire burns too close, discovers that his companion's feet are ablaze—only to realize that the man is a dead Confederate soldier whom the "sting of fire could not reach" (*Sword*, 340). The novelist also gives Vespasian responsibility for the security of the supply wagons during the Battle of Chickamauga, Calvin's actual assignment. Seth Hartzell, one of Calvin's first cousins, who appears as an almost mythical character in the autobiography—as one who has many "thrilling adventures"—most likely served as a prototype for Champ Seacrest, the hero of *The Sword in the Mountains*. Seth also influenced the MacGowan sisters' creation of a kind of mythical character type, Hank Pearsall, who appears in *The Last Word, Huldah*, and several western short stories set in Texas. This character embodies "values represented by the West—democratic freedom, openness, tolerance, natural virtue"—as contrasted with eastern values of "aristocratic control, limitation, intolerance."[6]

John Calvin Hartzell wrote his memoirs by hand in response to a "round robin" request signed by fifty family members (see fig. 4),[7] addressing the memoirs to nephew Wilbur Johnson Hartzell. The author dated the first chapter of the manuscript January 1, 1896, and worked on the project until sometime after January 21, 1898, the date recorded on the first page of the final chapter. (A brief addendum is dated April 22, 1898.) According to Loren W. Collins, the Hartzell descendant who provided me with a copy of the document, Josephine Virginia Hartzell,[8] daughter of Wilbur Hartzell, typed the manuscript sometime in the early 1940s with six carbon copies, which she distributed to relatives. The original manuscript, unfortunately, has been lost.

DEERFIELD AND NORTH Benton, near the Mahoning River about forty miles southeast of Cleveland, were rural farm communities that changed very little during the first half of the nineteenth century. The Hartzell/McGowan agricultural community consisted of a dozen or so families. In his memoirs, John Calvin described daily rural life in the 1840s and 1850s in minute and graphic detail—sheep raising, maple sugar production, educational and religious practices. During this time, the membership of the old Presbyterian church was torn apart over the slavery issue, a new church was built in Benton, and a small band of worshippers who stayed in the old church styled themselves Free Presbyterians, adopting the principles of the Declaration of Independence, in John Calvin's description. His father,

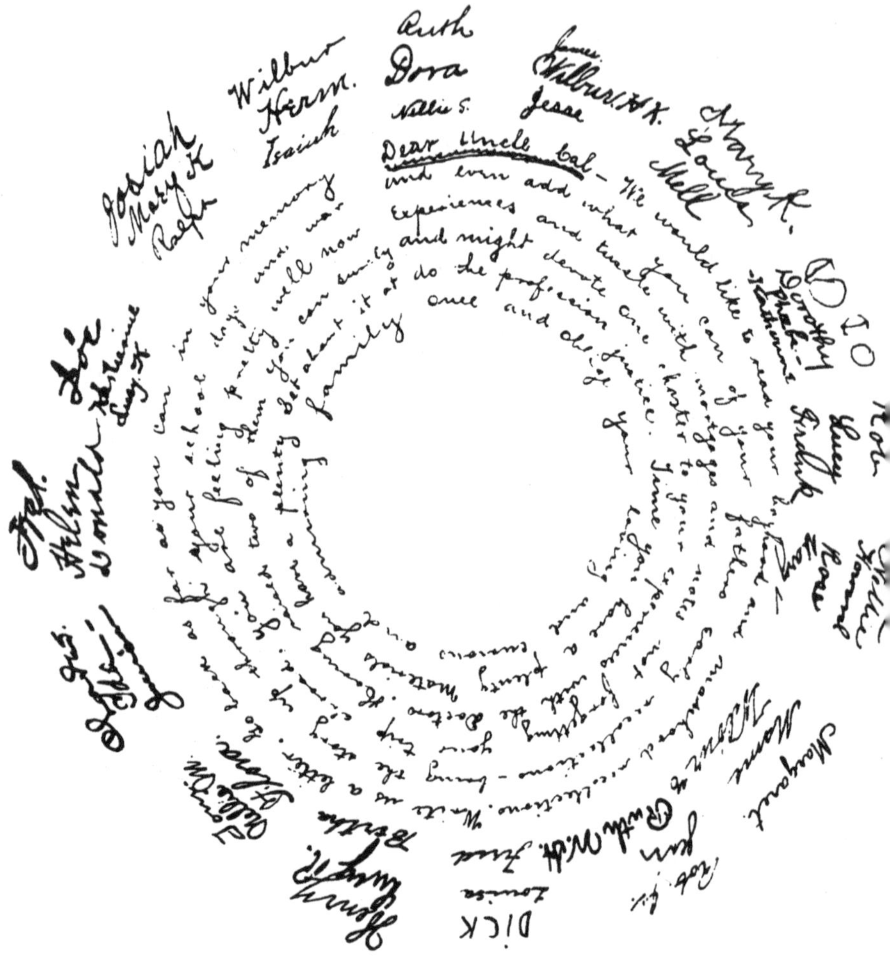

Figure 4. The round robin requesting John Calvin Hartzell to write his memoirs, signed by fifty family members. A transcription of the text precedes chapter 1.

Frederick, was "one of the foremost champions of those truths in [the] community" (chap. 5). Frederick's farm also became a station in the Underground Railroad for runaway slaves, as did Samuel McGowan's place in Orland, Indiana.

In spite of Hartzell's strict Presbyterian upbringing, by his own admission he was not particularly devout or religiously observant during the war. Chaplains, Hartzell notes, were "scarce in this army" and religious services rare. The 105th had no chaplains on duty during his service. "We have some good, religious men with us," Hartzell continues, "but our way of living isn't conducive to deep spirituality." John Calvin could not "join war and religion and make a good job of it." With some sarcasm, he concludes, "We've just got to wait until we whip these rebels, then go to church and be good ever afterwards" (chap. 12).

Hartzell's education was limited to three-month sessions (between harvest and spring planting) in a one-room school and in 1851 a brief stint, made miserable by homesickness, at the Albany Manual Labor School in Athens County, Ohio. His account of a school that combined labor and studies may be unique as a memoir of a white student enrolled in an integrated school in the North before the Civil War.

John Calvin's memoir is nostalgic about a past that reflected belief in the essential dignity and worth of the individual, a belief strongly held during the nineteenth century. By the mid-1890s, Hartzell felt the impact of the Industrial Revolution in the dominance of large corporations and the rampant growth of the iron industry in eastern Ohio. Hartzell describes the rural economy of his youth, the kinds of homes people inhabited, the types of farm buildings they constructed, the use of space, the natural environment and its gradual change, the process of assimilation by the Pennsylvania Dutch, and the educational and religious practices of the community. He devotes the first eight chapters and part of the ninth to these experiences of childhood, in part to show how they prepared young Northern men for the coming struggle. Especially in their religious and educational training, including school debates sponsored by literary societies and often based on American historical subjects, young men in the North learned patriotic values such as the principles of liberty and freedom that would make victory for the North possible. John Calvin was no exception.

Hartzell's family is of Pennsylvania German-Swiss origin. From the Zurich region in Switzerland, Hirzels (the name "Hirzel" means little stag) emigrated to the Kraichgau area, south of Heidelberg, Germany, and settled in villages such as Reihen and Sinsheim. In the late sixteenth and early seventeenth centuries they came to America, where the name changed to Hertzell and then Hartzell (Hartsell), and settled in the land between Lehigh and Easton in eastern Pennsylvania in 1738. They fought in both the Revolutionary War and the War of 1812 and eventually, in the early 1800s, migrated to the Deerfield area in eastern Ohio. The Hartzells, an enterprising family, prospered as farmers and soon became important contributors to the community.

John Calvin's older brother, Josiah, was sent to Amherst College in 1850 and graduated in 1854, later receiving degrees of Master of Arts and

Doctor of Philosophy from Amherst. He studied law in Toledo, Ohio, and was admitted to the bar in 1856. He practiced law for two years in Davenport, Iowa, and then moved to Canton in 1858, accepting the editorship of the *Canton Repository*. Retiring in 1876, he became a leader of the Republican Party. Uncle Jonas Hartzell moved to Davenport, Iowa, and became a well-known preacher for the Campbellite denomination. Other Hartzell/McGowans made valuable contributions to society. For example, Calvin's first cousin, John Encil MacGowan, after practicing law with Josiah Hartzell in Iowa, enlisted in the service as a private, mustered out at the rank of colonel, served as provost marshal of the Kentucky/Tennessee district, and was editor of the *Chattanooga Times* for more than thirty years. John Encil's brother Jonas McGowan graduated from the University of Michigan with a bachelor's degree in 1861, was commissioned as a captain in the 9th Michigan Cavalry, and participated in the capture of General John Morgan near Salineville, Ohio, where he was severely wounded. He served with General Burnside until his discharge in February 1864, received a law degree from the University of Michigan in 1868, and served two terms in the House of Representatives in Washington, D.C. (1876–80). Also on the McGowan side, Irvin E. McGowan invented the modern process of mass producing precision piston rings, thus making possible multicylinder engines; he was also a pioneer in the streamlined travel trailer industry. Other prominent Hartzell descendants include Josiah's son Charles, who was Secretary of San Juan Island; Joseph Crane Hartzell, Methodist Episcopal Church Bishop of Africa (1896–1916); and playwright Dorothy Heyward, who collaborated with her husband, DuBose Heyward, on the play that inspired the George Gershwin opera *Porgy and Bess* (produced 1927).

WHEN FIRST COUSINS Josiah Hartzell and John Encil McGowan traveled to Davenport in 1856 to set up a law practice, John Calvin accompanied them and wrote of these experiences in his memoirs. Josiah got John Calvin a position in a store in Davenport owned by a Mr. Leslie. The following spring the two young lawyers, Josiah and John Encil, "settled down to wait for business, but," as John Calvin wryly notes, "business seemed too tired to catch up with them" (chap. 8).

Shortly after the author's return home from the West in 1858, financial misfortune overtook his immediate family when his father, Frederick, generous to a fault, supported an ill-conceived project, a store run by his nephew Hartzell Schaeffer in Beloit, Ohio. Schaeffer managed to operate the store for about three years before declaring bankruptcy. To secure creditors, Frederick lost his home and farm. In his memoirs, Calvin writes, "I stayed home . . . and worked hard to help get a start for another home which we might call our own, and during the few years we were together there I learned to love [my father] with a perfect love. Our great misfortune showed the man in a new light—scales fell from my eyes. While he lived he impressed deeply into my mind this: 'A good name is rather to be chosen than great riches'; and to that end have I labored steadily" (chap. 9). Before Frederick died in 1868, he called on John Calvin to assume the family financial affairs, to pay all remaining debts, and to become a member of the free Presbyterian Church, all of which his dutiful son did.

In August 1865, John Calvin Hartzell married Louise Ann Lowrie Thompson, daughter of John and Mary Wilkinson Thompson. They had six children—Thomas B., Mary, Ruth W., Lucy, Bertha O., and Frederick W.[9]

Details of John Calvin's life after his discharge from the army are sketchy. Following the war, he pursued the vocation of farming, specializing in the raising of stock. Accompanied by his brother James Robert Hartzell, he traveled to Europe twice—the first time to Scotland and France and the second to the Shetland Islands. On the first trip, the brothers brought back Percheron horses, establishing the breed in the community. The second visit resulted in the introduction of the Shetland pony to the county and the state.

John Calvin was an active member of the Grand Army of the Republic (GAR), the Military Order of the Loyal Legion, and the Presbyterian Church. His ready sympathy, appreciation, and desire to be helpful, combined with his sense of humor, formed a unique personality. Wherever he went he was the center of the group, always ready to recount stories and amusing incidents. Albion Tourgée put it best: "He was an inveterate wag who could always be counted on to find something funny in the most lugubrious circumstances."[10] At each reunion of survivors of the Thousand and at GAR gatherings, he was expected to provide stories and humor and never failed to meet expectations.

IN THE NARRATIVE, addressed to his nephew Wilbur Johnson Hartzell ("Willie"), John Calvin refers to himself as "your uncle"; his father, Frederick, as "your grandfather"; and his mother, Mary, as "your grandmother." Why does he single out Wilbur rather than one of his own children? Dr. Thomas B. Hartzell, his eldest son, would seem to be a good candidate. Perhaps the sibling rivalry between Wilbur's father, Josiah, and John

Figure 5. John Calvin Hartzell, date of photograph unknown. This photograph accompanied the typescript copy of the memoirs.

Calvin, as revealed in several places in the memoirs, explains his choice of Wilbur, thus opening up the opportunity of getting back at Josiah. Or perhaps Wilbur was the leader of the round robin request, as seems to be indicated by the letters between uncle and nephew appended to the memoirs.

Hartzell's memoirs impart a strong impression of his personality, especially his sense of humor, which usually targets the narrator himself as the butt of the joke. The personal perspective is also evident in Hartzell's narrative point of view: he frequently imagines that he is interacting with his nephew in the dramatic present, as if the events are actually taking place as he narrates. He takes this approach in chapters 3 through 6 to relate boyhood adventures and to describe the Hartzell farm community. During the siege of Chattanooga, recalled in chapters 11 and 12, he again enters the dramatic present to interact with Wilbur (whom he imagines as a boy) and twelve-year-old camp follower Dick Cobb, living the daily life of the soldier through his routine military duties and reacting to the miserable conditions in the hospitals he visits. Often the dramatic present mode reveals the confusion and uncertainty of the moment as well as the common soldier's inability to understand, let alone to control, the events in which he is immersed.[11]

The dramatic present provides a sense of immediacy, of unfiltered experience. Elsewhere in his narrative, Hartzell writes from the vantage point of the historical present, that is, the time when Hartzell was setting down his memoirs, 1896–98; for example, in chapter 12 Hartzell notes that Chickamauga is now a national park and that monuments attest to the reality of battle sites. He occasionally steps back even further from his narrative to provide statistical summaries, such as comparisons of the Civil War with Napoleonic wars, lists of generals involved on both sides, and numbers of dead and wounded. These retrospective sections provide a more analytical view of the war, in contrast to the passages of vivid description that often reveal the confusion of events as they unfold.

To the precise, accurate, and realistic details he records of farm and military life, Hartzell adds a philosophical viewpoint, probing the significance of the events in his narrative. He often discusses the causes of the war, seeing the preservation of the union as the primary goal: "Duty called every man to defend our country's flag" (chap. 14). It is a war of rebellion by the South against the prospect of an "undivided country, rich and vast beyond comprehension" (chap. 14). Hartzell also sees slavery as the "cause of the war" (chap. 11), but more often mentions disunity as the root of the conflict.

Hartzell skillfully delineates scenes and characters. In every chapter, he uses verbs and verbals effectively to vitalize his sentences, as in chapter 4: "Here on this bank the wild grape vines and twists and tangles in sheer wanton idleness, curling, embracing, and knitting tree to tree and covering all with the foliage their broad green leaves furnish in such luxuriance." Using vivid language and metaphor, he pays minute attention to detail; in chapter 8, for instance, he describes the trail of tobacco juice on Captain Hubbard's face: "There was a crease ran from each corner of a wide mouth downward and a little forward, until the view of it was lost under his chin, but could be accurately traced by a little brown rill of tobacco juice bordered with fine bits of quid, held in check by a short growth of stumpy beard. The lighter juice kept true to the crease[s] until they met under the chin, and from there fell in beads to his shirt front." Hartzell uses military imagery in drawing domestic objects and routines; for example, he describes wool buying and selling as "all the skirmishing and schemes of both buyers and sellers, the advancing of pickets and videttes, and the cautious laying of parallels and breastworks, till the final struggle" (chap. 2). At the same time, he is keenly aware of the challenge of finding words to express emotions and feelings of great complexity and depth—as Hartzell says on the eve of the battle of Chickamauga, "I stand almost dumb in trying to give you the faintest conception of the events of the next forty-eight hours" (chap. 11).

Hartzell's style notably depends on photographic-quality mental images as acts of memory. His narrative is primarily the product of memory, the source of the stories he recounts of boyhood and wartime. Actually, his memory is rather remarkable. There is no evidence that he kept a journal or diary during the war or before it (unlike Tourgée, Cumings, Ayre, and Morse, who all kept diaries of their experiences in the 105th OVI), yet he recalls the most minute details of events and scenes that go back thirty to fifty years. He relies only occasionally on research.

The approach may be the result of the development of photography. His manuscript is interspersed with many individual and group pictures of family. Unfortunately, the copying process makes the pictures of very poor quality and too faded to reproduce. But Hartzell's mind operated like a camera and recorded scenes and stories with such clarity that one could almost draw pictures of the farming community he grew up in as well as of the scenes of battle at Perryville, Chickamauga, Chattanooga, and Missionary Ridge. At Chickamauga, Hartzell writes, "a number of fine, young officers, leading their men into that roaring, seething cauldron of war, passed me and were soon lost to sight in the smoke of the volcano, and I took such note of them as to remember distinctly to this day how they looked" (chap. 11). John Calvin describes the siege of Chattanooga as "another of the indelibly penciled pictures that hang on the wall of my memory" (chap. 11).

Like Stephen Crane, in his novel *The Red Badge of Courage* (1895),[12] and Ambrose Bierce,[13] in his contemporary writings on the Civil War, Hartzell analyzes the psychology of battle. Approaching "with hesitation" the subject of "how a fellow feels in action," he admits his inability to do it justice. For one thing, "there are many phases of it, from the wretched agony of waiting under fire, to the galling torture and the crushing, humiliating, agonizing disappointment of defeat." When all goes right, John

Calvin writes, "the blood rises up. . . . A feeling of ecstasy, born of the roar of battle and smell of burnt powder, takes hold of you, and each man feels invincible, and in such a state of mind danger and death have no terrors." This feeling, he claims, is unrelated to anger or fear or "any other petty condition of mind" (chap. 13). In such a state, men armed with sticks and stones would behave with the same valor as men armed with Spencer rifles, and Calvin believes they would have gone to "certain death, to a man, without thought or protest." He concludes, "This I call the exultation or ecstasy of battle."

The role of regimental band music was important to both sides during the Civil War, and Hartzell makes a number of references to the bands.[14] They bolstered morale, entertained the troops, and provided the cadences for close order drill as regiments marched into battle. One of the most interesting functions of regimental bands was assisting the movement of heavy artillery over rugged, dangerous mountains. The scene described by the author (chap. 11) was so intriguing that Alice MacGowan incorporated it into *The Sword in the Mountains*.

Hartzell's memoirs reveal his interest in military strategy. Gerald I. Prokopowicz, in *All for the Regiment: The Army of the Ohio, 1861–1862*, in large part a study of strategy used in Kentucky and Tennessee during the early years of the war, notes that "the training of the Army of the Ohio consisted almost exclusively of close order drill, performed by individual regiments. Little training took place at higher organizational levels. Brigade and division officers rarely practiced maneuvering their units. . . . Brigades, divisions, and the army as a whole remained mere organizational abstractions."[15] By drilling four to eight hours a day, companies could instinctively form the line of battle in combat, which enabled every soldier to fire his weapon simultaneously, resulting in maximum firepower.

This strategy was the regiment's greatest strength and at the same time its greatest weakness. Hartzell was aware that in the line of battle, an infantry soldier, even an officer, has no sense of the whole, "knows nothing of the movements of the army he is with, not even of his own brigade or regiment. He is like a checker on the board; he goes where he is sent, and stays until he is moved or gobbled up" (chap. 9). John Calvin acknowledges here that the soldier's ignorance of the tactics or strategies of the other regiments of the army can have a negative effect on the morale of the troops.

The skirmish line was another military tactic that Hartzell's Company H would have learned. Some regiments supplemented training in close order drill with skirmish (open order) drill consisting of skirmish lines with soldiers singly or in small groups spaced several yards apart, usually placed some distance in advance of the main body of the regiment. The usefulness of skirmishes became clear by late 1862, and the tactic was used increasingly thereafter (Prokopowicz, *All for the Regiment*, 50).

Much of the pride and cohesion in the regiment, Hartzell believed, was reflected in the way it went through the manual of arms (chap. 13). Using religious imagery, Hartzell describes the veterans of battle-tested regiments as "evangelists" who persuasively preach a gospel of victory for the North. An observer would never forget the preaching of these evangelists, he continues, and "these preachers are all coming back, thirty or forty regiments of them," to claim the victory. Prokopowicz stresses that training for company soldiers never went beyond "small-unit close order drill" (*All for the Regiment*, 184). If a regiment "proved amazingly resilient," it was nevertheless "incapable of following up any of its limited battlefield successes" (ibid., 188). This dichotomy was inherent in the army's social structure—a decentralized group of military communities with no structure beyond the regiment. The infantry regiment, then, became the basic unit of command and for most soldiers "the source of their identity" (ibid., 28).

During the Battle of Perryville, Prokopowicz observes, the 105th Ohio, a recently organized regiment with less than two months of training (August 21, 1862–October 8, 1962), was inexperienced in close order drill tactics and lacked the unity and cohesion these drills gave to veteran regiments. Moreover, the luckless 105th did not have its own regimental flag. Most regiments carried two flags, a national flag and a regimental flag, which was frequently a modified state flag with the regiment's name prominently displayed and past exploits colorfully embroidered. These guidons were large and colorful, visibility being important to identify and locate the regiment in the surging battle lines. In addition, flags bolstered the soldiers' courage in battle, as the phrase "rally 'round the flag" suggests. Because of the tactical and morale-boosting value that flags offered the regiment, protection of flags and guidons during battle was usually assigned to a unit of soldiers. In the Battle of Perryville, the 105th Ohio, lacking its own flag, instead carried the flag of the 101st Indiana, which was given into its custody when the Indiana regiment was being disciplined. The 105th Ohio chose to keep the Indiana colors encased throughout the battle. This circumstance no doubt added to the confusion and the lack of cohesiveness in the 105th during Perryville (ibid., 174–75). By the time of Missionary Ridge, although the 105th still did not have its own regimental flag, it carried the national flag.[17]

Following Perryville, the 105th would have acquired skill in close order drill, for the Army of the Ohio marched in pursuit of General Braxton Bragg's Confederate army to Murfreesboro, Tennessee, via Nashville and then made passage of the Cumberland Mountains and Tennessee River to Chattanooga.[18]

IN 1861 THE core of the United States Army had signed up for three-year terms of service. The year 1864 became a climactic year in which the northern army was in danger of collapse. For Hartzell this crisis became the central drama of the final chapters. Given the wretched conditions of the common soldier, Hartzell writes, it would appear that "nothing would induce" soldiers to reenlist (chap. 13). Amazingly, 136,000 three-year veterans reenlisted for a variety of reasons—the thirty-day furlough and the four-hundred-dollar bounty helped, but pride in the regiment also was a significant factor. Though bounty men grew wealthy dealing with "this class of cattle," the "great heart of the nation," John Calvin writes, "was loyal to the core" (chap. 14).

Hartzell certainly believed his military service was the highlight of his life. "I rejoice that I was permitted to bear ever so humble a part in securing the unity of our great country, and to share a little in the suffering of its noble sons" (chap. 14). He continues, "In my story of the war I have tried to show you . . . the life of the man with the musket, for it fell to my lot to be almost his constant companion, often his messmate and bedfellow. From February 14, 1864, to June, 1865, I slept most of the time in old fields and forests, my head pillowed on a haversack crammed with money, which could have been his [the common soldier's] by any act of vile treachery; he stood a sentinel faithful to his trust. The bad element was very small comparatively."

Two essential keys to understanding the romantic nineteenth century are beliefs in the perfectibility of man and in the worth and dignity of the individual. The concept of perfectibility was alien to Hartzell's Presbyterian upbringing, based on the teachings of his namesake, John Calvin (1509–64). As pointed out earlier, however, John Calvin Hartzell readily accepted the concept of the worth and dignity of the individual. In the end, as is evident in his memoirs, it was the loyalty "to the core" of the common soldier during the war that affirmed and bolstered his faith in the individual.

Notes

1. Albion W. Tourgée, *The Story of a Thousand: Being a History of the Service of the 105th Ohio Volunteer Infantry* (Buffalo, NY: S. McGerald, 1896). In addition to Tourgée's *Story of a Thousand* and his diary ("A Civil War Diary of Albion W. Tourgée," edited by Dean H. Keller, *Ohio History* 74, no. 2 [1965]), published memoirs about the 105th Ohio include *In Memoriam: Henry Harrison Cumings, Charlotte Cumings* by Rev. J. N. Fradenburgh (Oil City, PA: Derrick Publishing, 1913), which includes extracts from Cumings's diary of his experiences as an officer of the 105th, 1862–65 (pp. 35–163); *The Civil War Diary of Private Josiah Ayre*, transcribed by James Glauser (1975? held by Cleveland Public Library); and *The Civil War Diaries and Letters of Bliss Morse*, edited by Loren J. Morse (Wagoner, OK: Heritage Printing, 1985). These are day-to-day journals, whereas Hartzell's account, written thirty to fifty years after the actual events, relies on memory.

2. The title page of the surviving typescript reads as follows: "Some Autobiographical Writing / by / JOHN CALVIN HARTZELL / Captain of Company H., One Hundred and Fifth / O. V. I. / and / JESSE HARTZELL / Twelfth Ohio Cavalry / -o- / Done in response to a Family Round Robin / -o- / Volume One"; the present edition omits Jesse Hartzell's contribution. (Volume One comprises 166 pages; Volume Two begins at chapter 10, and the pagination picks up at page 303.) Biographical information in the editor's introduction has been compiled from John Calvin's memoirs, cited here by chapter numbers in parentheses, and from the obituary of John Calvin Hartzell published in the *Alliance (Ohio) Review*, April 27, 1918.

3. Tourgée, *Story of a Thousand*, 237n.

4. Charles I. Switzer, "The MacGowan Sisters: Early-Twentieth-Century Popular Writers," *Journal of Popular Culture* 34 (Summer 2000): 85–103.

5. Alice MacGowan, *The Sword in the Mountains* (New York: Grosset & Dunlap, 1910).

6. Switzer, "MacGowan Sisters," 97.

7. *Webster's Third New International Dictionary, Unabridged* gives several definitions of "round robin," including at least two that apply to the request made by Hartzell's family: "a written petition, memorial, or protest to which the signatures are affixed in a circle so as not to indicate who signed first"; and "a statement signed by several persons." In this case, the handwritten request itself was in the form of broken concentric circles, reading from the outside in, and was surrounded by the signatures. The round robin is reproduced in figure 4 from a faded photocopy. A transcription of the text immediately precedes chapter 1.

John Calvin Hartzell's response to the request was matched by at least one other family member, Jesse Hartzell, thus exemplifying a third definition of "round robin": "a letter sent in turn to the members of a group . . . each of whom signs and forwards it sometimes after adding information or comment." In an undated note appended to the typescript, John Calvin's nephew Wilbur Johnson Hartzell, who was evidently the moving force behind the project, mentions other family members from whom he had requested contributions.

8. Josephine Virginia Hartzell, b. 19 May 1905 in Minnesota, d. 10 Jan 1983, Patchogue, NY, was the daughter of Wilbur Johnson Hartzell and his second wife, Florence Wright.

9. For detailed biographical information, see note 1 to chapter 1 of the memoirs.

10. Tourgée, *Story of a Thousand*, 237n.

11. David Madden, former director of the United States Civil War Center, praises Daniel Sutherland's *Seasons of War: The Ordeal of a Confederate Community, 1861–1865* for the author's "audacious decision to use the present tense." Hartzell anticipated Sutherland's use of the dramatic present by a century. David Madden, "The Civil War as a Model for the Scope of Popular Culture," *Journal of American and Comparative Culture* 23 (Spring 2000): 3.

12. In Stephen Crane's *The Red Badge of Courage* (1895), the hero, Henry Fleming, engages in a mental battle between fear and, initially, "romantic" courage. As he enters his first battle, his romantic illusions are soon destroyed, and he runs in panic. Ironically, he receives his "red badge" of courage when he is accidentally struck in the head by a fellow soldier's rifle butt and subsequently fights bravely, becoming, at least temporarily, a hero. On Crane, see Ken Chowder, "A Writer Who Lived the Adventures He Portrayed," *Smithsonian* 25 (January 1995): 109; and Christopher Bentley, *The Double Life of Stephen Crane* (New York: Alfred A. Knopf, 1992).

13. Ambrose Bierce served with distinction in the Civil War, in the 9th Indiana. *Ambrose Bierce's Civil War*, edited by William McCann (Chicago: Gateway Editions, 1956), also reveals the horrors of military engagement. In the Battle of Shiloh, Lieutenant Bierce, while leading a skirmish line across an open field, was ambushed by the rebels. "Then—I can't describe it—the forest seemed all at once to flame up and disappear with a crash like that of a great wave upon the beach—a crash that expired in hot hissings, and the sickening 'spat' of lead against flesh" (18).

14. William Rosengren, "Regimental Bands in the Civil War," *Journal of American and Comparative Cultures* 24, no. 2 (2001): 191–205.

15. Gerald I. Prokopowicz, *All for the Regiment: The Army of the Ohio, 1861–1862* (Chapel Hill: University of North Carolina Press, 2001), 46–47.

16. The Ohio Historical Association Collection of Civil War flags does not include a regimental flag for the 105th Ohio.

Dear Uncle Cal—We would like to read your boyhood and manhood recollections. Write us a letter. Go back as far as you can in your memory and even add what you can of your father[']s early recollections—bring the story up through your school days and war experiences and tussle with mortgages and notes not forgetting your trip abroad. You are feeling pretty well now and might devote one chapter to your experiences with the Doctors. Having raised two of them you can surely do the profession justice. Time you have a plenty[.] Materials you have a plenty[.] Set about it at once and oblige your loving and curious and admiring family[.]

[This round robin (see fig. 4) was signed
by fifty family members.]

CHAPTER ONE

⌒⌐⌐⌐

House of Seven Gables

JANUARY 1ST, 1896

My dear nephew:

In answer to the Round Robin request I can tell you very little that is out of the ordinary experience of human life.[1]

I was born November 27th, 1837, the year in which Queen Victoria began her reign, and spent my boyhood days in the midst of a colony of Hartzells. The farm was entered by your great-grandfather, and was the birthplace of your grandfather, your father, and all your aunts and uncles of the Hartzell tribe.[2]

I grew up among Hartzells; went to school with Hartzells, and to church with Hartzells. In fact, both the school and church, as well as the cemetery, were on our old farm, so that we were fully equipped for life and death.

To the East and joining our farm was the home of your great-great-grandfather George; farther East and joining him was his son-in-law, Uncle Billy Lazarus, and next Peter, his son; then Thompson Craig, Jacob Sheets, David and Tobias Hartzell; South and adjoining were George Hartzell and Henry, Old Abram and Young Abe; West, uncle Billy Hartzell, uncles John and Sam Macgowan.[3]

But this is confusing—all things have a beginning, a middle and an ending. I can give a little view of the first and second, but the end no man knoweth.

The family had in itself everything needful for the comfort of life—such as saw, and grist, and fulling mills,[4] school, church and still house. The farm on which I was born was, and is yet, a lovely old place, the entire North line being the Mahoning River; and the farm was bisected by an eccentric—now innocently babbling, dodging and darting brook, and now a roaring. bellowing, fearsome, rushing flood, carrying everything before it—Island Creek. The two streams joined on our farm and our home was near the banks of both. I could hardly have chosen a more satisfactory place to be born, and, if I were to be born again, I would choose the same old place. Yet those two streams were like Alexander, the coppersmith. They did me much evil and caused me many stripes, luring me from my tasks on the farm, from school, and even on the Sabbath day my vagrant thoughts were led away from the serious matters of the sermon, so that before the opening services were closed I was transported in mind to their cool shady banks, lying in the shade or wandering along their margins, watching the fish, muskrats and cranes, the squirrels, groundhogs and chipmunks. Oh! a boy could always find plenty of fun at our old place. There were skating in winter, fishing in summer, and swimming-holes to spare; and in the spring, when the sun dissipated the snows, the river and the creek were sure to go on a bender; and the ice gorged, and trees, logs and all sorts of drift were caught in the flood; and the water backed up all over the bottom land, and the old sugars and sycamores that grew too near the banks swayed, toppled and fell in. Oh! there was excitement those days, and the like I shall never see again. Then after the flood went down, there stood the old guard of trees—old monarchs, with the bark ground off and the fibres of the wood all fretted and torn by the ice and drift, from the side whence the flood came—there they stood, the remnant of many a forlorn hope, and there some of them stand today.

My grandfather's house was brick, and stood (built 1810) near a fine spring. A little below his own house, and near to it, he built a small frame-house for one of his sons (Jonas, I think). The house had a spring under it and an apple tree over it. After Jonas was gone and your grandfather married, he took possession, as, being the youngest son, it fell to him to care for his father and mother, and they remained in their old home until death claimed them some ten years after I was born.[5]

Grandfather was a kindly, reserved man and loved quiet, so we were not allowed to go romping around their house, and he never took an interest in any of our childish schemes, so that, while I remember both him and grandmother very well, the impression left on my mind regarding them is of a quiet old couple in the gloaming of life, content with each other, and the company of older people than we youngsters.

Among my first recollections is an old trundle bed made of poles with the bark on. Its place in the daytime was under mother's bed, and at night it was drawn out, and sister Lucy and I slept in it. Another is of the ripe apples plunking on the roof of our house after night; and another vivid memory is of the old fire-place. Big and roomy it was for back-log and fore-stick, with andirons, crane and reflector. This last was for roasting meat and, I think, baking. It was, say, two feet or more long, of bright tin, open on one side, and the top extending outward and upward. The open side was turned towards the fire, and the projecting top caught the heat and directed it towards the contents of the pan at the bottom. I also remember that the brands in the fireplace were always carefully covered at night, so that in the morning, by raking off the ashes, we had a fine bed of coals, and with a little dry fuel we soon had a roaring fire. Sometimes, however, the fire went out, and I was hustled unceremoniously out of bed, and hurried off to uncle Billy's or uncle John's for fire. I mind me well of one such time I was started with a warning not to allow the vegetation under my feet make much advance towards maturity. I started off, but had not sensed the warning at its true value. I heard a pleasant call: "Oh! Calvin, come back, my son". Returning, I received an assistance to my understanding in the form of a good whipping; was started again, and this time successfully. I am sure the grass made no great growth under my feet that morning.

In these days I got many a whipping, and, tho' the stripes fell on back and bare legs, I always in the summer time wore my trousers rolled up to the knees, and rarely more than one gallus to my tow linen pantaloons. Thus my wardrobe was never cumbersome and always convenient about the water. I could wade or, when the water was high, swim, rolling my shirt and trousers into a little bundle, and, with the "gallus" tying the bundle to my head, would go sailing; visit the boys on the other side; and have never since found in clothing a device so handy, comfortable and cheap.[6]

Father was gone a good deal of the time, buying stock; and when he had a lot of sheep or cattle to bring home he took me along to drive. On the outward trip I always rode behind his saddle. He loved his horse; always kept a good one, a square trotter; and rode fast. As I sat behind him holding fast by two straps and the rear of the saddle, and old Aaron reeling off about eight miles an hour, my thoughts were not pleasant, and I wouldn't write them down if I could. Everyone knew him and he was a welcome guest wherever he went.

One summer day I shall never forget. Old Aaron's sharp back seemed to be slowly but surely working its way up between my shoulders as he kept up his steady, cruel clip. I heard a cheerful voice call: "Hello Fred." That sound always brought old Aaron to a halt. A pleasant invitation to "light" and sample some honey came from the owner of the voice (Daddy Kean), an old Scotchman. The invitation was hearty, and the honey plenty, and I certainly availed myself of it, neither knowing nor caring for consequences. But soon, as we got well under way again, I became a bundle of anguish and misery, and how I ever got through that day I cannot tell. Those rides when they were long, were sad to bear. What with the sweat of the horse which smarted and often galled my sore legs and the galls and misery of it all,[7] I was always glad when they came to an end and I could walk and drive the sheep.

That old horse was a good one—long, raw boned, docked and nicked large, but fine bony head and great brown eyes.[8] He could leave a long stretch of road behind him on those trips.

I had an always interesting companion in Turk, our old dog. He was a big, jolly old fellow, black cropped ears and a stump tail. He never had occasion to fight on the road; his dignity froze any big dog that approached him in hostility, though he would often unbend and allow some friendship with deserving big dogs and be real pleasant with the little ones. He was a good dog and knew his place. On week days he always went with father, but on the Sabbath day he stayed at home, knowing the day without being told.

What threshing was done was mostly with the flail, the men who wielded the flail getting one bushel in ten of the cleaned grain. One day one of the threshers sitting on the box in which we mixed feed for the horses with old Turk between his knees held by the ears in his firm grasp, said to father who was sitting beside him: "Fred, I can hold Turk so tight that he can't bite and you can't make him bite." Father unseen reached a short fork lying in the box and used for stirring the feed, ran the fork under the straw, unnoticed by John Rieger who held the dog, and gave old Turk an awful jab. Turk twisted out of John's hands as though he had been greased, took the fellow by the front of his shirt and vest and dismantled his whole port bow above the water line—at which I was most pleased. That Rieger family I never could abide. They were the sons of a tanner who lived in our district. They were John and Ben and Bill and Adam and Dave and Joe and Neal and Sol—all came to our school; always fought the small boys and were generally bullies. Yet, when the war came on not one of them went for a soldier. So old Turk knew just what he needed and gave it to him.

We also used to cover the barn floor with bundles of unthreshed wheat, untie them, and put four or six horses on the floor, walking in pairs round and round, with one or two men in the center who kept the circle in the center cleaned, continually throwing the full heads in the track of the horses, and when the top was pretty well tramped off the men, each taking opposite sides of the floor, commenced with their forks to carefully turn the straw over, so that the bottom became the top. Mostly the horses were kept moving all the time, but if there were six of them and two men, they were sometimes taken off the floor for a few minutes and the turning was soon completed. If there were only four horses and one man there was no stop the whole day, except when the grain was all tramped off one floor the horses were taken off while the clean threshed straw was stored in the shed or stacked and the grain raked clean. When it got deep on the floor it was shoved to one side; then the same process commenced again, stopping at intervals to prepare the wheat for its final storage in the granary or winnowing it through a wind-mill. Clover and timothy seed were threshed the same way, and clover threshing was very tedious; in fact, it was all tedious for the boy who rode the horses. The lead team always required a boy to guide it and keep the procession on the move. The horses of the following teams were coupled together and the leaders tied firmly to the tails of the teams in front by a stout strap or rope. This work was usually done in cold weather, and I have ridden around that old barn floor by the week, thinking, wishing, hoping, longing for a speedy deliverance—but a boy never paid his keeping anyway—so I only got relief when I could fool some other boy by telling him how nice it was and getting him to take my place. You could never fool a farmer boy that way though, nor a town boy more than once. When such luck came I took a little diversion out of sight of the barn and gave the other boy time to enjoy the ride—I was generous with all my pleasures.

When I grew big enough to turn the wind-mill I did that too. It was better than turning the grindstone, because there was no one to bear on, but there was no end to it. Like the water in the creek, the grain was always coming all day long. The old wind-mill said "crank a-lank-lank, lank-crank, a-lank-lank-lank." The boy who could turn that old mill all day and not long for "sweet fields beyond the swelling flood" has more patience than your uncle. Later the threshing was done by a one-horse tread power. That was the dawn of a better day for me.

Your father being the first born, our parents designed him for the pulpit, and he was early sent away to school. There was one brother between us, Joshua—of him I have no recollection as he died in infancy. So that I was the oldest boy at home, and all the boy-work fell on me for most of the year. Your father is four years my senior, and Jess is eight years my junior. Lucy and Tommy came between Jess and I. Tommy died in his babyhood; I recollect him well; a pretty little fellow with a curly tow head. So you see by this that I came in for a good many odd jobs beside the regular farm work.[9]

One of these jobs was turning the grind-stone on harvest mornings before breakfast, to grind the scythes, and sometimes the grinding had to be renewed after dinner. Oh! how those fellows imposed on me. How they bore on hard when, in sheer desperation, I would try to turn fast so as to come to the end of it. I have got their old mugs indelibly photographed on my mind—old John and Jerry Snider, and Gib Hoadly, and a lot more of them. I could say hard words about them yet, but it wouldn't do any good and show an unforgiving spirit. Oh—how I used to follow those men in the meadow as soon as I could lift a fork, and spread the swathes all through the hot harvest days, and help rake it up with a hard rake into windrows and, in order that a boy might not be idle, follow the load with a rake to gather up the vagrant straws as they fell from the load. My dear, but those were long, hard days, but the river in the evening set all things even. At such times father used to take me on his naked back, swim out into the middle of the stream and shake me off. He was a strong man—six feet one in his stocking feet—and a grand swimmer.

Another job I very much hated was pulling flax, for we made our own linen, or, at least, prepared it for the loom. The flax was pulled, tied in small bundles and, when fully dry, was carried to the meadow and evenly spread and rotted, then taken up into bundles again, broken so that the woody parts fell away and left only the fibre, which was scutched and hackled.[10] But the process is too long and tedious to describe. After the pulling of it was done my part was finished, and the rest was done by old fellows who went from house to house, and were experts. I can hear the old flax-brake going yet, all day long. Old Seth Layman who followed the business used to make his bargain either by the day or the job, and when I was a little fellow like your Jamie[11] I was always around him, for he was a pleasant sort of a man. He told me that when he worked by the day the old brake kept saying all day long: "By the day, by the day, by the day, day, day"; but when it was the job it sang another tune, like this: "By the job, by the job, by the job"; so jolly and hearty, and for nearly sixty years the song of the flax-brake has come to me whenever I see men at work.

I used to wear trousers made of tow or the coarser parts of the flax, and those trousers were like Bud Means' bull dog—when they got a hold "Heaven and earth couldn't make him let go"; as if I were climbing a tree or over the fence or through the barn, and got caught on splinter, limb or knot, those trousers could be depended on to do their duty.

Your grandfather never left home without leaving work enough for all the small boys about the premises, such as picking stones. This had to be done every spring, and I often used to wonder where all the stones came from, for, if we picked them ever so clean one spring, there seemed to be just so many more the next.

Family worship—there was one rule in your grandfather's house from which there was neither variation nor shadow of turning, and that was family worship. No morning sun arose on his family that we were not all assembled in a solemn and orderly manner—not only the family, but the man-servant and maid-servant and the stranger within the gates. The exercise began with singing:

> "Lord, in the morning, at thy voice,
> The cheerful sun makes haste to rise,
> And like a giant, doth rejoice
> To run his journey through the skies."[12]

I give this one only as a sample. We had many tunes and were all early taught to sing, being, I think, good singers; at least, we were often put forward to help at school or church. After the singing a chapter was read, then all kneeled in prayer, and as the morning, so the evening. No force of business or care of any kind was allowed to interfere, alter or cut short any part of this simple, yet solemn and dignified, service, neither noise nor confusion being permitted to mar its even course. Occasionally at night, one of the tired youngsters might fall asleep and, with head pillowed in arms on the chair seat, remain kneeling when the prayer was finished. Then fingers would be pointed, and the faintest, little bud of a giggle—which under any other circumstances would have burst its bounds—could be traced on the faces of all the youngsters, but no notice was taken by the elders, except that mother took charge of the sleeper and soon the house slept the sleep of the just.

CHAPTER TWO

◗◗═◗

Dipping Candles; [Trapping, Fishing, Hunting; Orchard and River; Maple Syrup Production]

DIPPING CANDLES: During all my days at home our ordinary light in the evenings was from the open fire in the fire-place; a lamp, which was a low oblong stone pitcher with a strip of cotton for a wick and any kind of melted fat; or from the candles made in molds or dipped. When the beef was killed in the fall and the tallow rendered, then we made our winter supply of candles; hundreds of them stored away, and we never went to spelling-school or any kind of an evening meeting without taking a candle. Every family that had any standing brought a candle, and thus all the homes and public places were lighted.

For dipping candles the necessary paraphernalia was perhaps two dozen rods, quite thin and three feet long, plenty of wicking, and a great kettle of melted tallow. The candle wicking was cut to proper lengths a dozen or more looped on each rod and separated an inch or inch and a half. The wicks were then saturated with the warm tallow and the rod placed away that they might cool, the same process being followed until all were stiff with tallow, then repeated until the candles were large enough to use when they were packed away. The weather had to be cold so the tallow would harden rapidly. To be fully up to the times a candlestick and snuffers were thought to be needed, though not really necessary, as a block of wood with an auger hole in it answered very well, and the snuffing could be done with the fingers. The vision, as I look back over half a hundred years, of the old home in the evening, when all the family were gathered round the big fire-place, father and mother sitting on either side of the stand, one reading and the other patching, mending or knitting, while the children play on the floor or the wide hearth. The great fire-place with its roaring fire and sputtering fire-stick, with a glowing bed of coals and the gray ashes underneath, crane with hanging hooks and boiling pots, and the firelight casting shadows over the room, the single candle on the stand—comes back to me, a scene of peace that passes the understanding of these later days.

We youngsters never had money, and, indeed, had no great need for it. We neither wrote or received letters, while envelopes had not been born. Postage was six cents, and usually the person who got the letter had it to pay; but the getting of a letter was an event in any family and, as a rule, it went the rounds of the entire community, I think. I never saw a lead pencil in school, and the only pens in use were goose quills, part of the teacher's qualifications being to make and mend the pens. I recollect the first Five Cents I ever earned. I helped my uncle John[1] all through sheep shearing. We were continually bringing the washed sheep to the barn to be sheared, and, when sheared, took them back to the pasture on the different farms owned by him. I helped him for a week, and when I started home he called me back and gave me Five Cents. No boy ever ran faster, or felt prouder, than I did with my first money.

The first great cross I ever met with was this way: The boys on the north side of the river made a business of trapping. Muskrat skins brought from seven to ten cents, and their catch often paid the tax on their farms; so as I grew stouter I thought I would make some money too. Father never looked with favor on any of my schemes in that direction, so I had to make my traps out of his sight. I finally got a big box trap made, carried it to the river, and baited it with sweet apple. The next morning, bright and early, I went to look at my trap, and, lo—it was sprung. Oh! the joy of it. Think of the fish hooks; or the value of it would buy a quarter pound of powder or a box of caps. No treasure I ever sought for seemed half so valuable, while all triumphs of later days pale in comparison. And yet it was only the pleasure of anticipation, for I hadn't my rat actually in hand, but I knew how to take him, for I had seen it done many a time, so I lifted my trap carefully and carried it carefully back a rod or two from the bank, cut me a stick with a short fork on the end, turned the trap on its back, and lifted the lid just enough to let in the forked end of the stick. Now the problem was to set the fork astride the neck of the rat, drop back the lid, seize him by the tail, then hit him on the back of the neck with the stick, and the rat belonged to your uncle. But, alas, he didn't, for in the fierce excitement of the moment I let go of the lid; it fell open, and in two jumps mister rat was in his element, ruddering his way back to the bosom of his family, "tho' lost to sight, to memory dear."[2] Then your uncle lifted up his voice and wept, draining the bitter cup of grief to its dregs. Since that day I have had many disappointments and losses, but none so hard to bear as this.

As we never had money, I was often in straits for fishhooks. Just one farm laid between ours and the village of North Benton where we went to post-office, store, smithshop and tavern. In my early days your grandfather's cousin Solomon, son of uncle Billy, kept the store.[3] I often rode a colt to the village on errands, and he would have me run the colt at his best pace from Dock Hook's to Hoadly's gin shop or grocery. The store was about the middle of the course, and I always had a fair company of admiring spectators. My reward was a stock of candy, with an option of a fishhook. Sometimes I took a few eggs in my pocket for a bass hook which was more expensive. I often traded apples for fishhooks, say, two or three bell-flowers or pippins for a hook, and, one way or another, I managed to get them.

All boys made their own skates; two files or other bits of steel, with a little shaping by the smith, were all that was required; the rest we did ourselves. Fastening the wood was an easy job. I made one pair with some thick hoop iron, but they were no good. Twenty-five cents was a big price to pay for skates.

The guns of that day were very highly prized by the older men. They always spoke of them in the feminine gender. Uncle John had one—a flint lock—and I felt safe that if all the fire in the country went out he could soon start a new one. She was a famous old gun, and was the main dependence of my grandparents for meat. That was long before my time, but as she hung in her hooks I admired and revered her, and I never knew her to be loaned to anyone. Uncle Abe also had one and took great pleasure in shooting squirrels for the sick, or the beeves or pigs for anyone in the neighborhood, but she never went out of his hands.

Until I was perhaps sixteen years old a few of these old fellows, with a sprinkling of younger men, used to meet Saturday afternoon on "Raymond's Bottoms"—next to us but farther down the river—a beautiful place, flanked by sheer bluffs on either side; and there they shot at mark to their heart's content. When I could slip away, and I most always could, for uncle Abe not being real pious gave way sometimes to practices which were not well approved by the more steady-going folk, kept me posted, and I was usually on hand and acted as marker. A cap box lid was tacked to the body of the tree, one hundred or more yards away, and when the shooting began I plugged the bullet holes with a bit of stick until a round was shot. Then all came up to take a look and decide who came nearest the center. A cap box lid was soon shot to smithereens, and then bullet patches were used instead. Sometimes a little purse was made up, but oftener not. "John Barleycorn" generally had a place in the match,[4] though no one ever became intoxicated, only just a wee thing good natured like, but nothing to detract from markmanship. Standing a rod or two on one side the mark, I have watched the muzzles of those old squirrel rifles when the last rounds were being shot just before the gloaming, and when, to a stranger, it would certainly have appeared, as the men toed the mark to shoot, that the marker was in more danger of being shot than the mark. But not so, though the muzzles of the guns seemed a little lost and would weave slowly up and down, yet, when the finger pressed the trigger the ball sped true.

Right here I must tell that some ten or fifteen years ago uncle Jacob Sheets, then perhaps eighty or eighty-five years old, a fat, heavy old fellow who walked with a cane, was sitting in his dooryard on a splint-bottomed chair watching two grandsons shooting at mark with his old squirrel rifle, but as they succeeded in blowing holes through the air only he said gruffly: "Gimme that gun"; and as he sat, shoved his spectacles back—they always hung way down near the end of his nose—and shot, set the gun against a tree, gathered up his canes and hobbled into the house. The shot was a fine one, and one of the boys said: "Grandpa, I'll bet you can't do that again." "When you beat it, I'll try," he answered. But they never did.

Old Uncle George who was the father of uncle Abe, and who lived on the next farm south, was a very particular man, exacting and high tempered. Uncle Abe loved his gun, and one Sabbath a wild turkey came up to the little ravine just back of their old log house. Bill, the oldest boy,[5] saw it and went in and told Abe how it was, proposing that Abe get his gun and go back to the bake-oven which stood near by and shoot the turkey, saying: "I'll manage father." As soon as Abe was safely out—the wind was up—Bill said: "Father, do you hear the wind? It will blow the house down. Do you hear the trees cracking? There! do you hear that?" Uncle George was scared, but the turkey was lying, quiet, under the old bake-oven. The above is only legend, but, knowing all the persons, I can truly say such a thing might have happened.

My grandmother lived some two years after grandfather's death. She was feeble most of the time and craved game, so I was often sent to ask uncle Abe to get squirrels for her, and of course at such times I was at liberty to go along. He always cut a tough switch, with a hook at the end, to string the game on, and I carried it, and never allowed a squirrel on the string which wasn't shot through the head.

I early had a gun, an old breech burned rifle barrel that had the breach cut off and a new breechpin. It was a cheap affair, to be sure, but I was proud of it and shot many a ground-hog and fish with it too. The great trouble was to keep it out of sight of your grandfather and get powder and caps.

Those old rifles, bullet pouches and powder horns that came to the shooting-matches were, many of them, real works of art. Bits of silver, bone and the like were curiously inlaid in the stocks, and the horns were cut and carved with various devices, while pouches were fringed with buckskin, and I thought them all too fine, longing for the day when I might be a proud owner. Your grandfather never owned or fired a gun that I recollect, and just the same with your own dad; books ruined them both that way.

I think now I must tell you about the Fall with its apples and nuts. On the bottom lands of both the creek and river grew the nuts. Today it is the same, only young trees have taken the places of many of the old ones. I always had a yoke of calves and a sled or some other contrivance so we could get the nuts home without labor, and my! oh my! what fun it was, and what piles of nuts we did gather. We left the walnuts on the ground in heaps, flailed off the hulls, picked out the nuts and stored them away for winter. It was then that for a month or more our fingers, and, in fact, the whole hand, were about the color of a second-hand saddle-flap, and what rubbing and scrubbing Sunday morning to get the stain off. The butternuts made less trouble, and often we had so many heaped up that some were left out through the winter. Did you ever taste a walnut that had passed the winter under snow, before it had become rancid in the spring? If you didn't, there is one good thing you have missed.

Granddaddy Lazarus had a cider mill—we had one, too, but it was crazy with age as I remember it—so we took our apples to Lazarus' mill. Two, great wooden nuts, with depressions in one and long wooden cogs in the other, and a hopper to hold about two bushels, a sweep high over our heads, and a long, piercing screech followed by a thundering, trembling groan, composed the entire outfit. The neighbors for a mile around knew when cider making began and when it ended. Of course it was slow work, and we all had free use of the old mill, taking our turns with it. There were acres of clean, grassy sod all around, and the apples were heaped in great piles, with rye straw and barrels, each to await its turn; and the glorious smell of that apple-yard as it lazily blended with the soft air in the mellow hazy gray of Indian summer. Well, boy-words do a great length in giving expression to one's thought, but just here is one place mine fails, else I should go on and tell of the great wooden screws, the pummice laid up in rye straw rings, and the great, glistening, trickling rye straw cheese, oozing, bubbling and bursting at every pore as the great screw came down slowly, slowly, slowly, until the stream of cider at the scupper dwindled and finally trickled in drops, telling that the rosy-cheeked apples had given their all.

The eager, little, bare-footed boys and girls, the men all bespattered with the rich, juicy, sticky cider, the hospitable, big-bellied, old gourd. There were acres of apples and often many piles were left over covered with snow until spring; and that cider made from those frosted apples, if you have never tasted any, then you have missed another good thing.

Our cellar was filled with apples, and during the winter, until May when the cellar door was opened, the mellow, spicy perfume of them made the boy "fairly dribble at de mouf," as in trembling, eager haste he tumbled down stairs and scrambled up the bins filled with rambos, pippins, bellflowers, russets, greenings and many more. Often those who had no apples made cider in shares. Two men, Kibler and Forney, made up an orchard for uncle John; the apples came from his "Walker place." Your cousin Seth[6] and I (your grandfather was Seth's guardian) were waiting our turn at the press while Forney and Kibler were just finishing loading. Each had a wagon and his own barrels, but Kibler's were the smaller, and as each rolled his own barrels into their respective wagons Kibler protested against the unfairness of the division, but all the answer he got from Forney was: "No, no, Kibler, part about, Kibler, part about"; moral: "Git a plenty while you're a gittin."

To describe Indian summer as it was in our old place with its hills and valleys, golden trimmed foliage of the forest, and winding streams, "apple and peach tree fruited deep," "when the frost is on the pumpkin and the fodder's in the shock,"[7] when the heat of summer has slackened its grip and bid good bye, and a boy is beginning to look up the missing straps and buckles of his old skates, and the bobolinks and thrushes, wrens and chippies are going or gone with the stray woodpeckers, robins and blue-jays holding on waiting for the surly blasts to come and bridge the river with crystal and bind the mire like a rock—just betwixt and between—I think the good Lord tried his prentice[8] hand on one of the other months and then set to work and made October.

Our old spring was in a depression back of the house where, in fact, a spring might be had in any spot or at any time, and in my boyhood days there were two or more. One was a plank box, say, four by six feet and two feet deep. All over the bottom of it the gray sand was continually boiling up with the inflow of the water and was a pretty sight. The other was just a piece of hollow log, called a "Gum," and it was most used, though only a few feet from the big spring. Two or three rods to the west grew a mighty willow. Tradition said that a short time after the first immigrants came uncle John went back to Bethlehem, Pennsylvania, the old home, on business, and when he started on the return trip broke a willow twig which he used as a horse whip, and when he got home stuck it into the ground. It became finally a monster. About eight feet from the ground the top had been cut off, and from the stump set out a great number of mighty limbs, forming a low, broad, symmetrical top. That old tree gave us much pleasure. On the stump in the center the falling leaves made just the place for hens' nests and the hens knew it. The limbs—well, a boy could climb fast, run along on one, reach up and swing to the next; in fact, if he reached the old willow he couldn't be caught. Another willow grew below the spring, but the big one was the favorite. The water from the springs formed what we called the spring race, and for a rod on either side the ground was soft, cozy and cool, just the place for big, fat, fish worms, so there was never any time lost in getting bait. How many suckers were lured to the frying pan by those, big, fat, slidery worms. A little farther down the race was the old still-house[9]—only its foundation was left in those days—and perhaps eight or so rods below that the race fell into a sort of lagoon which had once been the bed of the river but was now filled with water most of the year and grown up with rushes and covered with lily pads. Before losing itself in the lagoon the race made a fall of about two feet over a dam made by the roots of an old elm, with a smooth velvety grass carpet under its shady top, and here was a spot where I had great pleasure. The little water-fall was utilized to drive an infinite variety of flutter-wheels,[10] and mornings and evenings as I went to pay my duty to the river the busy, sputtering, little wheels as they went dancing round and round filled my heart with pleasure.

The old orchard grew on the sunny slope on the north side of the race, though a few trees grew on the south bank, and in the fall the old race was full of apples, and the muskrats in the lagoon had their parties and picnics by moonlight, sometimes going so far in their folly as to fall into the spring, when they left a tribute in fur to your uncle. That old lagoon was full of mystery. In the summer turtles lay on the logs, and big bull-frogs kept up their "ah rum" all night long, and the little frogs and the big frogs would break out in harmonious concert at proper times and improper times and any time. Seemingly each little croaker was bound to outdo his fellows, and the rout of it and confusion of it was music to my ears. Here the cow black birds held their political conventions; the crane, shite poke[11] and the wild duck retired for rest and reflection; while the mink, weasel, groundhog and skunk made it a regular health resort.

I should just like to roll up my trousers once more and wade into it, feel the soft, cozy mud squash up between my toes, pull rushes, and get a big handful of skunk cabbage to rub under your Aunt Lucy's nose, and then see her run and tell "Pap." And here under the old elm in the gloaming let us lie down flat and quiet to listen to the music of my old flutter-wheels, let us keep eyes on the lily pads—there! don't breathe! see that rat—and there is another and another! How quiet they pop up. See the pretty wake they leave. They are coming right towards us, going up to the sweet apple tree. Pretty little fellows, aren't they? There now, what did you snap that twig for? Down they go. They are modest and don't long for our company. Do you hear the woodchucks clucking, and the whistling wings of the ducks as they come home for the night? And now mother calls from the spring. Come, get up, it's time to go home.

The upland of the farm on the north broke off with a steep hill which was covered with a growth of trees, lime, butternut and many others. Here grew spicewood, which we used in the spring to make sugar water beer. Sassafrass, too, grew further up the river, and that was a necessity in beer making. Here also were sunny patches where bloomed the early flowers. At one place the river struck the high bank nearly at right angles, and here on a sunny day one could look down and see the fish—bass, pike, sunfish, suckers, silversides and all the rest of them—a favorite place for shooting fish. Just across the river from the high bank was a great sycamore. The water had cut under the roots and the body hung out over the river, and in summer many an hour I spent rifle in hand, watching the fish below. There were many great trees growing close to the banks that gave good points for the fisherman. These high banks, where too grew wintergreens, were out at intervals by sharp gorges which had served in the long ago as water sluices or scuppers for the tableland. These were thickly wooded, and here grew slippery elm, black haws, wild plums and wild grape vines. Down one such gorge gurgled a merry, laughing brook. It ran past the school-house, and on its steep, wooded sides we played "I spy the wolf," and in all our games like "prisoner's base," "fox in the morning," etc., if a boy could get into this gorge he could give his pursuers a good chase. The brook, when it took a tantrum, would fret and worry and tug until a tree would give way and the long roots would strain away great patches of earth, leaving exposed the rock and shale, a streak of which was soap stone, and this we school boys used to work into slate pencils. These pencils were articles of barter and trade in the school, a good bought slate pencil being a most valuable treasure.

The river running east formed the north line of the farm. Island Creek running north cut it in two. Two-thirds of the farm, all the cleared land with the buildings being on the west, and all on the east side of the creek was timber with banks or bluffs fifty or sixty feet high. On the west the tableland sloped gently down to the creek, its shining green face turned to greet the very first ray of the morning sun with a kiss. Along this creek bottom, for the whole length of the farm, was the sugar camp. Some sugar trees grew in the forest on the upland on the east side of the creek, but we had plenty without, and the sap from the trees on the lower level was accounted superior, and truly those trees were fine specimens. The old camp was like a fine open park. Very few other forest trees were allowed to remain, and the ground was completely covered with sod; and we, your grandfather, your great-grandfather and your great-great-grandfather no doubt, worked it, making sugar and molasses. I have heard the old folks say that our people made and packed it to Pittsburg and traded it for salt, and a legend tells that your great-grandfather took the deed or patent for this farm and left it in pledge for a barrel of flour.

As soon as the warm sun in the early March began to melt the ice and snow, and sap-suckers began to bore holes through the bark, making wet places underneath, and a stray crow or hardy robin came back to tell spring was coming back, busy times began. Our three months' term of school was over. The sugar troughs were turned up, cleaned and stood up against the trees facing the sun. New troughs were dug out, and we young folk were sent to examine the old spiles,[12] sort out the imperfect ones, and make new ones. These were made from the elder stocks that grew in plenty everywhere. Such stocks as were suitable were cut to eight or ten inch lengths, the pith pushed out, and pointed at one end to enter the half-inch hole made by the bits. Then back-logs from twelve to twenty-four feet long, and shorter wood to feed the fires was gathered. Sap barrels, strainers, skimmers, kettles and so on were all gotten in readiness. Now some bright morning we would start, I with a half bushel basket of spiles and father with a half-inch auger. He bored the holes, placed the heavier troughs; I drove spiles and placed the lighter ones. After about two days of such work we said the camp was open.

We had a great store-trough and five or six kettles for boiling. The kettles were taken to the creek and scoured. Then a long, strong pole was placed in two forks and securely propped against two trees. A long, wooden hook hung from the overhead pole for each kettle, and now we take hand spikes and roll up a great log on either side of the kettles, fill them with water, start fire, and then the campaign was begun to last for about a month. In a good run we got from twelve to twenty barrels a day, and the gathering and boiling of this was no small job, I assure you. Do our utmost—boiling day and night—we could scarcely keep even at times. The gathering was with oxen and sled, with two barrels on a sled, each person being armed with two buckets. We had to cross the creek a half dozen times each trip, and, when the water was high, the task was not a light one. Sometimes a barrel would be washed away or the sled turn over—then we got wet all over. We had wet feet all the time anyway, as the best sugar making is always the very nastiest weather. Snow, frost and sunshine, with a good dash of rain, make up the ideal sugar season. Those days when a boy got wet feet he sat down on a rock or log, held his foot high in air till the water ran out of his boots, then went to the fence or a convenient tree root, pulled them off, wrung out his socks, and then went ahead all day. Nothing worse than sore throat ever came of it, and a rag and slice of fat, pickled pork made everything right again. I usually rode the near ox crossing the creek or coming home with a load.

From the time the first batch was emptied into the syrup tub we had plenty of sugar and taffy, and always ate so much of it that we thought that was what kept us so healthy. If you never stood over a foaming, bubbling sugar kettle with a tin of cold water and paddle, and let the hot, thickening syrup dribble into the tin, then pour off the water and find it half full of an amber filigree work, beautiful to look at and of all things most ravishing to the taste, then there is one more good thing missed. Set your teeth down hard on it and it cracks and snaps. As you press harder and harder the sweet goodness of it begins to spread and broaden till finally it trickles in a little stream down your throat, filling your whole body from the soles of your feet to the crown of your head with sweet, ecstatic bliss.

The camp or boiling place was a board roof, the top end of the boards resting on a pole, the other end on the ground, the open facing the fire and the creek. With plenty of straw and some old bed covers, plenty of eggs to boil and a loaf of mother's bread, I have spent many a happy day and night over the kettles, telling and listening to stories or the never ceasing purl of the water as it went laughing by to join the brimming river. The monotony of it was broken only now and then by the leaping of fish, or the awful cry of the screech owl, or the solemn "who who" of the horned owl. The neighbor boys often came and staid late. There was the syrup tub free to all, and the "minutes winged their way wi pleasure." "Kings may be blessed, but we were glorious, o'er all the ills of life victorious."[13] When day began to break, with the oxen to the sled, we started the same round again—up the creek and down the creek—gee! whoa! haw! Buck and Berry! Uncle Abe's camp was the next on the creek above ours, and he had a boy, Warren Clark,[14] just my age. During sugar making time we were much together, and "many a canty day we've had wi ane nither,"[15] for this was the time to secure stores of bark and log torches for gigging which came a few weeks later.

Uncle Abe and aunt Peggy were childless except such unfortunate human flotsam and jetsam[16] as they could pick up, though in that they were always successful, and so kept a full table. When the sugar making was over then came the farm work—plowing and planting—with always an eye out for the first run of the fish which came along about the first of May when the dogwoods were in blossom.

CHAPTER THREE

⌒⚫⚬

[Gigging Fish; The Farm Community]

I THINK THE sport we boys enjoyed the most and kept up the longest was gigging.[1] Our torches were prepared long ahead of time, in fact we always had our eyes open for the long, shell-bark hickories and kept them in mind. The torches were carefully laid about eight inches thick and six or eight feet long. We usually burned two, which would take us about one mile up the river, while some of the best parts of the river we gigged over a second time, winding up about midnight.

You say you want to go along some night. Well, you may if you will tote the fish. Here is an old bag. See! I'll put an apple in the bag, and 'twill make a lump in one corner of the bottom. Now we will tie the two ends together, leaving the mouth open. Now put it over your head; let it rest on one shoulder—so—and hang under the left arm, mouth to the front. See you don't yell every time you take a fish off the gig, or you will get the handle of one over your pate. Don't stumble, keep hold of the fish, keep back of the giggers, and be quiet. Don't splash as you walk. We shall carry one torch up a half mile and hide it before dark. We shall start in here at the mouth of Island Creek. This riffle[2] right above here is the first above the slack water of the carding dam,[3] and one of the best. In the dead shallow water, as we approach it, we may pick up a few bass. It's getting good and dark now, and we'll start a little fire to light the torch by. Here come the boys, some in rags and some in tags, old sheep-wash clothes, boots that neither hold the water out nor in, and each armed with a four pronged gig. They stick the gigs in the ground and stand round the fire, and, to look at the party clad in every variety of cast-off rags, old wool hats faded and limp with age, they are indeed an ill looking squad, fit for treason or thievery, but really they are only a party of honest farmer boys bent on having a good time and a mess of fish.

So after the hearty salutations, jokings and gossip are over, the torch bearer lays the end of the torch in the fire. Soon it flares up bright, and when he throws it on his shoulder the light of the great blaze as it moves along, throwing shadows in every direction, the darkness of the night, the solemn croaks of the bull frogs and the pipings of the little ones, the gurgle of the hurrying water, and the leaping and darting of the playing fish, make a scene not to be forgotten, while the keen, pleasant excitement of it has few equals here below.

And now for the water! Once in we form in line, torch in the center, two giggers on either side with intervals, say six feet, between, boy and bag in the rear, and you have the whole outfit. Now slow; slow and steady is the word. Bass are shy, so lift your feet carefully, and don't breathe. Keep your eyes peeled. There! Click goes the left-end gig, and a black sucker goes into the bag. Pound and a half black one is good enough. Over a little under this old maple tree. Click, and splash! You didn't get him. Oh! wasn't he a fine fellow. It takes close calculation and much experience to gig bass in water a foot deep; but we pick up a few along, and now we come to the foot of the riffle and can hear the fish holding high carnival. The bright light blinds them for a moment, and the gigs must do their work in that moment or it's too late. Now hold down the torch and slacken that withe,[4] it's too tight, the torch burns dead, knock the coals off with your gig handle, and loosen up the bark a little. Now she flares up fine. Look sharp now! Can you see the fish as they play around the gravelly bottom? No? Well you will learn after awhile. Now here we go, and click, click, click, click, goes the steel on the stony bottom, and boy and bag are everywhere, while big ones come so fast that there is no time to yell, and the bottom is too slick. There you go! Hold onto the mouth of the bag. Here is one; sock it in; and here's another and another. And here you yell like a Kickapoo Indian and scream with fright; and say: "The nasty, yellow, red brown, copper colored, twisting, slimy, slippery thing! It just wriggled through my hands! Ugh! What was it?" Only a water dog.[5] I just thought I'd scare you a little. It wouldn't hurt you anyway. Come on till we strike the slack water above, and then we shall go back and over that best part again. "Ouch, I'm afire." A spark or coal has fallen on some fellow, and in the joy of the moment is overlooked until the sting of it says, "I'm here"; but a handful or hatful of water fixes the matter, and we're off again. Sometimes we can see two or three torches at intervals way up the river, then we go ashore, sit down and wait half an hour—then set in again; and so it goes until both torches are burned and we are all tired. So we empty the bag and find maybe seventy to one hundred fish. We divide them, pack off home, tumble into bed, and are asleep by the time our heads touch the pillow, and it seems less than two minutes when I hear the call to get up and go for the cows. Such short nights don't grow any more. Then we clean the fish and have two great platters full for breakfast, nice, brown, fresh and crisp. Your uncle passes up his plate for a second helping, while your grandmother's smile recognizes the fairness of it, and when the lad leaves the table he has a sense of fullness under the apron.

"Backward, turn backward, oh! time in thy flight,
Make me a boy again just for one night."[6]

And I'll go a gigging.

In those days, too, seining was very common, and Saturday was usually the day for it. The seines were forty or fifty feet long, with cork and lead lines. A brail or smooth shaven stick, with a slack of rope tied at each end, is fastened to either end of the net; then a man takes hold of each brail, holding it upright; another steps in front and catches the rope, then the four men, with the net stretched between them, start to drag it up stream, with two or three following to lift the lead line when it catches on brush or snag, while half a dozen or more others go up the stream a short distance and, with long brush poles, whip the water, making all the noise possible and driving the fish towards the seine. Then the net is hauled in and, as it approaches the shore with its burden of fish cooped inside and darting this way and that in vain attempts to escape, the sight is one which the ever present small boy does not soon forget. After each haul the fish are sorted, the small ones being thrown back into the river. This operation is repeated until the seiners are satisfied with the catch, when the fish are all collected in one pile and one man chosen to divide the lot, allowing an equal share to the net. If there are twelve men, thirteen piles are started, always with the finest fish first, one at a place, and round and round they go until the big pile is gone and there are thirteen in its stead. Then the man who made the division is blindfolded; another steps forward and, with a stick in his hand, touches one of the piles, asking: "Whose is this?" The blind man calls the name of some member of the company, whereupon the man whose name is called steps out and claims the pile, and so it goes until the thirteen piles are disposed of. I never owned a seine or had an interest in one, but the noise of the seiners had a powerful attraction for me, and at times I found a convenient opportunity to retire without any great ostentation, going slowly and unconcernedly down through the orchard until I broke over the hill onto the bottom land amongst the ironweeds and milkweeds or wild cotton; then I let out a few links of speed "and the landscape sped away behind" like forty.

Nicknames were more commonly used then than now, and boys among boys were known only by these handy titles. Mine was "Fissle," as I went barefoot spring, summer and fall until cold weather set in and generally had one or two toe nails off, an assortment of stone bruises and a collection of thistles, which I called "fissles,"—hence the name—in my feet, to say nothing of thornes and ground itch between my toes.[7] For this last very common affliction a bit of woolen yarn tied round the toe was worn constantly as a remedy. Many times my feet would crack or chap in muddy weather when it was cool—little fine cracks—and oh my! they did get so sore and would bleed in the mornings.

In the evening I would come in, get warm and dry, curl up anywhere and go to sleep. Then when bedtime came we all had to wash our feet, and what a miserable, unhappy operation that was! After we were through washing and wiping mother gave us a lump of sheep's tallow to rub them with. Mine at times would be as black and hard almost as a turtle shell. Sunday morning there was always a cruel time of foot washing, but then it is to be remembered that if I had had shoes I would not have worn them unless compelled to, for how could a boy who wore shoes run or climb? As soon as I was big enough—and that was pretty soon—to drive up the horses from pasture, that was my duty, and I soon became an expert in climbing on their backs. If I could get hold of the mane I would wet the balls of my toes, set them above the knee joint of the fore leg, and in some way wriggle up till I was fairly seated. Now, how could a boy do that who wore shoes on his feet and had neither halter nor bridle? In those days I went to both school and church barefoot. My first Sunday shoes were mother's old ones. We had each just one pair of good, stout, cow hide boots a year, had our own leather tanned, and old Johnny Craft was the shoemaker for the whole neighborhood. Our boots were all made in the fall. We had our feet measured for them about cornhusking time, and then the old shoemaker would promise them "next week," when I was always on hand promptly, though neither he nor I expected anything to come of it for the first six or eight times. After that I became more urgent, so that after a week or two more he would cut the uppers out and tree them. Then the skirmishing grew hot. He would do a little with them each week, and pull them out from under his old bench to convince me that they were on the way. After a long time I got them. Then I felt in my pride that swelling of the heart that I ne'er shall feel again.

Many and many is the time, while waiting for my boots, I've gone through the thick hoar frost for the cows, and how glad I was to find them lying down so that I could drive them up one after the other; then run and stand on the warm spot where they had lain to warm my feet; and I doubt not that most farmer boys of my day could tell the same story.

Saturday evening was the regular time for greasing all the boots and shoes with tallow or neat's foot oil which we made from the feet and leg bones of the cattle killed on the farm for beef. The bones were all broken and the whole mass thrown into an iron kettle filled with water and thoroughly boiled. An oil raised to the top, which was skimmed off, put away and considered very precious.

When my grandfather died I was about nine years old and can remember well the long funeral train as it wound through meadow and bottom, up across Island Creek, through the woods, and up the hill to the old cemetery which was on our farm. Soon after that we moved into the old brick house to care for grandmother. The brick house was two stories high and much more commodious than our old one. It faced the south, with a nicely sloping dooryard in front reaching to the highway and bordered by great lombardy poplar trees; and flanked on the west by a locust grove. A tight, well-made wood house and a long shed opening to the east where bees were kept. Here stood the old flax-brake[8] and many odd tools, and many odd jobs were done here. On the east were other locust trees and what we called the little barn, where cows, calves and young stock were kept. To the east and adjoining the house was the wood house, a long, stout, one-story building, with double doors so teams could pass through with great loads of wood, and in winter when sledding was good it was filled to the beams with dry logs of beech, hickory and sugar. No fuel but wood was used or known about, and it took all the spare time in winter to prepare it for use.

To the north of the house and adjoining was a big kitchen where all the housework was carried on, and near the east door of which stood the old brick out oven, a great balm of gilead tree and a pear tree. Near the west door was a smoke and dry house lined on the inside with brick and mortar. A great locust tree or two grew near, and close to the west of it a number of pear trees.

On the west side of the old house was a garden, and that was a garden to look at. As you entered the paling gate,[9] to your left hand grew a large stock of lovage[10] which always gave toll to the hand of the passer. Right in front of the gate and running clear across the garden were two flower beds, and these were a blaze of glory from the earliest spring to the latest fall, filling the air with the perfume of pinks and roses, hollyhocks of all kinds and shades. Hardy pinks bordered both beds; sweet williams, gorgeous peonies, poppies and many others of which I never knew the names; but I do know that these flowers were the pride and delight of both your grandmother and mine, and visitors always admired them. Dill and sweet fennel, rue, wormwood, hoarhound and catnip, our medicine supply, mostly came from the garden, besides a barrel or two of sauerkraut and sichlike family supplies.

The partitions of the old house were altogether of boards, planed and matched. The east half of the lower floor was one great room with a very large, open fireplace and wide, hospitable hearth around which there was always room for one more, and he was always there. If I could only tell of all the things to which this open-mouthed, old fireplace was witness, I could make a big book. Here ministers, elders and wise men of the east gathered and laid solemn plans for widening the borders of Zion and strengthening her states; here the children were instructed in the catechism

> "Till, faith, I'd grown sae gleg,
>   Tho' scarcely langer than your leg,
>   I could screed you off effectual calling
>   As fast as ony in the dwalling."[11]

Questions of baptism, fore-ordination, election, falling from grace and the like have been gravely and solemnly discussed around this ample hearth,[12] and at the close of the evening sittings we always heard, in song or prayer, how

> "Guiltless blood for guilty man was shed;
>   How He, who bore in Heaven the sacred name,
>   Had not on earth whereon to lay His head."[13]

The west half of the lower story was divided into two rooms, one a fair sized sitting-room and back of that the bed-room. The upper story had a hall with rooms on either side and a narrow stair which led to the garret. This was a most wonderful place, I do assure you, with its wealth of odds and ends, a play house and fairyland for all children. All kinds of dried herbs hung from the rafters, and it was the hiding place for most everything. At either end alongside the big chimneys there were little windows, and no finer place than the old garret could be devised for a boy to retire and read stories. 'Twas a sort of haunt for us all, where we could entertain our visitors, and the pleasures of it never cloyed.

There was also a little room at the head of the stairs where sugar was kept in open barrels. Lord keeps aye free a' temptation. I'm afraid that from your daddy clear through down to your aunt Rosy, each one of us would plead guilty in the matter of sugar, and if you only could know how good it was I am sure you would condone the sin of it.

Over the old front door was a transome with a deep shelf or recess, and here was an interesting assortment of valuables to be found. It was a place to deposit everything from pocketbooks to tools and nails, and when all other parts of the house refused to give up the coveted articles that old transome came often to the rescue.

Near the south-east corner of the house and in front of the wood house, its branches reaching over the roofs of both, grew a monster apple tree, and on it grew as many different kinds of apples as there were colors in Joseph's coat,[14] but the finest of all were wine saps. In the late summer as they ripened they cracked open on the tree, and the bees were busily humming all day long in the top of it, burrowing in the sweet lipped cracks. Under this tree was that old instrument of torture—the grindstone—in the turning of which I did penance for many a sin.

In the north-east corner of the house was a door opening on the path to the spring, and it always went by the name of the "spring door." As you went out this door and turned sharply to the right you entered the wood house by a small door, and here is a little spot I have great cause to remember. High up, but in reach of your grandfather's long arm, ran a heavy beam, lying close to the brick wall, and here was always kept a well-seasoned assortment of whips. This was our clearing house, and the whips were used in the adjustment of all balances. Many's the time I've retired from the sordid cares and duties of life and betaken me to the solitude of the bottom land, there to hold sweet communion with nature, and have been overcome by the enticements of the old canoe, or the rod and gun. Oh!

how the minutes winged their way with pleasure, until, like the truant that I was, I turned my footsteps homeward, slinking along the old spring race in the friendly shadows of the apple trees and the willows and the old house, up the spring path, to be met at the spring door with a smiling invitation to the clearing house. The smile told me much more forcibly than words that the balance in the clearing house was heavy against me, and I soon realized that

> "Pleasures are like poppies spread,
> You seize the flower, its bloom is shed;
> Or like the snow-fall in the river,
> A moment white, then melts forever."[15]

And another old truth was borne in upon my mind with great power, this, that "now no chastisement is for the present joyous, but grievous"[16] but it was no less true then than now that "What can't be cured must be endured."

CHAPTER FOUR

❧

[Shearing, Butchering, Threshing; Lazarus's Mill; The Still-House]

To THE WEST of the house, and some two hundred feet beyond the garden and on the top of the slope, stood the old barn, and a rare old barn it was! The inner part was built of peeled hickory logs, with a big bay on the west side. On the east was a horse stable with a big mow over it and between the wide threshing floor above which was a scaffold. Sheep sheds were on three sides of it and open sheds to the front. On the side next the house the shed roof sloped down to within six feet of the ground, and we used to run up that roof, clear to the top, to take the fresh air. These sheds in the winter were filled with sheep.

Besides these we had two other barns, one on the south side of the farm opposite uncle Abe's, where we also had a tenant house, and the other about half way between. Then on our old north place across the river was another good sized barn. These were all filled with sheep in the winter, so you see that on the side of your dad you are descended from the shepherd kings. Indeed at that time our income was nearly all derived from sheep, and I have known your grandfather to pay a hundred and fifty dollars for one sheep and thirty dollars each for twenty head bought at one time. That must be fifty years ago, and what he did was common to all our old Hartzell kinsmen. I can well recollect that wool brought as high as fifty-six cents per pound, and buyers were as plenty as frogs in the old lagoon; while to tell of all the skirmishing and schemes of both buyer and seller, the advancing of pickets and videttes, and the cautious laying of parallels and breastworks, till the final struggle when the wool was all bought up in a day, except here and there a stubborn old fellow or a very fine clip held on, though more often to loss than profit. Then came the sacking of it, which was always a happy time for me. Sacks eight feet long and three feet wide, with a strong hoop in the mouth and swinging loose at the bottom. It was great fun to get into and tramp them full, when they were weighed, sewed and dropped on the floor.

The piles of wool when ready for market were white as snow, but first came the sheep washing. There were a few choice places along the river where pens were built in May, and when the water was right the washing began. Three or four men, clad in rough old clothes, went in, while one man stayed in the pen to catch the sheep, one by one and hand them into the water. Sometimes we built a shute just wide enough for one, and so steep that the sheep would just slide down into the water sort of easy. These places were always occupied, and flocks waiting their turns, and these times were great ones, for your uncle was equally at home in the water and out. Often one of the bolder sheep would dart into the water and swim for the other side, and then there was yelling and swimming and scurrying, for every sheep must be washed, there was no escape. Sure as fate they had to go down into the water and come up out of the water, though for the most part we were Presbyterians in faith, and only held to the above in the matter of sheep.[1] Sometimes the water was cold, and some of the more soft-hearted owners would provide a jug, and warmth and cheerfulness came with it, but I have often been in when the chattering of teeth made sorry music, and our bodies would be blue with cold below the water line. I recollect one time as the jug was tossed from hand to hand, it slipped and went to the bottom. Men waded to their necks to find it, but I got it by diving. Your grandfather never furnished, neither would he tolerate any liquor around either in harvest or at any other time. He was the only man of the many who could say so much and speak the truth, and this was his principle from boyhood. I have heard him tell how at public gatherings, log rollings, raisings and the like, his comrades would try to run him down and, when successful, would drench him with the bottle for holding to such audacious principles.

Well, the sheep were finally washed, and then came the long siege of shearing. The old barn floor would hold from six to eight shearers and the wool of one day's shearing, and the steady clack of the shears, as they went click, click, click, clip, clip—all day long for a week or two, made music which brought peace and plenty. I soon learned to shear, and the first money I ever earned through hard work I earned by shearing sheep at three cents per head. As soon as we finished I rolled up my kit[2] and started, and could make one dollar a day at it.

That old barn, if it could talk, would tell many a tale of fun and frolic, for it had more places to hide—sheep racks, horse mangers, oat bins, hay mows, straw sheds and a lot more. Those old logs were hard as flint and slippery as glass, and many an unhappy hour I spent mowing back hay under the roof of it on the hot summer days, and how often I have looked wistfully down to the hay wagon to see if the load was nearly off.

On one side of the horse stable door was a log with a wide yawning crack in it, and this was our bank of deposit, and was always known in the family as the "treasury crack." There your grandfather always kept a stock of pipes, old pipes and new pipes, pipes with long stems and pipes with short stems, and in that old treasury crack and the transom over the door could mostly be found any small thing of value about the place. So take it for all in all, the old house and the old barn and the old farm steading were altogether commodious, roomy, rangy, friendly, hospitable old buildings for their day and time, and did not belie their looks.

Their great questions of the day were viewed and discussed intelligently in the great room of the old house, and, while the local horizon was very limited fifty years ago, I believe that the men who compared notes in yonder old room could not be matched in mental breadth by any like gathering of men in their class today. The isolation of the farmer did not cause mental stagnation and dry rot, but rather gave free opportunity for good mental digestion. The strong food of that day was the Bible and the constitution of our country, and no set of men was more familiar with either of these than your Hartzell forefathers, and the angry winter's storms which howled around the old house and down the wide, deep-throated old chimney caused a sense of contentment to circle round the hearth. With equal assurance of hospitality came the birds back to the old barn in the spring; the swallows to the same old nests on the same old pole rafters year after year; while the wren and the pewee and sparrow, each and all, knew the shelter of the old cracks and crannies of the sturdy old logs, and seemed all to delight in singing, "home again, home again from a foreign shore."[3] What places those cracks and knotholes were for bumblebees' nests! And how many wily tricks have been played to get the school boys as they passed to examine cracks that were loaded! And how many battles have been fought with the little, yellow soldiers around the old barn. Alack and

Alas! The boys who fought those battles soon had other battles to fight, and today all that remains of many of them is scattered from Antietam to Vicksburg. All that they had to give, they gave—the last full measure of devotion that the land we love might be and remain one and undivided. "Greater hath no man than this—that a man lay down his life for a friend"—and that they did for you and for me and all who are to come hereafter.[4]

Butchering was one of the interesting events of the year to me. The kettles were filled with water, for scalding, the night before, and long before daylight the fires were lighted, and as soon as uncle Abe could see through the sights of his gun things began to crack and blood to flow as the squeals of the dying porkers rent the air. Almost any farmer could dress a pig, but when the yearly killing of eight or ten came around the neighbors turned in and helped each other; and here comes old Kibler—regular on all such occasions. He has no brains to speak of, but a mouth like a rift in the rocks or hole in a brick wall—handy about tobacco and to eat or make a noise with. But he could stick a pig or prepare the casings, chop the meat for sausage and stuff it with a neatness and dispatch born of long experience, and in this he delighted. The chopping of the sausage meat was done by two men armed with light cleavers. It began in the evening by candle light and usually lasted until quite late. The old skillet was on the coals all the time filled with little meat patties, and all ate, tasted and gave most solemn judgment as to the seasoning, pepper, salt, sage and the like. It took many skilletfuls of patties and much deliberation to come to the right conclusion on this very grave matter, and here old Kibler came out strong. After about the fourth skilletful his judicial opinion was formed, and there were no exceptions taken and no appeals.

My fun was to blow the bladders, put in beans or corn and a handle to make rattles for the youngsters; carry water, run errands and be in the way generally. 'Twas a long, hard day's work, but good humor prevailed and made the time pass pleasantly, and when the old smoke house was full of nice round shoulders and hams, the barrel full of pickled pork and jars full of long coils of sausage, the future seemed assured. The pig had filled his generous mission and is surely entitled to honorable mention in these chronicles. Our pig was a fair kind of fellow and could "eat his peace and accumulate much grease," shedding his blessings long after in doughnuts, mince pies, hams, sausages, schnitts and knep,[5] soap, bristles, etc.

The pig of today stands at the spout; wrecks and swallows railroads, grabs this way and that for wheat, corn and coal, bonds, gold—everything in sight—monopolizes the whole trough while the ten thousand stand around to get a whiff of his breath, and beg this lordling of the earth to give them leave to toil. No, I'll not disgrace our old-time pigs by the comparison. Of course those days we didn't know much about angel's food, ragouts and bedeviled things to eat, still we lived well enough and some good things are nearly forgotten. There is the old dish of schnitts and knep, dried sweet apples with the skins on, a ham bone and dumpling—boiled in a big iron pot and served hot. When a man was filled up on that he was fit for anything his hand found to do.

Come up to the big barn. You hear that steady thump, thump, thump, thump, all day long? Well, come and see. Two sturdy fellows stand face to face. See the quick singing tree of the hickory flail? At every thump the creamy wheat rattles on the barn floor like hail on the ice. It takes muscle to make that music from early morning's ruddy light till the last fiery glow in the west shoots between the lowest logs of the old barn. Ask them how it is, and the answer will be "schnitts and knep, schnitts and knep."

Do you see the regular, curved, rhythmical swing of those four old grain cradles[6] as the tips of the fingers show over the standing wheat in the old hill field over there? No haste, no dallying, but with slow, steady tread they sweep round that ten acre lot, and before sundown every golden head that bends and sways to the wind will be laid low. Pick up one of those cradles and try it. It's easy to look at. Guess not—well you are right. I see you notice those shirts saturated, dripping, the trousers reeking, and the deep, bare, hairy breasts streaming with sweat. No, these men are not here for their health. It's the fifty cents a day they are after, and schnitts and knep is the motor.

Do you hear that chopping in the woods across the creek? The men are making rails up near the old graveyard. Let's cross the hill field and lower meadow and go over the creek and up the old woods road, and watch them a bit. Here are the big oak and hickory, and here are the men at work with maul and wedge and ax. Up here is a great old oak lying prone, cut in eleven foot lengths for rails, and here are two men with heavy knot mauls and wedges trying to open the butt cut.[7] This is hard work; at every swing the breath comes out with a short, sharp grunt, and the brave old oak groans and writhes as wedge is followed by wedge. The fiber of the wood, heart and sap begin to part and snap. No, let up now, till finally the sturdy old log parts in the center, the two halves fall apart, and the hardest part of it is done. I tell you, my boy, the very smell of those freshly split rail cuts makes a fellow hungry, but both heart of oak and hickory had to yield to the man with the maul fortified by schnitts und knep, flanked by apple butter and sort of held in place with a plate of lye hominy. Boys raised upon and nourished by such food make a safe guard for the colors, and whether you look at the dawn's early light or the daylight's last gleaming you will see the flag floating high in the air while there is life enough to hold the staff.[8]

One day in the long ago a dutchman by the name of Schneerly was thrashing with the flail, of course, in the old barn, and had earned two bushels of wheat. He wanted to take it to mill to be made into flour. In those days we had long linen bags, home-made, to hold three bushels or more. When the wheat was measured up your grandfather said to the man: "There is old Fan. You can take her and pack it over"; but the dutchman said "no," and asked "if I carry over three bushels, will you give me the extra one?" "Yes." The sack was filled, and your grandfather saddled old Fan, the man shouldered the sack, and they started off together to uncle Peter Lazarus' mill, the old brown one that kept up such a merry clatter only a mile off to the east. It's a pretty road, let's go too. Come on! Here just below the barn the road curves a little to follow the trend of the hills and get down to the creek by an easy grade, and just here in the curve is the old water trough. Part of the generous surplus of the old spring is carried over to the road, and many a tired and thirsty horse as he slaked his drouth with clear, cold spring water, if he only knew would doff his cap and say: "Thank you," to your grandad, but how could he know when your grandad didn't advertise.

But, come on! Here we go down a gentle slope, and half way down it we begin to meet the old videttes of the sugar camp.[9] We don't need the countersign. Hurry up! Here we are at the creek; roll up your trousers; the water isn't deep. Here, see the big white sycamores, ghostly old sentinels of the forest that have been standing their watch since the Mayflower landed her first living burden at Plymouth Rock. Here we start up the big hill—half way up the hill—here is a sort of bench, and here is fine old cucumber[10] and a tall hickory or two. Off one of those hickories I shot my first owl with my rifle. He was a big fellow; as he came flopping to the ground with a broken wing I rushed up and grabbed him, when he bit me till I howled, and clawed me with his long talons till I was bloody as a butcher, so that with prayers, kicks, struggles and many tears I got clear of him, when he turned on his back and guarded every point of approach with beak and talons. Finally, I despatched him with a long pole, and when I carried him home I took my trophy in one hand and my gun over my shoulder, and from that time on my gun was allowed an honorable place.

Your daddy never took an interest in such things that I can remember, still I think even then he would have known which end of the gun to have pointed at the mark on account of the round hole in the muzzle and because of his knowledge of books which tell of such things.[11]

Now we shall follow the bend to the top of the hill. This big, red oak on the north side of the road is just half way up, and from here to the top it's pretty steep. At the top the road winds along the high bluff that flanks Raymond's Bottom where we used to go to the shooting-matches. Listen to the chipmunks! They're singing their evening songs and taking their last scamper before going to bed. Aren't they pretty, striped, little fellows? There is a happy colony of them, and they have an ideal home. See the hanging birds' nests. Orioles are at home here, and these nests hang here from year to year. Any winter day you can come along under the hill here and count a dozen vacant, swinging, swaying, little pouches—the summer home of the pretty "Flash of flame that shook the dew from his wings and sang in the morn so sweet, over the wheat, over the wheat."

Here on this bank the wild-grape vines and twists and tangles in sheer wanton idleness, curling, embracing and knitting tree to tree, and covering all with the foliage their broad green leaves furnish in such luxuriance. Here I saw once upon a time, before I owned a gun, a flock of wild turkeys running along this edge of the hill, a dozen or more, single file, and they seemed to have very urgent business down the river, as they ran very fast. But come! Make haste! Here is a little over the head of a deep, rocky ravine which opens out just above the cow ford. That's where the water is over your head, and where we swim the horses in harvest time in the evenings to take off the sweat. It's the old swimming hole with its dry, shady bank under a few stunted, starved, spruce pines looking so tired, and just ready to let go and fall on a fellow's head. Below here again used to be an old spring with huckleberries, blackberries and wintergreen.

But there they are just turning the bend out of sight, the horse and rider, dutchman and sack. Here just to our right is a little notch out of the woods, with an old deserted cabin in the clearing, where used to live an old, black man, but that is long ago. Now we'll strike a trot to catch up to them before they reach the mill. Here to the right lives Deacon John on the very spot your great-great-great-granddaddy first camped, and here is the old cider-mill, and old uncle Fred Lazarus on the right, and John, his son, on the left just opposite, and Peter, the miller, under the bluff.[12]

And here we are at the old brown mill, and here is uncle Peter on the platform in front of the mill door, and over his head dangles a long rope with a hook at the end, used in pulling the full sacks up to the second story. Here comes the man with his three bushel sack and his mounted guard, and with firm tread mounts the four or five steps to the platform, and uncle Peter points farther up, so the man with the sack mounts the ten or twelve steps to the second story, and has fairly earned his extra bushel of wheat.

This mill is on Mill Creek, and a mile farther up is uncle Jake Sheets' saw-mill.[13] He died at ninety and remembered well the wailing and mourning of the people at the death of Washington. He married your grand-aunt Betsy,[14] and tradition has it that while Jesse Grant, father of the General,[15] ran the tannery at Deerfield, he and uncle Jake were rivals for aunt Betsy's smiles, but our old people didn't tell tales out of school, so I can't verify this. Uncle Jake had a cozy old place up there. Mill Creek cut the farm. There was a nice water-fall on it and an old saw-mill with a single muley saw set in a big stout wood frame. It was slow but sure and gnawed up in its leisurely way many a big tree.

Uncle Jake's mother lived with him in one part of the house. Over her room was a loft with a vinegar barrel in it, and in this barrel was a wooden spiggot. Jake Winans, his grandson,[16] and I, of the same age, were visiting there and exploring the upper regions of the house, when we came across the spiggot which was a new and mysterious piece of machinery. We could start the vinegar all right, but no persuasion would stop it, and the stream soon found its way through the ceiling into grandmother's room against her protest. The men were sent for, and your uncle, well knowing that he could be of no service in such a case and that his further presence might be an annoyance, quietly retired to his home and friends, and gave his entire attention to business until after church on the next Sabbath day. A glance at the fine old faces of his uncle and aunt revealed to his alert mind that the dreadful crime had not been published. Once more I could look the world in the face, though the hint of it for long years afterward sent me into retirement.

I thank the old still-house for many things. Uncle Jake's people lived some seven or eight miles to the south, but I can readily believe that the attraction of the still-house would reach that far and farther, though miles of unbroken wilderness filled with wolves and bears lay between, for afterwards I marched days, weeks and months through Kentucky, Tennessee and Georgia, with wild mountains on every side and forests everywhere, yet applejack and the fruit of the still were ever present, though I never saw a still in my whole life.

Uncle Jake used to tell me of the route blazed through the forests, and how on one trip he shot a black bear about half a mile south of Beloit. Uncle Henry's first wife was his sister, so that made them double brothers-in-law, and yet for all that there was never the greatest cordiality between them.[17] Uncle Jake told me that when uncle Henry was sparking his sister they lived in a log house with wooden pins driven into the logs for clothes hooks. Uncle Henry came in one night with a long sort of wamus or hunting shirt on his arm. He hung it on one of the pins over some other garment, and when he started away reached for his wamus and stripped the pin. That night uncle Henry had a woman's nightgown, and the old lady had none, and when the old fellow told it the crack in his face curled clear round behind both ears, though he was then past eighty and should have been thinking of other things.

Old Doctor Dellenbaugh, one of the first doctors I ever heard of, was a brother-in-law to both, having married a sister of uncle Jake. He was a juriscopist[18] but had another shorter title which I should not like to write down. Anyway he had a big practice, so people thought when Doctor Dellenbaugh came into the house with his pill bags death just grabbed up his old scythe and dart, broke out of the window, door or anywhere, jumped the back fence and cut for the woods. Like Jack Hornbrook he had:

> "A doctor's saw and whittles
> Of A' dimensions, shapes and metals,
> True sal-marinum of the seas,
> The farina of beans and peas,
> He hast in plenty;
> Aqua fortis, what you please,
> He can content ye."[19]

But the doctor had one fault, maybe two, though if he had I never heard what the other was, but of the one,—John Barleycorn[20] and he lived too good neighbors, and often the old Doctor got the fling. It came about in that day that a great temperance wave rolled over the land. The Doctor was converted and gave John Barleycorn the go-by. Then he joined in to rescue the perishing, and in this had an always ready helper in your grandfather, who was always a great temperance worker; so the two joined forces and preached temperance from school-house to school-house. For a long time the work prospered, until one cold day your grandfather met the Doctor in a state—"the dog had returned to his vomit"—and when your grandfather, in astonishment, inquired: "How's this, Doctor, I thought you were lecturing on temperance, and here you are drunk again?" Then the Doctor replied: "I yust dell you how id vas, Vret. I zaw id vas no use, und de only vay vas for de riches to gid ad id und dring id all ub from de boores zo de boores gouldn't git any." I tell you this to show you the straits to which temperance people were put to work out their reform.

Now let's go back to uncle Peter's old mill again. Here we are at the fore bay. Now see when he raises the gate the water rushes onto the wheel, and as the buckets fill the old wheel begins to turn and the hopper starts up its song and the merry clatter is begun. Up in the mill are a dozen little groups of sacks awaiting the farmer boys with their pack horses. How many, many times I've packed two sacks of wheat, riding on the top, balancing, shifting my weight from side to side to keep the sacks from sliding off, and clutching the hindmost sack with one hand and the horse's mane with the other, straining with all my might coming up the hill to keep them from going off over the horse's tail. Down hill I could make the horse hold his head high by tugging at the bridle, so making a hill or dam of the horse's neck, which prevented the sacks from slipping forward. Here are big bins of wheat—uncle Peter's toll—a good place to play.

> "Rickollect the dusty wall,
> And the spider-webs, and all!
> Rickollect the trimblin' spout
> Where the meal comes josslin' out—
> Stand and comb yer fingers through
> The fool-truck an hour er two—
> [. . .]
> Rickollect the flume, and wheel,
> And the worter slosh and reel
> And jest ravel out in froth
> Flossier'n satin cloth!
> Rickollect them paddles jest
> Knock the bubbles galley-west,
> And plunge under, and come up,
> Drippin' like a worter-pup."[21]

But, come now, let's be going down the creek. See what a smooth, slippery, rock bottom it has! Here on the left is the high bank, and half-way up a ledge of hard sandstone sticks away out, fretted and worn with age into many graceful shapes with curves and waves. Up there on the top are wintergreens again, and now we come to the mouth where the creek is lost in the brimming river just below the carding dam. The water isn't very deep on the breast of the dam, and we are barefoot. Roll up your trousers again, and we can wade over on the dam. No? The roar of it won't hurt you. Well, then, here, get on my back and I'll tote you over. Now be careful and don't choke me; keep still, and I'll carry you safe over. So, here we are. It isn't so bad when you get used to it. Now, we'll cross the bottom to the foot of the bluff. Yes, this is the race. It takes water up there just below the rocks, and there is a water gate to regulate it. Isn't it a fine little race? See it skirts the bushy, rocky bluff covered with a low growth of water beech, haws and wild plums, winding in and out, the overhanging limbs and foliage hiding it here and there, a deluded wayward little stream. But when we go a little farther we shall see that this little stream has a mission, and that's why it hurries so. Here we come to Bill Barr's fulling mill,[23] and here our silly little stream leaps against the breast of the big, rough-looking wheel, and round and round it goes and creaks and groans and pounds, and still our little stream leaps and dashes and pushes the protesting thing.

Now let us go back a little. At sheep shearing time all the tags and bits of wool are taken and picked and cleaned and such other wool added as will be needed for the household supplies in the coming year—for stocking yarn, blankets, linsey-woolsey[24] for the dresses of the women and wamuses of the men. Now the whole is tied up in a sheet or sacked, a lump of soap rolled up in a burdock leaf,[24] and the boy is started to the fulling mill. Our old friend Barr empties the wool into a big hopper and turns on soap and water and sets two, great, wooden mauls going, raising and falling alternately on the woolen mass with a heavy bump, bump, and whole is churned into a white frothy foam. This is scouring. From here it is taken and dried, then passes over an endless apron to the carding machine, where it is pulled, hauled and twisted until it comes out at the other end a long, white, fluffy roll, when it is ready for the old spinning-wheel that stands, in the summer, in the little room at the head of the stairs with the sugar barrel; so you see that our sly, hurrying, little stream has its mission. "Never does the streamlet glide useless by the mill."[25]

Over across the river, just in sight, lives Thompson Craig, his wife Katy, sister to uncle Abe.[26] Bill Barr married a Linton, and they are mixed up with the Hartzells too some way, but this leads to the indivisibility of matter and endless tangles like the wild grape vines on the hill; so now let's go back up the north bank of the river. We will follow up the race to the rocks. There the water hugs the bank so closely we shall have to scramble over the hill and down again just below the cow ford onto a fine bottom. You can see here old lagoons where the river has changed its bed in the long ago. The river must go on a tear two or three times a year. It grows restless with its mild, low, purling, gurgling music, and when thaws dissolve the snow hordes or the fall rains come, then she growls and fumes and roars and rips up the bottom lands in great deep trenches and sings another tune. No use talking temperance to her now. She's got too much water on her stomach already and is humping herself to get rid of it.[27]

Now here we come to Taylor's right on the bank, and at the foot of it lies the old dugout canoe—what lots of rides I've had in it—but we'll go on up the river to old Jimmy Carter's. He has a lot of big boys, though we never had much to do with them, they being mere Methodists, but they were all fine giggers, and Jim always made my ground-hog skins up into whip lashes for me, so I like them pretty well and would go in only I'm afraid of old Mary. She has a great lot of geese, and they wander along the river, and we kids have to have pens to write in our copy books at school, so I have to catch her geese to get the wing feathers or quills for pens. Then Mary tries to catch me, but I don't intend she shall, so let's go along up a little farther above the ford, get some sassafras root, and then home.

Up here lives John Diver[28] who cheated an Indian on a horse deal, and whose brother, blind Dan—he lives a little father on—was shot by Mohawk, the Indian, in revenge. He was wearing his brother's coat, and had just entered his door to take it off when the bullet whistled through, striking him across the nose just deep enough to take both eyes. There are a lot of these Divers, old and young, and I hear that in the long ago they became mixed with the Hartzells.

But now let's cross the river to the south side and across the flat above that high bank, and now we are in our school district. Here live Whites. Thank goodness! They are no relation, except we could go back to Adam. Here are Ebenezer and Ad and Dave and Lucy and Susan. Eb went to the war in an Indiana regiment and got to be major and was killed. Ad studied medicine, went into the army and died. Across there lives old Jimmy Bryant. He sent four boys to the war. One was killed at Chancellorsville, and the rest, I believe, got home.

Now home, past uncle Billy Hartzell's, over Wolf Trap run and by the school house. So you see we started east to the mill, then north down mill creek, then east to the carding mill, then back west on the north side of the river way past our place, across the river again to the south, back east again to the west side of our place, and home by the old barn. And now mother has a hot corn pone in the dutch oven for supper. I'm hungry and tired, and the cows are to get up and milk, and the pigs to feed. You say you will help. Well, go up to the barn, let out all the horses but old Finn, put the bridle on him, ride up the creek and get the cows.

CHAPTER FIVE

~~~

The Calves; A Trip for Whitewash

The Calves

ONE TIME IN the dim past we had a sick calf, and, as it seemed past hope and quite worthless, your grandfather sold it to me for five cents. With good care I finally won it back to health, and from that time I made many excursions among the neighbors to find a proper mate for him. At last I found one at granddaddy Lazarus', which I bought for three dollars. How I ever got the money to pay for him I don't know. Anyway I got him home and soon had a nice little team. The next spring one day I had my calves yoked up, and Seth and your dad were together some place between the big barn and the garden. They ranked as big boys and I a little boy, your dad being just home from foreign school. I wanted to show my things too, so I drove my calves around in style, and at last brought them up close to the big boys so that they might look them over. The chain was still hooked to the ring and dragging on the ground. Finally I thought I would unyoke them, so took the bow off the near one, and while I was replacing the now empty bow the off steer made a dart, taking yoke, chain and all. He went so quick that the chain flipped around one of my ankles and hooked, and then away we went round the lot, an excursion by lightning express. Of course he yanked me down and dragged me, forked end first, lickety bump, round and round a two acre calf lot, out by the brick pond, past the old cider press, down by the orchard, up by the old smoke house and pear trees, I thumping and bumping, grabbing and yelling, till at last I got hold of the chain with one hand and pulled myself up in sitting fashion, and while this position did not expose so much of my body to be bruised and fretted by the lumps and chunks and stones which lay in the route chosen by my calf, still it was doubly oppressive to my now limited bearings, and though my patch-reinforced-tow-linen trousers did not rip nor tear, the rapid grinding movement soon made an unhappy breach in them. I tried to pull myself forward to get enough slack on the chain to unhook it, but failed. Then as I was flying by an old peach stump I let go the chain and grabbed the stump with both hands. By this skillful move I snubbed the motor, but the calf bellowed and tugged and pulled till I felt I was being raveled out like an old stocking. I roared for help and, looking around, saw those two idiots writhing and tumbling in delight at my calamity, like a pair of "blathering, blustering, drunken blellums."[1] At their leisure they came and freed me from my toils. Of course my wardrobe was something worse of the little exercise. My trousers, what was left of them, were mainly a hole with some linen fringes, and my body was all wounds and bruises. Willie, you think your dad is an angel,[2] but I know better, for that calf was as gentle as a lamb and never would have done me that way if your dad hadn't jabbed him with pen knife blade or something stirring.

That same summer your dad and I made a little cart for the calves, and you know the tongue must be split and spread to rest on the axle of the cart. So we got a hickory pole and split the butt, yet spite of all we could do the split would run too far up the pole, and so spoil the tongue whenever we tried to spread it. Things were in this shape when one morning your grandfather went to Benton to old Sam Foy's blacksmith shop to see about a new wagon we were getting made. Your dad and I went along— cross lots by uncle Abe's and old Ricker's tan yard. When we got to the shop the smith was forging a lot of rings, and we saw at once where one of them would be useful. I touched them a little with my toes until I found one cool enough, and afterwards, as we boys were trudging along behind your Grandfather on top of a rise just opposite uncle Henry's old house, I found that miserable ring in my pocket, took it out, and your Dad and I were quietly talking of the good use we should find for it on our cart tongue, and were making no noise to disturb anybody at all, when your Grandfather, who was a rod or two in front, turned round quick, and a glance told the tale. I clutched the ring and was putting it in my pocket when he said quick and sharp: "What have you there, my Son?" I saw the balance was against me. There was an old beech tree whose long branches reached quite out into the road, and, as he took out his knife and looked up, the beech limbs seemed to say: "Here we are, we know that boy." I took a double dose of the same old medicine, though with many loud protests, and when I had finished the last, bitter, burning dregs of it your Grandfather said: "Now take that ring back to the shop and don't let the grass grow under your feet. I trust you won't forget this." And I haven't. If you could have stood there that hot, dusty summer morning on the brow of the little hill with your venerable Daddy and Granddaddy, you would have seen through a long, trailing cloud of dust a little, dark, plunging, leaping, flying object, straight in the center of the highway, you would have justly said: "That is the flying machine," though it was only your Uncle obeying the commands of your grandfather. I really don't blame anybody for that licking; the occasion seemed right for it and all the circumstances convenient. The old beech tree rather invited it. How could it be otherwise, and I have long expected it as one of the decrees of Providence, and "The Lord loveth whom he chasteneth."[3]

A Trip for Whitewash

In those long ago times still bright in memory's early rays "when all was fair and new," we often had no lime to whitewash at the spring cleaning time, so we used to use a sort of white clay which we got on old Uncle Abe's place just south of the old grave-yard; and now your Grandmother wants some, and if you will get that little, old, splint basket with the oak handle you may go along if you want to. Well, here we go down the road by the little barn to the old water trough, and now here at the creek we turn up and go through the bars. Do you see this big, old walnut tree? The top has been broken off long ago and about twenty-five feet of the stub stands. How thick is he at the butt? Three or four feet, you guess, and that isn't far from right. You see here at the ground some beast of a fellow, maybe an Indian, long ago has made a fire, burning and charring it. A big patch of the bark is gone, but growth upon growth of new wood has formed and slowly worked inward until it meets in the center of the scar, making a complete curtain for the old wound. Trees are kinder and more skillful than people. See, there is a long scar left, and that is rather ornamental, but if you get down on your knees—here, put your head close to the ground—and look in, you can see the old burned patch. Put your arm in, reach up and around, and you find a pocket. Well, that pocket is always full of hickory nuts and shells and dry grass and cotton from the cotton-weed pods, and here, I think, is where the King and Queen of the chipmunks have their winter palace. One spring day when I was a little fellow like you, as I was wandering along the creek looking for fish and muskrats, I thought I would put my hand in that same hole and see what I could learn. I lay flat down to get the full length of my arm. When I had it in up to my shoulder I felt some little thing, warm and soft, that screamed out in a sharp little "chit-it-it-it" and then if your uncle had had just a little of wit or good manners he would have taken his hand out and said: "I beg your pardon; I didn't know anybody lived here." But he hadn't, and just grabbed the little thing round the body tightly and dragged him out. So just to teach your Uncle a lesson, the little fellow set his long teeth into my thumb, biting it through and through, and when I tried to shake him off he was just like Aunt Jemina's sticking plaster,[4] so I jabbed my hand and all into the creek here and held it under water. When I let go then my thumb began to swell, and I ran home to your Grandmother, who put some fat meat on it and a rag round it. But how sore it did get! The pencil I am writing with this minute touches the scar of it, so that's what makes me remember this old walnut, and whenever I see a chipmunk, and he jeers and guys[5] me about my old hat or my one gallus or anything, I say: "You go long and tend to your own business, and I'll tend to mine." That's the way I got most of my education, and what a fellow gets that way stays by him.

You see the old stump hates to give up life. It has started a lot of limbs up there where it was broken off and every year gives us a few walnuts. Here by the creek at the old ford are two pretty fair sized willows, one on either side. Along the lower side of the fence, on either side of the road, is a row of willows. These are to hold the fence when the water is up, and keep the rails from floating away. A flood gate hangs across the creek, fastened to the willows above the ford, and here between the old walnut and the creek was our last sugar-camp.

Now we go along up the creek, the green, springy sod under our bare feet, with here and there patches of spring beauties garnished with the long, dark leaves of the shy leek,[6] and the crowfoot[7] peeping from under the warm shelter of the sugar leaves where they have been piled up in the eddies along the fence by the hoarse, hurrying, ripping, biting winds of winter. Do you hear the soft, cooing purling of the creek and chorus of the blackbirds, thrush and plover[8] that join to swell the merry refrain? Did ever the foot of King or Queen tread on more luxurious carpet, or their ears enjoy more beautiful music? I tell you, Willie, my boy, when you get to be an old fellow, and have rumatiz and miseries and specs and things, you will, when you think of this, sigh and say:

> "Oh the days gone by! Oh the days gone by!
> When the bloom was on the clover and the blue was in the sky,
> When life was like a story, holding neither sob nor sigh,
> In the golden, golden glory of the days gone by."[9]

But here we come to the bars of the lower meadow, and here let's turn in a bit. It's a beauty spot of maybe three acres, sort of cove hidden by tree crested hills and shaped like a horseshoe with open heel to the creek. Just inside the bars is a walnut tree and a pile of old, fire-marked stones. Some day, long ago, those old sugar trees have paid tribute here. Just over the fence, a little nearer the creek, we used to have a camp. Now let's sit down on this stone pile and see if we can waken up the past and run back a little while. Just why we called this the lower meadow, I can't tell. There are two, one just back of us, and both of them reaching nearly to the creek and fringed by the big sugar trees on the lower side, but this lower meadow is the fartherest up the creek and quite hidden from view of the house by the hill field. The other is spread out in plain sight of the house. This one, as you see, is very nearly level, with a sort of little gully running more than half way through, and here at the head of the gully is a clump of crab-apple and hawthorne trees. You see the tops mingle and the white and pink of the crab-apple blossoms blend with the milk-white bloom of the thorne, so when you come up the creek in the gloaming to hunt the cows, when the sweet perfume of them mingled with the lilies, sweet-williams, butter-cups and johnny-jump-ups[10] that grow everywhere, settles down, you blow the wind all out of your body, shut your mouth, and, with a slow, long drawn breath, your head and heart filled with bliss, you think of heaven and the angels and of the "Sweet fields beyond the swelling flood" and which "Stand dressed in living green."[11] Here you might come at early morning in the summer and hear such a chorus of bird music—blue bird and bobolink. Did you ever listen to the liquid notes of the bobolink? That was your Grandmother's favorite. Then there was the cat-bird or brown thrush. He is a notable singer, a real Melba,[12] and the robin when he is happy makes a good second; the saucy little wren, the silly pewee, the shy little chippy[13] and shoals and nations of the "bonny lark, companion meet, as upward springing, blythe to greet the purpling East."[14] And here grew all the flowers—crows-foot, wild potatoes, indian turnips, and the pretty, white-hooded blood-root, bluebells on the hillside—and here we used to string raspberries on timothy stalks, like buttons on a string, and when the stalk was long and fruit ripe the lower ones would squash so we had to eat them on the way home. I have tossed and raked hay in this meadow many a day, and when "the artist of the sky" shot his beams of light and heat straight down into it one thought of the burning lake,[15] but nearby was the merry creek piping its sweet little note telling of cool soothing pools o'er-shadowed by elms and sugars, beech and oak, and only one gallus button to hinder.[16] Two, sharp, steep-sided, little glens open out into it, and when it was wet, and the upper lands raw and bare, these scuppers vomited so much sand and dirt into it that the mowing of it grew to be a scandal to the mower and grief unspeakable to the boy who turned the grind-stone, so that finally it was thrown into pasture.

I would like to linger here, but we must push on up the creek. You see those great boulders in the bed of the creek. Well, often when high water goes down you will see that some of those big fellows have been rolled several feet on their way down stream. Now we come to a great elm at the foot of a little bluff. The current has been cutting and digging, sapping and mining, under this tree for many a day, patiently all the year round, though at times it tosses and tears away at a great rate, still the old monarch stands erect and throws over the spiteful little creek his long, protecting arms, and casts a cool shade where the vicious little imp may curl up and rest in a quiet pool, which in its whirling, purling, pitiless fury it has dug to undermine the staunch old friend that has stood guardian for it so long. The old elm with his great strength is too kind and gentle and harbors a wily foe. But now let us lie down under this tree and look into the deep water. The fish love this pool, and when the water rises in the spring the suckers run up the creek, then the water goes down suddenly and the fish remain; then they take to the pools, and Warren Clark and I have spent many happy hours gigging and snoodling[17] them in daylight. I have lain right here and snoodled many and many a sucker. You know there are different kinds of suckers among men and fishes. Now here, right by that big stone, lying perfectly still on the bottom, is a black or May sucker. You see he's dark; his head is flat on top, and he moves neither tail nor fin. I never caught one with bait. They never run in shoals like the white suckers, and are finer, not nearly so bony. Some people say when the good Lord was making fishes he had a lot of little bones left, so rolled them up and made a white sucker, but I never believed it. See the chubs and the silversides and the little pike and the swarms of minnows. I've watched this little creek since

I was knee-high to a duck, waded and paddled and soaked in it, fished in it with my first pin hook, have seen it when I could dam the flow of it with my bare foot, and again when it was too lazy to run and would curl up in shady pools and by morning would be an eager, rushing hoyden,[18] then a torrent reaching out and tearing off flood-gates, fences, everything it could grab, plundering and tearing up and carrying off like a thief, then when the tantrum had passed purl as contentedly as a kitten. With all it leads a most useful life, watering the cattle and sheep for miles along its course, and if it does go wild sometimes soon falls into its old pleasant ways.

It was here, when our forefathers came and clustered along its banks nearly a hundred years ago, it sang its songs to them living, and as they lie—husband and wife, father and son, mother and daughter, five or six generations of them in that quiet harbor just on the hill up there—the cheerful little song never falters, but says to the birds and squirrels in the woods, and to all the sheep and cattle that hear its music; "Come, quench your thirst, wash and be clean. Yes, men may come and men may go, but I go on forever."[19] And soon it will join the unknown, brimming river. Then comes more trouble than our simple, woodland stream ever dreamed of. In the first mile of companionship with its big friend it is dashed against a great wheel and compelled to toil unrecompensed, and so on in its whole course it is harnessed and harassed and churned, carries burdens of boats and people and lumber; now bears away all the vile offal of great cities, and dens and hives of unclean humanity, until it is lost in the vast illimitable ocean. Our little creek never thought of that when you and I lay watching the fish under the old elm tree. Nor more did we; but like the creek wanted only to hurry on and on to join the brimming, ceaseless river of life and be in the hurry and scurry of the swiftest tide.

> "Oh well I mind me of the days
>   Still bright in memory's flattering rays,
>   When all was fair and new;
>   When knaves were only found in books,
>   And friends were known by friendly looks,
>   And love was always true."

And now, Willie boy, before we leave this old elm tree, to show you what kind of fellow your Dad used to be, I shall relate that in the long ago Uncle Nick Eckis, your grandmother's brother, kept a store in Benton and had an ashery.[20] His son, Usebius Theodore—we called him Seve, though we had a more expressive name for him—came over one day to visit us, and your Grandfather set us to picking stone from a field between the hill field and the big barn. I was the littlest boy of the three, and the youngest, and how it came about I don't remember, but, naturally, those two, big fellows must have goaded me scandalously, when I gathered up my old cap full of rocks and soon had them on the run, over the hill field, across the lower meadow and up the creek till they reached this old elm, I following with my artillery in hot pursuit, too hot in fact, making the same fatal mistake that General Jubal Early[21] did in the Shenandoah Valley, for here the broken and defeated enemy turned and made a determined stand. Flushed and reckless with victory I rushed headlong into the trap set by my wily foe. And now what do you think those fellows did to your Uncle? They just picked me up and jammed me into this water-hole and drowned me just like I did the chipmunk. Oh! They did surely do me mean! Do you see that gravelly flat right over there? Well, there are plenty of rocks, and if I had just run across the creek there and taken my stand, they never could or would have gotten me in flank or rear, but you know that "of all sad words of tongue or pen the saddest are these: it might have been."[22] So General Jubal thought, and so your moist, cool, sad Uncle thought. And today it cuts me to the heart to show your Daddy as others saw him, so I'm only giving you a snatch of his ways. This little creek, if it could talk, would tell you how he pushed me off the sled when we hauled sap, and kept me off, and he laughed, and the creek laughed, and your Uncle wept.

Now if we turn round and look west, you will see just beyond the breast of the hill the top of our barn and tenant house, and straight south you see a little glen. Now we shall go up to the head of that, where there is a spring, and across the road is Uncle George's old log house and barn. A foot-path from the house door leads down to this spring, with stiles at the road crossing, and here is a cup for drinking. Isn't it a cozy place, sheltered by big beech and sugar trees, and soft, green moss dotted with spring beauties all round? Old Uncle George across the road there is your Great-grandfather's brother,[23] a particular, fault-finding, crusty, old fellow. I was always afraid of him. He told me once how he whipped your Grandfather. In front of his old house, and between it and the road, was a small field of an acre or so that was always sown to rye, and just west of the rye patch there was a line leading up to the entrance of the barn. When the rye was tall your great-grandfather sent your Grandfather, who was then, no doubt, a barefoot boy, over to Uncle George's on an errand, and he, I suppose, came up the creek and the glen, just as we did, instead of going a few rods west to the lane, dashed across the rye patch, parting the tall stocks with his hands as a swimmer does in striking out in the water. Old Uncle George showed me how. He said: "And then he makes dees vay," putting the points of his fingers together and moving his arms backward. That made Uncle George mad and he seized Fritz and gave him a good lambasting. The thought of it pleased the old fellow as he told me, and I pondered the meaning in my heart.

Straight west one-quarter of a mile is a cross-road and the south-west corner of our place, and our place forms one of the angles. There stands the old brick meeting-house. It was built long years ago by these old pioneers, who paid their allotment in labor and material. They had many trials, laid many plans and endured many sacrifices to complete it. Old George Taylor, who lived across the river where we saw the canoe, was an old Scotch-Irishman and a member, but had the fault of taking a drop or two more than was needed at times. When the walls of the church were up all the resources seemed to be exhausted, so they called a congregational meeting to devise means to go forward with the work. As they were gathered on a Saturday afternoon, trying to solve the heavy problem, old George Taylor, who was deviously wending his way home from the village, bethought him of the meeting and came in. He sat and listened for a time, then rose up and said he "would like for to inquire what had become of the means already subscribed." He had scarcely seated himself when Uncle George was up and, with a snort, said: "What is dat to you? You gif not to dat nor any ding else." Then came old George Taylor's quick retort: "That is true, sir, but I gave what is of more value nor money, I gave my advice." Uncle Abe told me this, and he was Uncle George's son.

Now let's get a drink, then go out into the road and turn east. On the right is Uncle George's orchard, and on the left is our place with an open wood of big beech and sugars with a tall hickory or two. Here we cross the little creek again on a foot-bridge and go up this rocky little rise. Here on our left above the road, the south-east corner of the farm, is the old cemetery, the last resting-place of all our Hartzell forefathers who lived and died here.

Now you can see what a perfect place it is. You are born at the house by the old willow tree, and go up the road west, to the limit of the farm, and there is the old school-house; get your education; then turn south a quarter of a mile, and there is the church; and when you are done with these and want a rest you go east a quarter of a mile, and there is the harbor where you can rest, while the brook and the birds will sing to you a sweet lullaby, and "sorrow and sighing shall flee away."[24] Let us go in and look about. Here, not far from the center of the old part where the graves are thickest, are the low, sandstone headstones, one to the memory of George Hartzell, born 1739, and the other "To the memory of Christina, his wife."[25] All about us are laid to rest their children: John, Joseph, William, George, Abram, Christina and others.[26] Here of the third generation are John, George Abram, William, Frederick, Jacob, Elizabeth Christina, Joseph, Lucinda, Peter, and many more, with aliens and strangers unknowing and unknown. They sleep the sleep that knows no waking, while our world keeps steadily rolling and whirling away, and we see alike the same kaleidoscope of bursting buds, waving fields, full barns, granaries and storehouses, followed by like frosts and snows and chilling blasts.

> "For we are the same our fathers have been,
>   We see the same sights our fathers have seen,
>   We drink the same stream and view the same sun,
>   And run the same course that our fathers have run."[27]

You see our old home was hospitable, both to the living and the dead. The birds by day, the brook and whippoorwill by night, sing the same songs to the home folks and to the stranger and alien.

Now let us go on a little farther. East and joining Uncle George lives old Uncle Abe. He is a sort of pompous, self-sufficient, old fellow and a good type of the old-time, thrifty, Pennsylvania dutch farmer. He has a red frame house and a cider mill after Grandaddy Lazarus' mill went down. His place is nice and tidy. The out-buildings are all neatly kept. He is hospitable, opinionated and proud to a degree. One of the first buggies or spring vehicles that came into the neighborhood was owned by Alonzo Strong, his nephew,[28] who lived a little farther east on the banks of Mill Creek. In going to Benton he had to pass Uncle Abe's place, and as he drove past the old man, who was on foot, the sight made his choler rise, and he remarked, with much feeling and emphasis, as he looked on the little, panel-bed sugar trough: "Now is der skribter fulfilled, ven beggers shall ride und brinzes go avoot."

His Grandson, Addison Miller, was a member of my Company, "H" 105th O.V.I., and at the battle of Perryville was shot through the lungs. When the news came old Abe met his nephew, young Abe, and immediately inquired: "Did you hear de news aboud Ad Miller, Abe?" "No." "Vy de ledder-head god shod." You see he was a democrat and opposed the vigorous prosecution of the war.

But come on now just back here on this place under a limestone ledge. We will get the whitewash clay and then hurry home or your Grandmother will give you an awful scolding for leading your Uncle to idle away this whole afternoon, and you won't get your supper, so we shall cut across lots, by old Uncle Abe's, through the graveyard, down the old lane, through the woods to the creek. You see the road on the south of our place was not used on account of the steep crossing at the creek, and this old road through the woods, north of the graveyard and so on down Island Creek, came out near the old water trough and was much used in early days, and still used in my boyhood days by funeral parties. Now across the lower meadow and the hill field; it's almost sundown. See how the swallows fly. They are taking their last romp before going to bed. Hear them laugh and twitter. And the whippoorwills—they seem to come right out of the high wood-crowned bank there to the right, and sail over the bottom land, calling "whippoorwill, whippoorwill." Now there's your Grandmother calling. She will whip poor Will if he doesn't do better next time.

CHAPTER SIX

◯﹏◞

[The North Place]

Your Grandfather wants us to go to the north place for sheep this morning. Do you want to go along? Well, take this salt sack, go into the smoke-house, and there you will find the salt barrel. Get about a quart in it. A funny salt sack! No, that's regular. One of my old tow-linen trouser's legs sewed up at the bottom, and that patch is just where my knee used to peep out to get the fresh air. Boys had better not ask too many questions. I must split some oven wood first. Drat this tough wood! You go over there, along the old orchard fence by the cider press, and see if you cannot find a piece of rail or plank. That'll do. Now let's cut before Mother sees us. Hello, Calvin, come back and mend the coal rake! There that's done! Now when I say "go" you cut down the spring race, and at the foot of the orchard turn to your left, on up under the hill, and stop at the first ravine. I'll take through the orchard to the old slippery elm and come down the ravine to meet you. Well, have you been waiting? I had to go back to fix the bread shovel. Now let's be off. We will cross the river here by this big, old, soft maple. The water is shallow on the riffles this morning. Now we go right up here a bit and come to Taylor's. Old George is dead long ago, and Hiram, his son, lives here in a double log house. Here are three crazy brothers of Hiram—John, George and Leander—pretty good old fellows to work; and here are Newt and Sol, the trappers, in one of these old houses. Up-stairs they have the skins hung. Come on, we'll look at them. Here they hang from a low ceiling, each one stretched on a pointed shingle by the nose, tail downwards. Strike this first one with your hand, that starts them to swinging, and the whole lot of them set up a dry crackle; they are so dry and hard, hundreds of them, skunk, rat and mink.

Now come, it's only a short half a mile to the south side of our place, straight north through the woods. You notice here are only oak trees, no beech or sugar north of the river except on the bottom, but dogwood, black haw, wild plum and hazel nut, all you like. Here's the school-house, and across the road there is our place. There is a thicket of an acre or more all wild plums. Here we come in the fall with the teams and haul home tubs and buckets filled with fruit. Then your Grandmother makes plum butter and jam and things. Over there in that little, one-story log house live a funny old couple, Billy Patch and his wife, quite alone. I go there to fill the water jugs when the men are harvesting. They have no well-sweep,[1] only a hook and a long cord, so that I make slow work of it. As these two old people sit at table they each have a pat of butter. Old Billy doesn't like his butter salted and his wife wants salt in hers, and why shouldn't they be pleased? Old Billy has a stiff, crooked thumb. He says that was done by the "bustin' of a gun." He is cross, and I never go there unless I am sent.

We'll get over the fence here and salt the lambs. There they are, call them up. Won't come for you? Well, just listen to me. Here they are. Now drop a few handfuls of salt on these bare spots, and look out for your toes or they'll make you howl. When a sheep sets his sharp hoof on a barefoot he feels heavier than he looks. Now just over the fence there are a lot of rams. Crawl up on that stake and rider fence. I'll jump down and give them some salt, and then, well, watch the matinee. Here they come, some thirty of them, and as they crowd around the salt the fun begins. Notice the long, rough, curly horns. Now the young fellows divide and begin to back off, a few feet at first, and as they make a quick dart with lowered horns and come together head on, you think one or two such blows would end it all, but they don't. The old fellows still stand there quietly licking salt, occasionally looking at the youngsters and giving a low blat like the rattle of sheet iron, until finally, as one after another they retire, leaving the field to one or two, an old fellow darts out and faces the victor, sends his challenge, backs off a few feet, then shoots forward, and the field is clear. Often the young one sets out at full speed to meet the old fighter, but just before the crash he steps neatly to one side, having learned prudence in former combats. And now come others of the old fellows, a regular tournament it is. The cracking and bumping grows terrific, and it seems as though none would be left to tell the tale of battle or bury the dead. The woods echo with the thunderous pounding. The sound of it can be heard for a mile around; and now all the fighters are vanquished but one old sir knight. There he stands, the hero of many a battle field. Your Grandfather sawed his horns off long ago, so there are only great, heavy, curved stubs left, not more than six inches long. He thought that the old fellow, shorn of his long horns, would feel the disgrace so keenly that he would retire from the arena and thus set a good example for the rising generation, but the sound of battle always roused him up. You see he fought several duels which had a fatal ending for the other fellow. He is heavy, short legged, deep bodied and thick necked, the wide folds or wrinkles in the skin of the neck reaching clear back to his shoulders. His head is bare, the result of many battles. Now watch how deliberately and grand he walks out and faces the victor, a noble old fellow too, sporting a pair of great, twisting horns with a little, dark blood seeping out near the roots just now. Our old Ivanhoe with his coarse, heavy blat sends out his challenge.[2] Both, with quick step, back off two or three rods and without further ado, like the two battering rams that they are, come together. The concussion as they meet seems terrible, but they keep right on repeating it until at last our old veteran comes out victor again, and they all run back to their salt. These fellows are practicing this way every day, and often in the quiet evening, or at midnight when you awake, you can hear the bump, bump, bump, coming from the field of battle; so now let's go. The other sheep are in the orchard between the barn and house. We'll take them out into the road and round home by John Diver's, Carter's ford and Uncle Billy's.

The next farm east of us belongs to Duck Foot (George Hartzell), and he is Uncle Billy's son.[3] His name is an heirloom, and I can't tell the origin of it. He lives in a low log house, and logs are laid on the clapboard roof to hold it down. He keeps a big-bellied bottle with tansy in it,[4] and I think the tansy grew there, anyway it's been there a long time. He puts some wild cherries into it in the spring, and, with good whiskey over all, he has either tansy bitters or wild cherry bitters owing to his sickness.

This road is straight and runs from the center of one township to the next—Poland, Canfield, Ellsworth, Berlin, Deerfield, Atwater, etc., etc.; and where the beginning of it is or the end I don't know, but I am sure it's a long way off.

Now let the sheep into the road. They know the way home, and you run after while I shut the bars. Can't keep up? Well, let them go; they'll soon tire out. Here on the left lives old Johnny Craig.[5] He is a deacon in our church and a strong democrat, so your Grandfather has many a bout with him on politics. I heard his conclusion after one of these duels the other day, when he said to settle the matter: "Fred, I was born a democrat, I've lived a democrat, and I'll die a democrat." So that ended it, and, indeed, what more could be added?

We will follow right on west to Kiah Batts. He is son-in-law to Uncle Billy Hartzell and has a little furnace where he makes plow points, so the farmers around get all their plow points and iron of him.

Here we turn south past Charley Carter's. In this little field with the high fence are two fawns. Pretty little things, aren't they? This next farm is John Diver's, and here we come to old Jimmy Carter's and the river. The sheep stop and bunch up. They don't like water, and we'll have to be smart to get them across. Give me the salt sack and I'll go ahead. If they don't follow me in I'll just take one of these fellows by the horns and pull him along, then the rest will string out and follow in single file. You stay behind to watch that they don't break away, and when they start keep them going. See how carefully they pick their steps and how timidly they look as they follow their leader. We're most of us like these sheep in our willingness to follow a leader, and the shepherd who has a good leader in his flock can take his sheep anywhere. If men only had leaders as good and as honest as this old fellow, there wouldn't be half so much trouble in this world. Well, we're all over and all right, and the sheep will run home. We often have great trouble with the young sheep and always try to have a good leader with them.

Right here Wolf Track Run adds its little mite to the river. This is Uncle Billy's land on both sides of the road, and there he is, a pleasant, cheerful, happy, old man leaning on his staff; and as he gives us his kindly salutation in German or very broken English we know without being told that here is a man who has not been soured by his long tussle with life, and if his old head is gray his heart is green, and if you and I toddle down the west as he has done there will be no chilly side of life for us, and our friends will sing:

> "Life's labor done as sinks the clay
>   Light from its load the spirit flies,
>   While Heaven and earth combine to say
>   How blest the righteous when he dies."[6]

But now the sheep are turning the corner by the school-house and will soon be home and into mischief, so we must follow them up. That old bellwether is always looking out for good things for his followers, and when he finds neglected bars or gates he has no hesitation in leading them into green pastures and beside still waters.[7] And now we are at home, and here is John Sheets[8] with a great lot of fish. Uncle John[9] has let the water out of his mill-dam. The fish were nearly stranded on the bottom, and they have so many they are dividing and sending around to everybody. That was always the way in those times with our people. No butcher's or meat bills, and when we killed a beef, calf or sheep our neighbors were always remembered and no books or accounts opened. Only that good, old law: "do unto others as ye would that others should do unto you," was ever present and uppermost at such times, while about the only duty of a justice of the peace was to make and acknowledge deeds.[10]

When I was yet quite a little boy your Grandfather owned a farm some twelve miles north of home, and we used to take the sheep there in summertime, and always took old Aaron to ride. When I got very tired I could ride behind, or sometimes your Grandfather would walk and then I had the old horse to myself, my feet not reaching below the saddle skirts. When he trotted there would be a long parting between me and the saddle. You see I wasn't big enough to fill Daddy's saddle, and the old horse could hardly have known that I was on his back, or if he did he just whirled in and gave me a little treat, which it was a sorry treat to me, and I relished it as little as Sancho Panza did his tossing in the blanket.[11] I never had been so far away from home in my life and everything was new and strange. I well recollect how odd it seemed that no matter how far we went everybody knew your Grandfather, and as meal-time came around there was always an anxious gazer in front of every house, and long before we came up a hearty: "Hello, Fred, dinner's waiting." Then the women and children came out and joined their earnest plea, and old Aaron had his oats or corn on the grass in front of the house, and the sheep had a chance to rest and nip the grass by the wayside. Your Grandfather would toss Billy or Bob over his shoulder and take Jenny by the arm, and we would all go in the house and gather round the table. There was friendly chat and inquiry and the children had to sing. That was the first thing your Grandfather found out in every family—who could sing—and, if no one could, he always set to work to teach them some little song. So the time flew by, and all too quickly the kindly good-byes were said and friendly warnings given to "Fred" never to pass by without looking in. Then Fred mounted old Aaron, and your Uncle, with the waist belt of his trousers punishing him with satisfaction, hustled up his now rested flock and wondered how big the world was anyway and if everybody in it knew his Daddy. But why everyone loved him never fully entered my head until he went away.

Skirting the south line of this farm, and cutting off a small corner of it, was a canal. On my first trip, as we crossed the bridge with the sheep, I could see two sturdy horses approaching on the narrow tow path—a boy on the hindmost—and they had many bright ribbons and things on their head-gear, gorgeous in their beauty, with skins of wild beasts as housings for the harness, and a long rope attached to a floating palace. As I leaned over the bulwarks of the bridge and watched the beautiful thing approach and pass under I was nearly overwhelmed with the sight of it, for upon the top were fair ladies and brave men, and they could pass down into the bowels of it and back to the top of it at will. Where did this beautiful and wonderful thing come from, and to where was it going? Was I in the body or out of the body? And was there anything in this world more beautiful to behold? As I followed the sheep to the pasture nearby my mind was filled with wonder and amazement, and for a long time afterward no boy of our school was so looked up to as me who had traveled far and seen many people and things. As much as to say: "Oh, you can't tell him anything. He has seen a canal boat with his own eyes and people from a far off country."

It wasn't long afterward that your Grandfather sold this farm to a thrifty Welsh stone-cutter, a very good and honest man, but after making one or two payments upon the land he fell sick—and was ill for almost a whole year. One spring day he and his wife came down to our house looking sad with sickness and discouragement. They stayed all night. At the breakfast table the man turned to your Grandfather and said, "Frederick, I shall have to give up the place; I can't go forward." Then your Grandfather rose from his seat, went to his old desk, took out the note due that spring, tore the name nearly off and handing it to him said: "John, I'll give you this, and now do you think you can make it go?" John took his hand, few words were spoken, but I think I know now what the poet meant when he said: "The quality of mercy is not strained, it droppeth like the gentle rain from Heaven upon the place beneath. It is twice blessed; it blesseth him that gives and him that receives."[12] This man died in a few years. His widow raised her numerous family on that farm, and the oldest son still owns and lives upon it. The family has been a very prosperous one. The old mother still lives, and as I meet one or another of them occasionally I think I see that the works of a good man do follow him. "For he did good and not evil all the days of his life and wronged no man in word or deed."[13]

CHAPTER SEVEN

❧

[Soap Making; Transportation;
Social Gatherings and Camp Meetings]

A PART OF the equipment of every farm in those days was the ash hopper, while the soap barrel had its abiding place, just as permanent as either the salt or flour, and was never moved or changed about except for grave reasons. Soap making came regularly in the spring as soon as the weather settled, and a whole year's supply was made at one time. The house-wife of that day prided herself highly on a nice kettle of light colored, thick, livery, soft soap, and indeed when the soap didn't come the trouble that brooded on the earnest, anxious face of the house-mother communicated itself naturally to the whole of her domain. So there was always some devious magic or spookery about the business, but when Aunt Peggy or Aunt Margaret or any of the neighbors came in and Mother's face lighted as she said: "Oh, come and see my kettle of soap." Then everyone, from Granddaddy down to wee Rob and Rosy,[1] knew that the dawn had arrived, and when Mother led her visitors back to the ash hopper and the soap kettle under the old balm of gilead tree, and thrust her big soap paddle under the mass, pressing its handle down on the rim of the old iron kettle, and the soap would spring up, tremble and sway and finally make a clean parting, then break into an infinite variety of lively, wriggling, trembling, dancing, independent squares and wedges and cubes, then settle back into a compact mass again, everyone knew that we had had good luck with our soap. Soap making was always discussed from the standpoint of luck. Every kind of waste fat around the farm was put away for use in its making, together with all bits of skin from the pork. The hopper was filled with fresh ashes after being lined with rye straw and some sassafras roots in the bottom. The ashes were well tamped down and gradually saturated with water; then when in a day or two the lye began to drip and the kettle was filled with lye strong enough to bear up an egg, the business began in earnest and anxiety increased until the old soap barrel was full. We made both hard and soft soap, but soft soap was the main standby for clothes washing, while to borrow or lend a bucket of soap was a very common thing among our people. In fact, I believe that if there had been a wall as high as the tower of Babel built around, say, five miles square of our old neighborhood, with neither sallyport[2] nor scaling ladders, we still could have gotten on finely, for we had everything and the means of making everything needful for our comfort and happiness. We were contented with what we had, and sang: "Praise God from whom all blessings flow," with more pure-hearted honesty than was ever inspired under vaulted dome.

In those old days there was very little litigation, and it was considered altogether disgraceful to go to law with a neighbor. The Justice of the Peace was the great law officer and did all the writing of legal papers, such as wills, deeds, etc. Few contracts or bargains were written. A person of any standing lived up to his word. Uncle Peter[3] was the J.P. and only law officer I knew anything about until I was quite a lad. His wife was Aunt Rachel, Uncle Sam MacGowan's sister. He was a good, Christian man and a terror to evil-doers, a threat of Uncle Peter's court being all that was needful to soothe and quiet the most litigious and bring peace. Though he was a man of most upright character he inherited a quick temper from his father, Uncle George, and they used to tell many stories of his profanity; as when one time the bees got after him, Aunt Rachel hearing him swearing and seeing the cause came to his rescue with the broom. As she battled the bees with the broom Uncle Peter kept saying: "Rachel, Got tam de bees, I pelieve dey will sting me to det." Aunt Rachel brushing away said, "Aye, aye, Peter, aye, aye," until he was quiet. Aunt Rachel lived to a great age, receiving a pension from the Government after Uncle Peter's death on account of his services during the War of 1812. Aunt Margaret, Uncle John's widow, who is still living, receives a pension on the same account. Men are still living who tell of Uncle Peter's authority in settling disputes, but so far I can get no word of a law suit. Personally, I recollect him well and the honor in which he was held in my boyhood; in fact, no one of the young folks ever thought of any higher arbitrant for earthly difficulties and disputes than Uncle Peter. He had a tidy little farm with a double log house, but never accumulated much property. The only cloud on his title at that time, as I remember, it was his being a Campbellite in religion, which was looked upon with a shade of suspicion, much as old travelers always regard any short cut or new route at the first opening.

Uncle John Hartzell had no family of which to speak, only two girls, having lived single until he was fifty, then marrying a girl of twenty-five. He went by the name of Bachelor John as long as he lived, this to distinguish him from Deacon John and many other Johns in the family. Whenever he wanted a boy he called on Fred, and I was detailed, so that one way and another I served the old Uncle a goodish bit, and I liked it, for he had a new one-horse buggy with springs under it, and as the work was mostly driving stock I often got to ride home in it, which was an honor not to be despised by anyone. I remember once we were driving by a wayside grocery, and he called me in and gave me a strong glass of beer, which I had gulped down, rose up to the top of my head and turned and came down through my nose in a very trying and painful manner. I was scared, and after that was shy of any kind of beer but the sugar water beer that Mother made, which I wish I had a barrel of it in the cellar now.

Uncle John kept telling me he wanted me for his boy, and one day I told him I was coming; so asked Mother for my clothes, which she made into a bundle and tied in a handkerchief, and I cut for Uncle John's—about as far as from your Dad's house to Myer's drug store. I went in, and Aunt Margaret took my bundle and gave me a little rocking chair. I sat there till noon, took my dinner and after awhile in gloomy silence until I could stand it no longer. So when Aunt Margaret was out I made a dart for my bundle and, when I had it secure in my hand, I bade her good bye; said I had made her a nice visit and hoped she would come soon and make us a visit. Then I turned on the current—about a million I think—and under my spurning feet and road like an arrowy Alpine river flowed, and I never was so glad to see Mother and the children, even cross old Sally Linton's foxy grin looked good, and I never wanted to be anybody's boy again (Sally Linton was our hired girl).

In the days before railroads came, and the price went up to fifty cents cash, a half dozen or more of our people would arrange to go to Akron together, each with a load of wheat; so they made the loads ready at night. The old tar bucket was filled and hung on the hind axle, a water pail and feed for the horses made ready, and early in the morning they set off—a long caravan—going to a far country like the sons of Jacob going down into Egypt after corn.[4] It took two days to make the trip, and when they came back your Grandfather always had a great load of bran which was waste and given away, though it was not considered worth hauling except by a few, but your Grandfather always took all the sacks he could get, and a clothes' line to bind them on, so always brought a great load horse. Soon others followed his lead. Then bran came more into favor and was sold for one cent a bushel and became an article of merchandise. All this time many were feeding brush to get their cattle through the winter. Each winter day they slashed down a lot of timber, and the cattle browsed off the small twigs and buds, and thus were brought through without hay or fodder. Sometimes a cow was killed by the falling of a tree, for when the cattle heard the axes going in the morning they would rush for the woods unless held back, and care had to be taken in falling timber.

I recall one time when the men were going away with wheat Uncle John wanted me to stay with Aunt Margaret, as she was quite alone, so I stayed with her at night. One night she was sick and got me up to go for old Aunt Mary, Uncle Billy's wife, a quarter of a mile away. Uncle John had a cross old dog named Rine, and I never went in or out of the house without first reconnoitering to see if Rine was about. As good luck had it, this time I got safely out and away, and soon had Aunt Mary up and ready with an armful of hoarhound, pennyroyal and such stuff;[5] but when we got to Uncle John's gate old Rine bounced out with a most terrifying roar and growl. Now Aunt Mary was a little woman and at that time must have been over seventy years old, so I gave up all for lost, but Aunt Mary scorned the danger, made a plunge for a pile of bake oven wood, charged old Rine and, with one heroic dash, sent him off the field in a most shameful rout. I was nearly scared to death and dashed into the cover of Aunt Mary's petticoats, where I hung till the field was quite clear. Since that day I have seen many acts of bravery, both by field and flood, but none ever impressed me so deeply as that charge on old Rine.[6] I remember Aunt Mary as a busy, helpful, little woman, full of courage and always ready. She rode horseback until quite old and was very nimble on her feet.

Horseback was the only and usual means of speedy travel. To be the owner of a good horse and saddle was a proud thing, and a new saddle was always commented on at church by the young folks. Your Grandfather always kept a good one which we boys were rarely allowed to ride. When we did ride it we always had to shorten the stirrup leathers, and the boy who forgot to or made a mistake in changing back those stirrup leathers to the exact place at which he used them, that boy, I say, had woe, he had sorrow, he had redness of eyes, and thereafter clung to the sheepskin or rode bareback.

Your Grandfather had an occasional partner, Caleb Steel by name, and the two made many forays into distant parts for cattle and sheep. I went along one time to collect and bring home the stock, riding a big colt called "Woolly John," a tall sorrel and very high spirited. Many's the race with the cattle and many the tumble I had with him. When the cattle were distributed in the different pastures we stopped at a store in Deerfield kept by one, Gibbs, and there Steel bought a big, dried codfish. I think the first I had ever seen. When your Grandfather came out Steel was mounted, holding the codfish in his right hand and low on the horse's side out of sight. I rode behind, and we had gone but a little way when I saw your Grandfather clap his hand to his nose and make a great ado about some vile smell. Then Steel brought up the codfish, and when your Grandfather saw what it was he said he wouldn't ride in company with such a man. Your Grandfather was on old Aaron, while Steel had a white mare on whose speed he greatly prided himself. They started off, neck and neck, like two mad men. People ran out on the road to watch; houses flew by; hills rose and fell; Woolly John stretched out his best and kept in good sight. The dried cod came down the white mare's flank at every stride with a whack. Down toward the river by the old stone mill is a depression, and as the racers sank out of sight they were too near even to tell much about the event, but in a few seconds Aaron's big head, with nose straight out in line with his neck, began to show on the rise, and at the top your Grandfather, turning his head quickly, saw the grey trailing in the dust, with the codfish waving in the air, and as he took off his old hat to salute his partner I felt like the chappie who roared out: "Weel done cuttie sark."[7] In hot weather they always rode in their shirt sleeves, with coat and vest made in a roll and buckled on behind the saddle. It was a great race, and I was always glad we beat; besides it gave me a glimpse of something I had not known or dreamed of, for you see they were both good men. Your Grandfather, though a young man, was clerk or you might say chorister, stood up and gave out the hymns in church and led the music; while Steel was a sober, godly member; and to see those two men ride a horse race was very startling to me, though quite pleasant withal, for I had been in the habit of giving any boy or man a tussle on the road if I was out of sight of home, but I felt it to be a sin which according to our catechism is "any want of conformity to or transgression of the law of God." This relieved me of any sense of guilt, however, and always afterwards I was nothing loath to try conclusions with any horseman on the road, and never wasted an opportunity.

Your Cousin Seth was with us much about that time. He was then a tall, unfinished fellow with red, curly hair and long arms and legs. When he had to move, one of his feet always appeared to say to the other: "Now, you just go ahead and I'll come on after a bit"; but when he once got those legs wrapped around the body of a colt he stuck like mistletoe to a Georgia chestnut tree, so that between us the colts were brought up to habits of usefulness.

The men of that day had as part of the equipment for horseback riding a pair of leggings which were most often squares of green flannel wrapped around legs and fastened with a piece of tape tied around the leg below the knee, the leggings reached from the knee to the foot, exposing only the toe. I think too almost every family owned a pair of saddle bags which were carried on the crupper in the rear of the saddle with loops running forward, through which the stirrups were dropped; thus the stirrup leathers held the saddle bags in place. When long journeys were made the saddle bags always went along, being very convenient to carry food, raiment or any necessity or luxury. They had an opening in the side and were fastened and locked very much as the U.S. mail pouch of to-day. The ladies all prided themselves highly on their side-saddles, and a girl of the better class usually had a side-saddle as a part of her marriage portion. Your Aunt Lucy,[8] when she was a girl at home, could ride almost anything in the way of a horse, but didn't confine herself strictly to the side-saddle or the conventional mode for ladies, and, being the only girl on the place at that time, was a tom-boy of the purest ray serene. Whether you made a reconnaissance to the front or rear you could be sure of seeing her somewhere, like the Cossacks after Napoleon on the Moscow campaign.[9]

In the fall when apples were ripe we had apple parings, and as early as I can remember had a machine to do the paring, a wooden wheel with crank and belt running forward on a smaller wheel with a fork to hold the apples. I was usually the parer as the young fry went from house to house in the fall evenings. The party generally formed circles around the tubs and cut and cored the apples after they had been pared by one or two machines. The parties usually held pretty late, and when they left there were enough to fill the dryers or make apple-butter. These schnits were often strung and hung from the ceiling above the open fire or other convenient place to dry, then were packed away with the strings in them for future use. These paring bees brought together merry parties, as did also the singing schools, but the most exciting events of all were the spelling matches when rival schools met to try conclusions. We used to go long distances, and the school houses were packed full. Two captains were agreed upon and a tally keeper. The captains chose sides, and as everybody knew everybody else they sang out the names fast and furious. Each person as his name was called lined up on the side of the captain choosing him. The names were called turn about until all were chosen; then the teachers commenced pronouncing the words. The tally keeper was busy as he made note of all the words missed on each side. After that was finished they all stood, and as the words were missed—each miss brought the misser to his seat, and usually it didn't take long to seat one-half or three-fourths of the crowd—then began the serious business of the evening, and excitement ran high as one giant after another came to grief and all were down but three or four. The silence and interest were painful. The candles, as the now tired teacher turned page after page hither and yon through the book, were forgotten, the long, black, burnt-out snuff reaching high above the blaze, and the tallow drippings down the wall. The room grew dark. Then in sheer desperation the teacher would go to Walker's old dictionary,[10] fire a twelve pound jaw breaker, and the suspense was ended. I well recollect that some young folks who were scarcely counted average in other matters could spell any word that was loose at both ends, so I conclude that spelling is a sort of gift like conjuring or fortune telling—everybody can't do it. With bright moonlight and good sleighing these spelling matches offered much pleasure, and young and old came out—sled loads and sleighs with bells and robes and laugh and joke, with merry hearts, all bent on having a good time, and none were disappointed except the boy who got the mitten, and he always came up smiling next time.

The camp meetings held by the Methodists and Campbellites[11] I think resulted in much good, social fellowship over a wide scope of country. They were held in the woods, and the Methodists built booths and brought bedding, and the meeting often held for a week. The first time I saw Garfield[12] was at a camp meeting, and I remember he created quite a good impression as a promising young man. The next time I saw him he was a Colonel, and he and Captain J. E. MacGowan[13] came to visit me at Murfreesboro, Tennessee, and we all took a soldier dinner off my mess chest; and the last time we had him to dinner with us soon after we set up house-keeping, all unawares that we were entertaining a future president, yet all the same we knew we were in the company of a mighty man and withal a good fellow, though we called him Jim.

During the winter there was kept up at most of the school-houses literary societies which attracted many, both young and middle-aged, never flagging in interest. Essays and declamation occupied the early evening. Then following the recess came a debate by an appointed class. After the class took one round the debate was a free for all, only order maintained, and parliamentary rules were followed so far as we understood them. These societies increased in interest. Tawney decision, Missouri compromise, Lecompton constitution, Kansas war, etc.,[14] afforded an infinite variety of constitutional questions, and many a brave lad, who soon after followed his country's flag at the top of the drum, drank in his first inspiration of patriotism at the "literary" in the little, old, red school-house. Fine debaters were developed, and many who were in time to become captains in both peace and war received their first mental sharpening in the literary societies of long ago.[15] These societies were kept up until the war broke out and have never since been resurrected in the country districts.

But I have forgotten to tell you about the old stage coach which ran from Cleveland on the lake to Wellsville on the river, bringing us the mails. It was kept up until the Fort Wayne and Chicago Railroad was finished sometime in the forties, and brought us our mail once a week from each way. That was a great event, and when we heard the drivers' horn we felt sure we were getting near to the heart of the universe.

Your Aunt Lide's[16] people had their brood at Smith's Ferry, some forty or fifty miles below Pittsburgh on the Ohio River, from whence some of the boys strayed to Indiana. I have before me now a series of letters written by these boys to their home people at Smith's Ferry, some thirty miles from where I am sitting. In date they range from 1815 to 1831, and were mailed at Madison, Jefferson County, Indiana. Each has a twenty-five cent postmark written with pen. In one of them the Indiana boy asks his brother to come and visit him, and says the trip will not take him more than four or five weeks, one way, which journey today would take perhaps twelve hours.

I remember well that your Grandfather went with our village storekeeper on a trip to Philadelphia, and while he was gone my pretty, little, yellow-haired, curly-headed brother Tommy[17] died, and we were overwhelmed with grief. How long he was gone I don't recall, but I've heard him tell of riding on canal boats, and they went all night, and in day times the passenger sometimes got out to walk awhile, from which you can see the utility of saddle bags.

I remember the big, old, covered, Pennsylvania wagons with four and five horse teams, feed boxes fore and aft, tar bucket and water pail, covered with dust and filled with boxes and barrels of goods, and the wide strap leather harness called quiler harness. Many of these old sets of harness were hanging in the stables up to and after war time, while the wagons in their endurance beat the "one hoss shay." When there came rumors of the railroad the teamsters, who were most important men, having seen much of the world, predicted that now the world would go to the dogs and the horse market be ruined, in which the farmers agreed with them, but the railroad came and the horses and the world jogged on just the same.

I have before me two bills of goods, just a running credit account of household supplies, of date 1827 to 1837, bought by Captain Wilkinson of Smith's Ferry. The Captain was a soldier of the Revolution of both the artillery and navy, being a Lieutenant of the latter; and in these bills I see items of tobacco and whiskey, which may be accounted for by the navy ration of that day. I give you some items: Postage on letter 18c, one-half pound of tea 75c, one-half bushel salt 37½c, one stone jar 75c, one yard check 31c, one pint flask 10c, one lead pencil 12½c, one and three-fourths yards muslin 45c, thirteen and one-fourth pounds of iron $1.06, one almanac 12½c. Calico and muslin range from twenty-five to thirty-three cents, with book muslin at fifty cents, salt from seventy-five cents to a dollar per bushel, whiskey 12½c per quart. This will give you some idea of prices, and when you recall that the goods were all brought from Philadelphia over the Allegheny mountains, in wagons, they were not so dear after all.

Our surplus sheep, cattle, horses, and hogs were all bought up by drovers and driven to the seaboard cities, Philadelphia and Baltimore, on the hoof, the trip taking about six weeks, and often a boy would get to go along, but not I. Those drovers were a hard-working, honest, jolly lot of men whose word could be depended on for any amount. Always on horseback, they carried great rolls of money back and forth on their long and often lonely journeys, and I never heard of one breaking up or anyone losing money by them till after the railroads came, when they all claimed that they made more money and got the stock through in better shape. After the railroad was finished I followed the business occasionally, but there was no money in it and much vanity and vexations. The old drovers have long since made their last trip over the divide.[18]

Some two or three years ago your Daddy and I went up to see the little invoice of select old fellows then living near the old hatchery. The first that we struck was Uncle George Lazarus[19] gathering elderberries along the banks of the same old Island Creek. We pulled the ponies in to the side of the road and went over. He seemed as chipper and witty as any sweet sixteen. Finally I asked: "Uncle George, how old are you anyway?" "Well," he replied, "if I live fourteen years longer I'll be a hundred." Then, with a droll sort of smile, he said: "I'm beginning to think it's just a little mean to live so long. It'll be so tough on the bell ringer."

Yesterday, February 24th, 1896, I was in Benton, stopped at the store to warm and found three, old grizzlies swapping jokes around the stove. Uncle George took the store dog by the tail and pulled him off the bench to make room for me, and I soon discovered I was reckoned the oldest man in the party. Uncle George says he got a finished education and the best kind of a licking in our old log school house, all in three weeks. He says there was a stick chimney in it that was on fire half the time. The boys brought their axes, chopped down trees for fuel; they all took hold of the limbs, and so hauled the wood to the school house, then cut off a big log and rolled it in. The benches were slabs with holes bored through them for the legs which stuck away up through the slab. They were all the same height, and only the feet of the big boys and girls touched the floor. Old Arthur Hayden taught, and he had the itch, so stayed after school to anoint himself—when Uncle George coming back after a book one evening caught him at it he got a licking. The windows were greased papers.

Uncle George said to Sol:[20] "Do you mind the Christmas we barred the door, and when we took away the prop the teacher fell in, and was mad and Henry[21] licked him?" Then we all chuckled, and these were George and Sol and Henry, Grandsons of your Great-great-grandad, and their combined ages would be about two hundred and seventy years.

Uncle George said the last time he saw old George Taylor was in our orchard. Taylor was coming up the spring race through the orchard, and as they were about to meet he fell down, and when he got up said: "I'm getting a great deal spryer than I used to be." "How's that," Uncle George questioned, "you're getting older?" "Yes," was the reply, "but when I used to fall down I blundered all around, and now I can fall flat quick."

At last Uncle George rose to go, saying: "I'm nurse now." You see Aunt Jane, his old wife, died a few years ago, and his Grandson has the farm and lives in the house with him. As he passed out he said: "I have three babies now, and I'm afraid they're going to come faster than I can take care of them." He says he helped fix up the first carding machinery just below Uncle Peter's old mill near the Mahoning on Mill Creek. The power was two yoke of oxen, but the high water soon washed it away, and he was glad of it. Then they gathered up the scraps and put up the fulling and carding mill of my day.

Uncle Sam MacGowan and Sol Hartzell both taught school in the old log school house, and the course of study was the three Rs, readin, ritin and rithmetic.

The last one of the old fellows we called on when we made the visit I told you about was Uncle Henry, then ninety-two or three. He wanted your Dad's opinion on politics, and claimed that since the democrats came in wool had gone off in price, and he was going to hold his for the next administration. When he was eighty-five or so we had a fine stable of French horses, and one morning he came hustling down some five miles, driving his favorite mare, "Hootch," came into the barn and said to me: "I can't make anything in sheep any more, I believe I'll go to breeding horses." He was a pioneer of the right stripe, totally without fear, with more courage than a dozen lions, good judgment and a keen eye to business to the very last, though altogether wanting in education, and we all loved to listen to his tales of long ago.

He showed me once a comfortable, old log house on the first farm he ever owned, and where he commenced house-keeping. He said he cut alone the logs in that house in one day, and on the next hauled them up with two yoke of oxen, one of which had never been under the yoke until that morning, and as he was yoking them he got a pretty hard bump in the side, but pushed on, and when the day's work was done went home, pulled up his shirt to show the place to your Great-grandmother Dorothea.[22] The spot on his side was much bruised, black and blue, and two ribs were broken.

Along beside this farm lay a great scope of lands owned by a wealthy speculator called Sim Jennings, and Uncle Henry agreed to clear twenty acres for him in order to make enough money to enter his piece. As he was working away an old Quaker land hunter rode through the timber and very cautiously took a good survey of this land Uncle Henry wanted, and rode off. Then Uncle Henry cut for home, on the way borrowing some money of old Judge Smith, got what he himself had, wrapped it all up in a linen handkerchief, and in the morning bright and early was off on foot— his money in one hand and dinner in the other—for the Steubenville land office, some thirty or forty miles away on the river. Races for land were common, but he was bound to win. As he approached a long hill down near the Ohio he saw the old Quaker half way up watering his horse in quiet comfort. Uncle Henry pulled his hat down over the side of his face and pushed past unnoticed, and as soon as he got by improved his pace by a few links. As he approached the town people by the way could see by his pace there was a race on hand and cheered him on. As he looked down the road from the top of a long hill he saw a whole family come out of a cabin below him and he roared out: "Give me something to make wind and muscle!" The man ran into the house, broke an egg into a tin of whiskey, and handed it to him as he passed; he took it down in a gulp, pushed on, reached the land office, made his entry, came back to the tavern just in time to see the old Quaker ride into the stable-yard; and our side won again.

His brother-in-law (he had three of them), John Smart, was a river man. He took flat-boats down the river, and finally died of cholera in Mobile.

Uncle Henry once took a trip to Missouri, going part way on the steamboat. It took fire, ran into a drift, but floated off, and burned to the water's edge. Uncle Henry was so strong, courageous and helpful in saving life that the passengers gave him a regular ovation.

My, oh! but he was a pusher and driver; had a big family of boys, and while they were with him they all earned their bread. He had many farms and teams, good ones, too. Breakfast was eaten before day, hamper packed with rations, and when the barnyard gate opened, and Uncle Henry mounted on old Puss took his place at the head of the column, it looked like a brigade engineer corpse train. Take him for all in all he was a wonderful man and, with education and cultivation, had been fit to lead armies, tunnel mountains, or any other great undertaking. He was at one time a partner with old Ossawattomie John Brown,[23] and bought wool with him.

When he was about seventy years old he felt a little grunty one day, and as he rode past Doc Cook's he said: "Cook, I'm wrong, and I want you to make me right." Then Cook gave him a lot of blue mass[24] and some other poison stuff, such as doctors keep, and, knowing his man, told him not to dare venture out before so long a time, but the same day—it was cold and stormy—he wanted some sheep brought home from one of his farms, so mounted and was off, got wet, cold and chilled, and always suffered with some dreadful misery in his legs, which were black and blue and yellow and red and all colors below the knees, with great running sores, sometimes better and sometimes worse. He had a new cure about every month or two, often invented them himself, and fattened up all the quacks within a hundred miles, and was finally cut off last summer at the age of ninety-four. On his last day his mind ran on the burning steamboat, and he said to his daughter: "Mary, that poor woman is all wet and cold, can't you get her some dry clothes and send her to bed?" On being assured that she would be attended to he went to sleep satisfied.

I think I might tell you that the very highest tide in footgear, in my boyhood, was reached when a young man had a pair of calfskin boots, with an abundance of red leather at the tops, the more red leather the better. We had our own hatters in those days, and a fine, lamb's wool hat added the last touch to a young fellow's dress. Such a chap was fit to go home with the girls. Some girls yet living used to carry their calfskin shoes in their hands on Sundays as far as our house, wash their feet, put on their shoes, and go to church; when service was over came back to the house, took off their shoes and went barefoot; and they were nice girls too.

You know all our beef and veal skins were tanned on the shares, the tanner getting one-half and we the other, so our foot gear was extraordinarily cheap. Shoemakers usually went from house to house and made up the footwear, but our shoemaker lived so close that we took our work to him. Many farmers had a stock of lasts and did their own repairing.

As I look around I see an old bayonet. Our people called it a bagnet. It is an heirloom, and the legend that goes with it is that in early times, in a circular hunt to destroy wild varmints, the hunters surrounded Atwater Township of Portage County, armed with tin horns, axes, guns, corn knives and weapons of all kinds, Uncle Henry, a lad at that time, took the old bagnet, fastened it to a stout hickory stick, and, as a young, half-grown bear tried to pass the skirmish line, jabbed him through and through, pinning him to the ground. Uncle said he bawled like a calf. We have no bears to punch now and find it makes a good poker.

Speaking of tin horns reminds me that there was a time when tin horns were held in high repute, and took the place of bells, gongs, fire alarms and such like noisy trumpery. A sound I long to hear is the winding blast of a long tin horn about dinner time. When the sun pours down all his heat, and you are dripping with sweat, gasping for breath, with stomach shrunk up to the size of a hulled walnut, the waist band of your trousers bagging and flapping both to the front and rear like the sails of a becalmed schooner—even the robins and pewees on the trees standing straight and stiff legged, with parted beak and drooping wings,—then your whole body, mind and soul are fixed on one absorbing theme, the old dinner horn. Will it hang forever by the spring-house door? But no, time at last sets all things even, and here comes such a blast of heavenly music as few men these later days have any conception of. It thrills your heart with delight, and the roll and echo of it, as the sound expands and diminishes, fills the whole being with sweet contentment. The tale that it tells is one of food, nourishment, milk and honey, cool shade, rest and refreshment, the old spring, the green sod and the perfume of the sweet locust blossoms blended with the odor of frying links of sausage! Oh! my dear boy, there was poetry in those days too, and your Grandmother knew how to execute the most ravishing strains of music that were ever appreciated by an admiring audience; and Oliver always wanted more.[25]

CHAPTER EIGHT

❧

The Underground Railroad; Bread Making; Old Time Sundays; In the West, etc.

NOWADAYS WHEN THE baker sets about making bread she uses a penny cake of some kind of modern, scientific mixture and does the baking in a fine range, but in the days of which I write the old "out oven" had its abiding place some ten or fifteen yards north of the spring door and only a few yards from the rim of the depression which contained the spring and formed the head of the spring race, and which no doubt was the inducement for the location of the farm buildings and probably the farm itself, for what could be more desirable than an abundant and unfailing supply of pure water? I remember it was not an uncommon thing for our old people of the neighborhood, who were sick, to send to our house for a jug of water from the old spring.

The old oven had different patchings and renewals. I think my first remembrance was of a clay oven—clay mixed with straw. This afterwards gave place to brick. In these first ovens the fire was always built in the back, where was a small hole, say, four inches square, to give it draft, the broad blaze rolling along under the dome to the front; but the last triumph of skill in out-ovens was built by old Jimmy Bryant, an old stone-cutter and mason, who renovated our oven and made what he called a squirrel tail oven, that is, having a draft flue starting at the back and following along on top of the arch to the front, where it terminated in a short chimney. The fire in this was built in front, the blaze following the dome to the back and bending down to the flue for exit. All around the rear of the oven grew broad leaved horse radish and sprouts of balm of gilead. Here the hens often laid and hatched, and here your Grandmother often came to pull the fresh green leaves and wet them with the spring water to lay over her butter or fresh meat in hot summer time. Here beside and a little in front grew a pear tree, and the branches of the big willow reached almost down to it. I have much reason to remember the old oven, as it was always considered the boy's business to get the oven wood, which seemed to me a grievous task. It took wood any length from two to four feet, all dry and split to small and even size, and to find free splitting wood often required a good bit of hunting. Usually the old fence rails were reserved for this, but in a big family like ours, with all its comers and goers, the old oven never had a chance to remain cool for long; then besides it was often utilized for drying fruit. I don't know how many loaves it would hold, but I think from ten to fifteen, and then the front part was always filled with pies and sweeties of one sort or another. A coal rake, which was a long-handled, wooden hoe and often burned out and had to be renewed, a broad, wooden bread shovel and a sort of mop was the outfit. Bread making was always a time of some anxiety with your Grandmother, for everybody forgot the oven wood but herself, and, as I never liked to cut a stick to be wasted, she was frequently appealed to to size the pile. Then the oven must not be too hot or too cool, and the bread must be just right on going into the oven. Folk nowadays talk of rising or yeast, but our old Dutch ancestors[1] called it "sots," and every household had its "sots crock"[2] which came into use in the baking; was, and for that matter still is, full of mystery to me. Often on bake mornings we would find the sots crock on the kitchen table bubbling over, and streams of white, bubbly, spumy, frothy stuff slowly making their way over the floor. This was troublesome but not altogether bad, only telling that the sots was just a little thing too good and needed to be checkmated or curbed with some other things, but I am getting where the water is too deep for me. I remember though we used often to borrow or lend a tinful of sots.

The bread was worked out, put into straw baskets, of which we had a dozen or more, then set away in some warm corner and covered with a blanket to rise. When the right moment came, the oven just hot enough and the bread just light enough, it was carried out and placed on a bench in front while the coals were lifted out and the floor swabbed. Then one loaf after another was taken out of its straw basket and thrust in the oven far back. The loaves filled perhaps two-thirds of it, and what space was left was filled with pies, custards, etc. Then the old, wooden door was put up and propped with the coal rake. When the bread was done the coals and ashes were all brushed off the bottoms of the loaves, and all set on edge outside the oven together with pies and pans of yellow custards with dark and light patches on their shiny skins, and the pies picked full of holes with a fork, and hot amber juice of apple or peach standing in bubbles over the holes.

These bread loaves, when they leave the shovel for the hot floor of the oven, widen out and take on a generous, comfortable aspect; and a fellow who never saw anything but this slick, shiny, baker's bread would almost certainly faint away could he behold and taste one of these loaves from your Grandmother's old out-oven. It was good the day it was baked and the day after, till it was all gone, inside and out. The crust was better than the inside, and the heel was best of all.

I wish you could have one loaf of bread, a stump apple pie[3] and a dish of custard from that old oven; then you all would agree the world lost a big lot when the out-oven went down; and if you could taste a peach cobbler baked in crock or earthen pan in such an oven, then turned upside down to cool and give the hot juice a good chance to soak into the thick, brown crust; then with pitcher of cream from the spring house. I say if you could but help eat the like of that you would never sing "I would not live alway."

Speaking of the old spring house reminds me that the crocks all had lids on, and we used to run in, take a lid off, blow back the cream and take a drink of milk. Of course, I don't say your Grandmother approved the custom or gave her consent, but all the same we did such things, and as far as I can see there was no great sin it it before the microbes came.

Well, after I went to the war, in the early part of our first campaign, my regiment was lying in the line of battle one awful hot, dusty day of August or September near the Kentucky River. Kirby Smith[4] was flailing our fellows out in front, and stragglers and wounded were coming back. We had no water, and the men of our regiment were straggling anywhere in search of it when the Colonel[5] said to Lieutenant Bard[6] and me to gather up the stragglers. As we went we came upon a nice, low, wide spring house filled with crocks of milk with covers on. Just looked like Mother's. I said to Bard: "Do you think it will be any harm to take a drink of this milk if we blow the cream back?" He thought not, so we each took off a lid, blew back the cream and took a good, long pull at it. The force of early habit and training hadn't worn off yet, but from that time on it did wear off pretty fast.

Out here by the out-oven we made the apple-butter, fifty or a hundred gallons, every fall. We never got too much of it.

Did you ever taste an indian turnip?[7] There is something interesting about the indian turnip. It's not sour and it's not sweet, it's not bitter and it's not bity, but there is a sort of gentle yet persistent determination that grows more intense as time rolls on, until finally I think I might say there is a sort of red-hotness, and the water starts from your mouth and nose and eyes, and you loll your tongue and run to the creek to try to coax the full current through your mouth, thinking the coolness of it will put out the fire, but in vain. Then you cut for the orchard to try a bite of apple, and that is another vanity, but when Mother gives you a tablespoon of apple-butter, and you hold it in your mouth for an hour, the fire will be put out, and you never will be at all curious about the taste of indian turnip again. After all it doesn't hurt a boy; it's part of a liberal education—a kind that abides.

Your Daddy says he remembers the old log school house, but I don't seem to, and all my school recollections cluster about a little, red school house with a big box stove in the middle and benches running around the inside so that the wall made backs for the older scholars; then a long writing desk made of wide, strong boards and fastened to the floor; in front of this other rows of benches and desks, so that the straight front of the writing desk made a back for the younger scholars. Thus the school faced towards the center of the room, and the classes swarmed into the center and formed a line.

My first school was the New England primer,[8] which, if I remember correctly, had some crude pictures—one of poor John Rogers, who was burned at the stake, and his family. He was the father of nine small children. A cut of a mouse with a cat in hot pursuit, and a legend: "The cat doth play and after slay." A dog after a thief, and a legend: "The dog will bite the thief at night." The alphabet and some short words, together with the catechism. Here I learned that "God is a spirit, infinite, eternal, and unchangeable in his being, wisdom, power, holiness, justice, goodness and truth," and have seen no improvement on the definition since.

As the school was mostly Presbyterian the minister came once or twice a year to catechize us. I recollect once I didn't have my lesson well, and as I was still on the front benches I hid my primer in my old cap, and so tried to read the long, hard answers, on the sneak. The minister noticed it and said, "Calvin, you don't even read them very well," which attracted the attention of the whole school and made me feel the little sneak that I was.

In truth they were tough for a little fellow, but a good understanding of them is useful all the way through life, and I think that more men who have been raised on the shorter catechisms have had a strong hand in guiding and controlling the interests and destinies of this land we love than all others put together.

We had three directors, though practically but one, Captain Hubbard[9] by name, a nosy, important, tobacco chewing, old Yankee. There was a crease ran from each corner of a wide mouth downward and a little forward, until the view of it was lost under his chin, but could be accurately traced by a little brown rill of tobacco juice bordered with fine bits of quid, held in check by a stout growth of stumpy beard. The lighter juice kept true to the crease until they met under the chin, and from there fell in beads to his shirt front.

At the beginning of school he always came with a roll of white paper containing the rules for the government of the school. These covered all the outgoings, incomings, shortcomings, lesson times, seasons, places, and every conceivable condition and circumstance of school life, with punishments, pains and penalties, numbered as high as twenty, taking possession of the child from the time he left his home until he returned, went in the house and shut the door. After that they wouldn't hold. At any disturbance he was always on hand, the rules were spread out before him, and the culprit tried by them, he being judge, jury, court house, jail and sheriff, all in one. I have vivid recollections of trials of this kind. Rule Eight said we should not go skating at noon. This rule a few of us boldly defied and broke. The minister's son, Gran Stratton (who followed Colonel Manderson as Colonel of the 19th O.V.I.), now of Spokane Falls; Jim Hartzell of the 7th O.V.I., now of Cape Girardeau, Mo.; Cals and Mart Lazarus of the 104th (the latter killed in action) and I were rebels. Old Ephraim summoned the parents, and the trial proceeded in a solemn and awful manner before the whole school, the parents being called upon to voice their opinions on the crime and its proper penalty. Uncle Henry was barbarous and called names. After it was all over, as a matter of form, the rebels were given a chance to rebut, but were so overwhelmed as to be speechless. Now in times past your Great-great-grandmother had given me some pointers about Uncle Henry's school days, and the time seemed ripe. I should get turned out of school and a licking anyway. Only courage was lacking, and at last, lest the trial go by default, I made an attempt at public justification of our acts, and had the right of it too, for we were always back in school promptly in time for books. I got my voice and crawled along carefully until I came to Uncle Henry, was gathering courage and doing him up to the evident satisfaction of all our side, when your Grandfather arose and, in a voice not to be mistaken, said: "Sit down, my son." The case was closed and we lost.[10]

Our school house stood on the brow of a little hill. At the foot ran a small, chattering brook which took its rise on the Sam MacGowan[11] place, then across Adam MacGowan's farm (old Adam was Uncle Sam's father), then through both Uncle John's "Walker Place"[12] and his "home place," then across Uncle Billy's,[13] then past the school house and following the west line of our old place until it fell into the river. Between the school house and the river was the deep glen where we spent so many happy hours playing "I spy the wolf," climbing the slim, tall trees and hiding amongst the branches. Girls could climb as well as boys, and it certainly was great fun. One game we had, that I have never heard of since, was called "whip jackets." We gathered a half dozen slender rods, bound them firmly together, then two boys, each armed with such a bundle, putting their left feet together stood facing each other, but in such a manner that each presented his back to receive the full stroke of his antagonist. Each grasped his weapon with both hands and at the word began to lay on with might and main. All was fair that went between the hips and shoulders. A circle of admiring friends surrounded the flagellants, encouraging them without stint or favor, and I have seen boys bear it and lay on without uttering a complaint, except the unbidden tears which rolled down their cheeks. The bout ended when either was willing to cry: "Hold, enough!" But both victor and vanquished were so thoroughly punished that crowing and crape[14] went together. The brook was infinite diversion when all else failed. I think our children learned well. The schools were good and taught by conscientious teachers. We had for our first arithmetic the Western Calculator.[15] Grammar I think was Kirkham's,[16] but grammar was as much a mystery to me as Mother's sots pot, so I just learned to repeat the rules, standing fair in my class, but never could see either use or sense in it. In arithmetic we had much mental exercise, which has stood me in good stead ever since—also in geography. Our schools were orderly. As we arrived we always made a bow with bared head to the teacher, while the girls dropped a "kerchy."[17] When dismissed we passed out in single file, stopping at the door to salute the teacher before leaving. We had "speaking days" when visitors were invited in while we roused the Romans and paraded the boy upon the burning deck, and "Ah! were you ne'er a school boy and did you never train,"[18] etc. Then too we made much account of music, learning many little songs by rote. On such days we all wore our best clothes; the big boys wore dickeys; and the parents came in their best. All men and boys of that day wore broad, full trousers, and when the style we wear now first came in the wearer was pointed out as a weakling or a sort of sissy man. Your Dad used to come occasionally on these days as a distinguished visitor, and he wore soft raiment and fared sumptuously every day. He also criticized my efforts shamefully and out of all reason, for when a boy is saying his piece, and right in the middle of it is taken with an itching in the back or on the leg, naturally, if he is a genuine boy, he is going to stop his speech till he has time to scratch the place, and then go forward and conquer, and yet for just such little faults as this, even yet, after more than fifty years have fled, he tries to humiliate me.

The teachers used to "board round" a week at a place, but as we lived so close I think they sometimes forgot and made a new start before they got clear around. We used quill pens altogether. Each scholar furnished his own goose quills, and the teacher made and mended the pens. We carried our drinking water from Uncle John's or Uncle Billy's, drawing it with windlass and rope in the old moss covered bucket. That and the old well-sweep were the only devices I recall for drawing water. Two boys always went on this errand, and then the water was passed in a gourd or tin to each scholar by one of us.

The rod or ruler or ferule were an important part of the school furniture, and no objections were made to their liberal use except by the victim, and that didn't count of course. I believe the teacher who couldn't take a back-seat boy by the scruff of the neck, draw him down over the writing desk and pat him with the ferule, would hardly have been counted capable. Another choice form of punishment consisted in bringing the culprit to the center of the room and there giving him a proper number of hot strokes with the ferule on the extended hand. This was about as hot as indian turnip, though I think the misery of it didn't hang on so long.

I don't know why—but true 'tis—that most of the time some of the scholars had the itch. Your Grandmother always made tiny little bags of sulphur, tied a string to them, and we carried them around our necks; and red precipitate and a fine tooth comb[19] had active missions to perform. But, as the auctioneers say, "I can't dwell." The very ground where stood the old log and the little red school house has been ripped up, and the glen where we played is spanned by a railroad bridge, and here comes a long train of cars loaded with coal, all unheeding of the past and careful only of the future and its dollars.

So, good bye old school house. Many a good fellow, who answered roll call and took his catechism and grammar with gad and ferule[20] inside your own walls, has answered his last roll call to the music of plunging shot and screaming shell. Within your walls we first learned of Bunker Hill and Valley Forge, La Fayette and the swamp fox, Paul Jones, and the Constitution and Guerriere, and patriotism was bred in the bone.[21]

Sunday was a long, tough day for all us youngsters at the old home, but on Sunday morning your Grandmother always made an egg pudding[22] for breakfast, not an omelet, but a sort of big griddle cake baked in a skillet or pan, then cut up like a pie. It was dusted both under and over with a little flour, and was so good that everybody wanted more. I never got enough of it in my life, and think the making of it is now a lost art. After breakfast came such a rubbing and scrubbing! I had to get down on my knees, lay my head on your Grandmother's lap, and no matter how much I had rubbed and scrubbed before she found patches of brown in all sorts of out of the way places; but, like all things else, this finally came to an end, and then Mother packed the great, big-bellied, willow basket with a lunch, for our sermons were none of your little, touch and go, fifteen or twenty minute affairs, but solid hour and a half and two hour ones, filled with strong meat and divided into heads. All I can remember of them is something like this: "and thirdly, brethren, I should remark," or "under fifthly I observe," or "ninthly and lastly, brethren, I would exhort you," and so to us uneasy, unhappy, wriggling youngsters the sermon dragged its weary length. The old people took it more comfortably. Grandaddy Lazarus had a heavy wool sheepskin, and it was mitigating in its effects. Sim[23] Hartzell and nearly all along the far end seats could lean their heads against the wall and sleep with much comfort, and as the years rolled round each sleeper's head left a mark that broadened with age and use and deepened in color from the center outward, rather uniform in size and pleasing in effect as they lay at regular intervals dark, round rings against the dead white wall. The heads of growing families sat on the outer ends of the seats next the aisle which ran down the center of the church from the pulpit to the double doors facing south. The boys sat next their fathers for the sake of order and discipline. The older worshippers who sat in the body of the church could, and did at times, lapse into slumber and enjoy a little repose. We had a men's side and a woman's side, and any man or boy who would have sat down on the women's side would have scandalized himself and whole of the church—the like would not have been tolerated. The communion tables and benches stood always in the center of the aisle. The pulpit was well up in the center of the north wall, being reached by a short flight of steps. After the morning sermon we had an intermission of about an hour, when, in summer, your Grandparents with the children, with man-servant and maid-servant, went out to the shady side of the church and took refreshments out of the big lunch basket. Then after a little chat among the elders we again returned to our places for another long sermon, reaching home from two to three P.M., there to read the bible verse about— every member of the household who could read—and to that reading there was no limit but darkness, death and blank despair. Many little tricks and devices we invented to switch off attention or give a new slant to the purpose of your Grandfather, such as closing the book at the end of the chapter, and getting up to stretch and yawn, showing signs of great weariness, but all to no avail, though there were rare occasions when he fell asleep himself. At such times your Aunt Lucy[24] with deft fingers made his head as comfortable as possible, and one after another we shied out and cut for the old barn or orchard or garret.

Our congregation occupied a wide field. From Dave Hartzell's[25] on the east to young Sam Miller's on the west was all of ten miles; nearly the same stretch from north to south. The east side kept up a prayer meeting, also the west side at the houses of members, the place of meeting being announced from the pulpit, as also the monthly concert, ladies' foreign missionary and sewing societies. All these various meetings were well attended. Prayer meeting was no more to be ignored than any other, and the people were always provided with seats by using boards laid upon trestles or stout chairs. The services held well into the night, the candles burned low, and we little folks grew tired and many of us fell asleep, often on our knees.

Communion days were great days, and all the arrangements thereto were made in stately solemnity. Sometime during the preparation, to each person entitled to come to the tables was given a token, a round bit of metal the size of a dime. These were taken up and given out each communion. The long tables with benches on either side, occupying the wide aisle, were filled several times, and as each table was served a very solemn and touching address was made by one of the officiating ministers, so that nearly the whole day was taken up, and it was a memorable event. Whatever may be said for or against the strict religious ways of our ancestors, good, self-respecting and intelligent, upright men grew up under them. So far as I can remember a lock to a house was a thing unthought of. Thieves could easily break through and steal, but there were no thieves. People mostly came to church on horseback or in big wagons. A few had panel-bed buggies. Some of the ladies had foot warmers (a small, square, tin box with holes in it, carried by a bail).

One awful temptation to we boys on the long summer Sundays was Hubbard's orchard. Near the center of it was an early apple tree, and as our first parents were tempted by apples and fell so your parents were tempted by apples and fell. Our old New England primer said: "In Adam's fall we sinned all"; and if there was such an apple tree in the garden of Eden there was a good excuse for it.

One of the characters of my early remembrance was an old Scotchman born and bred in Ayrshire. He made our house his home when within the bounds of our people, and many a night, sitting on a low stool by his side, I have listened to him read Burns and tell of his people, for he knew them and all the places with which that poet had made us so familiar. We all liked him very much, and your Uncle Bob[26] was named for him, James Robertson. He drew all his water from the pure wells of John Calvin,[27] and had little patience with such modern upstarts as John Wesley[28] and Alexander Campbell,[29] whose followers were beginning to infest our old neighborhood. Uncle Abe said he prayed for the howling Methodies and watherey Kamalites[30] as they passed our doors to follow their own vain devices. Uncle Abe tasted the humor in everything, and his keen scent brought it out of "death and Doctor Hornbrook"[31] so plainly that I soon fell into something of the same way and spent much time in the company of our favorite, carrying a pocket edition of it through the war.

In the early history of Ohio we had associate judges. One of the first of these for our county was a Scotch-Irishman, a Presbyterian named Porter. He and Uncle Abe were great cronies, and on one occasion as they met, in reply to Uncle Abe's: "How are you, Judge?" he said: "Well enough, but wull you believe it, Abe, they've turned me out of church." Uncle Abe said it was incredible, impossible, and inquired for what it could be. "Naethin under the sun, Abe, but I would take a drop too much now an then." Of course, he had Uncle Abe's hearty sympathy as of a brother who had a fellow failing. Judge Porter had a brother who remained in Ireland until such time as the Judge could forward his passage money. This he had paid down, the brother had taken passage for America, but for long weary months nothing had been heard from him, and the Judge was in great anxiety when Uncle Abe met him one day. After the usual salutations and inquiry the Judge said: "We are in great distress on account of Brother James; I greatly fear he's been lost, and as we went to our family worship last night I said to my wife we would have a word of prayer about James, and we got down on our knees, and wud you believe me, Abe, dem the word could I say."

All this time your Dad was going to school, finally entering the Western Reserve College at Hudson, which was thought to be the high water mark of education. One time there was to be some sort of a triumph in learning at which our candidate was to unfold his rudimentary wings and display his learning. Mother was to go, and the outcome of it was that I went along. So your Grandfather took us to Atwater where the cars came, and that was my first sight of the cars. The road, Cleveland and Pittsburgh, had been finished only a short time.[32] The engine was named "Clipper" in big, bold letters on the side. As I stood by the side of it two, quick, short whistles scared me so that I caught Mother's skirts and felt the last day was surely come. As the train sped away with us the engine gave a prolonged whistle which frightened your Grandmother as she clutched me in her arms, resolved that if we were to be massacred we should die together. Of this trip, my first journey to foreign parts, I remember only the wonderful big buildings and the railroad locomotive, while no man occupied so high a place among mere human beings as the engineer of the "Clipper" in my estimation.

All this time the political ferment which led up to the War of the Rebellion was in an active state. We kept an underground Railroad station, and often had runaway slaves, men and women, concealed about the place in the day time, your Grandfather forwarding them to the next station north during the night, for you must know that in those days, to feed or shelter a poor black man in his search for a land where all men are free was a most serious crime.[33] Our old Presbyterian church was rent; a new church was built in Benton, and a little band of worshipers styled Free Presbyterians occupied the old church on our home place. Their foundation principles you will find in the opening lines of our Declaration of Independence. Your Grandfather was one of the foremost champions of those truths in our community, always stood by his guns, both ready and willing to meet all comers. Those were both serious and troublous times, and my recollections of them are vivid, but as they are easily come at in the history of our country I shall say no more concerning them.

About this time there was a Manual Labor School started in Athens County, near the Ohio River, open to both white and black.[34] Your Grandfather took two shares of stock in it, and took me down. That was my second trip to foreign parts, and must have been at least a hundred miles from home. As to color the school was about evenly divided. I was left to board with Mr. Mosher, an old Dutchman, and when your Grandfather left the world grew dark, and I was as one without hope. I think I cried steadily for two or three weeks, when a beautiful girl—a real angel as I now think— who has long since gone where sorrow and crying are no more, took notice of my woeful plight, came and sat by me in school, and I laid my head in her lap. While the scalding tears fell gently upon her apron she took me by the hand, soothed my sorrows and led me to believe that I might live to see home and friends once more, notwithstanding the great distance that separated us.

Students were allowed five or six cents an hour for work. I was allotted a piece of ground to clear of small trees and rubbish, and here I spent most of my time. Board was a dollar twenty-five per week, and I paid that and beside made enough money to pay my postage. I have no recollection of either studying or learning anything at this school. I was to go home in the Spring, and as the time approached my spirits rose. When the time came to leave I cut for the Ohio River, started to Wellsville on a little steamboat that kept getting stuck all the time, though finally we arrived. As there was no train to leave for some time I started to walk to Salineville, some twelve miles up the railroad towards home. There lived my good angel who had preceded me. I covered that twelve miles in good time, and when I arrived was met by kind friends, and the world did seem to be a jolly place after all. Here I saw for the first time your Aunt Lide,[35] and the good angel was her sister, Rebecca Thompson.

At this time your Father was in his first year at Amherst, while I was about fifteen. Two years soon passed, when, returning, he went very soon to Toledo, entered the law office of Bassett & Kent. After being there some time, for some reason he sent for me. Your Grandfather took me to Atwater station, got me a ticket to Toledo, gave me Five Dollars, and told me if I was a good boy he might send me more; if not, what plan or scheme was in my head I knew not, and as far as my recollection serves me your Dad's head was just about as vacant as my own.[36] All I recall is that when I arrived in Toledo he had a box of very good cigars in his room, and I fell to, this part of my education not having been neglected.

We soon packed an immense trunk with books and started west. The first, dirty, nasty, little town we struck was Chicago. The houses stood upon stilts, all underneath being vacant, except when occupied by pigs and rubbish. We staid all night at a little Irish tavern and slept over the barroom. The clerk gave us a candle and told us to leave our shoes outside the door. In the morning we had to pay a quarter each to get them. Mine weren't worth ten cents before they were blacked, and had never had an introduction to blacking. We were glad to get out of Chicago, our next stop being at Davenport. From there we took stage coach, I think, and started for Sunset. The stage people weighed the baggage, and as your Dad's trunk was a whole freight car over weight, and our finances very much frazzled, it was good business to keep the stage people a little blind about the weight, or overweight of that trunk, so we always tripped lightly up when loading time came, seized it by the handles and chucked it on with an air that said: "Oh! it's only feathers, a few pillows and such like." We rode day and night. The coach was full outside and in. I sat on the seat with the driver, and it was fine in the daytime. The horses flew, "the landscape sped away behind like an ocean flying before the wind," and my heart was gay until night came, cold, chilly night. I had no overcoat, in fact I never had one up to that time and for long afterward, so to keep from freezing I crept into the boot, a leather arrangement under the driver's seat, filled with all kinds of plunder. Here I lay nights and was knocked and banged about most unhappily. One day we arrived at a little hamlet called Newton, where one or both of us took sick. When we got straightened up your Father started back to Ohio. He had met your Mother, I think, and was in love. He just had to go. Some of you boys know how it is yourselves. He got me a place in a store at Davenport, corner of Front and Brady Streets. Here the Indians came to trade, and I got a birch-bark canoe, used to carry it to the river and soon learned to paddle it myself.

Sometime, I think, in the spring of the next year your Father, Mother, John MacGowan and Aunt Melvina[37] came—two young lawyers—and settled down to wait for business, but business seemed too tired to catch up with them. Uncle Jonas Hartzell[38] lived there then and was, I believe, the foremost preacher in the place. There was a great, steam flour-mill, and teams came from far and wide, loaded with wheat and corn. The streets were blocked with wagons from morning till night. The flour-mill bought all the wheat and made their own money to pay for it. The bills were on the face beautiful, and read "Burroughs & Pettiman will pay on demand One Dollar or Five Dollars." The country was full of it. The millers put up their flour in barrels that were made in the mill. The hoops were made from ash and brought from Ohio.

Your Dad sent me back to Toledo where, some twelve miles out in a great black ash swamp, lived a merchant, Vrooman by name. In the midst of the great woods he had a store where he traded all kinds of goods for barrel hoops. They were put up in bundles of a hundred each, and were legal tender for all debts. At the back of the storeroom, which was a long one, there was always a barrel of whiskey standing on end with the head knocked out, while a friendly tin cup hung over the chime.[39] His customers came with ox teams, stopped in front and, without a word, opened the door, marched to the barrel, with the tin cup helped themselves, and then were ready for business. Here were acres and millions of hoops, and it looked like a vast, modern lumber yard. I was to get three carloads, and as they had to be hauled to Toledo through an almost bottomless mud I had to wait. Sundays all the countryside gathered here to loaf. Horse-racing was the amusement. Mr. Vrooman soon asked me if I could ride, and I told him I could. He had just bought a Kentucky stallion, bright bay, big head, a lean, hard-meated fellow, cross as an old tiger, with a coat like silk, and veins about the head that looked like little ropes under the skin. He told me when the race was to be run, showed me the course, and wanted me to put the horse over it until he became perfectly familiar with it; so early mornings, before anyone was stirring, I gave him a turn or two until he seemed to know exactly what was wanted.

The day came, and with it a lot of backwoodsmen who, as they approached for the race, lined up on either side of the track. The horses were brought out, a score made across the road, and there we stood, tails to the score, ready at the tap of a drum to wheel and be off. When the signal came my horse reared up and wheeled so that when his front feet struck the ground he was in line, and away we went. I was a light, slim lad, weighing perhaps a hundred pounds, shirt and pants my whole outfit for clothes, with a strap tight buckled round my body, and a blanket strapped on the horse for a saddle. The other horse was a lithe gray, and while I had never seen him before I knew he was an old favorite. As we got away in good style a yell of delight came from the crowd, mostly encouraging the gray. It was neck and neck with us for one-third of the course. I had neither whip nor spur, and the event seemed doubtful. If we won, I was to have Five Dollars over and above the joy of it, so win I must. I lay right side of his neck, slapping him with my hand and reasoning with him energetically, when he seemed fairly to shake himself loose from the earth and fly, and our side won. Ah! that was a great race and can't be described. It was one of those sights that must be seen to be appreciated.

CHAPTER NINE

~

[Adventure in Iowa; Financial Difficulties; Enlistment; Battle of Perryville]

DURING THE TIME I was at work for Mr. Leslie, corner of Front and Brady Streets, I think the first railway bridge ever built across the Father of Waters was finished.[1] The steamboat people didn't like it, so one day they gathered a lot of steamboats at Davenport and Rock Island, maybe twenty or thirty, and, passing single file through the draw, like a flock of big geese, went up the river as far as Moline, made a graceful turn and started back.

The leader was the "Effie Afton." As she entered the draw she struck the pier on which it rested, and remained there, took fire, and set fire to the bridge. Two spans and the draw toppled and fell into the river and, being of wood, floated. Great excitement prevailed. A half dozen or more boats settling their noses against a floating span would push it down the river, all the time blowing whistles, calliopes, and making all the noise possible. The shores were lined with people on either side, some cheering and some cussing, altogether making such a scene as remains in my mind vividly as though it was yesterday. The point the river folks tried to make was that they held the bridge an obstruction to navigation, while the fact was that the railroads were hurting their business, taking both the freight and passengers that they wanted, for you see before the railway came freight went by boat to New Orleans and thence to the east by salt water. A great law suit followed, in which Abraham Lincoln was one of the attorneys; the river men were beaten and the burned spans soon replaced.[2]

Before the bridge was built great companies of Mormons used to land from the ferries, old Grandfathers and Grandmothers, middle-aged men and women, and children, hundreds at one time, all Europeans of the lower classes. Their bedding and clothing tied up in bundles was dumped from the boat on the wharf, and soon as they were landed push carts were provided, baggage loaded, and immediately they took up their weary tramp, like a herd of so many cattle, for Salt Lake, being always in charge of a smart young fellow who did all the business.

Your Father and Mother came in the Spring and went to housekeeping, but boarded with Mr. Leslie who owned the store, and acted as general roustabout and stable boy, opened and swept the store, swept the Campbellite church of which he was a member and Uncle Jonas Hartzell was pastor.

Will Grant, your cousin, about my age, came out about this time; but here I must dwell—to tell all the story would tax your patience and be of no use—so I shall close this part of my yarn soon. Two boys like Will Grant and myself would naturally get into much mischief. I remember one time we took two of your Mother's best sheets, made sails for our old skiff, and had a day's pleasure on the mighty river. We sneaked the sheets away and sneaked them back. When we took them they were clean and white, fit to grace the bed of a king. When we sneaked them back they weren't. We both felt bad, and your Mother felt bad too. Just why we weren't both naturally skinned alive is one of the mysteries that sort of bothers me yet.

Somehow your Daddy got hold of some timber and grass land ten miles or more down the river on the Illinois side. He was having the wood cut off, and we went down to help one winter. The hands at the camp sent us once to Rock River, a town half way between the camp and Rock Island, for a jug of whiskey—at that time twenty cents a gallon. The snow was very deep, just a wall of it on either side the beaten sled track. Following the track we saw in the distance what we thought to be a dog sitting in the road, but as we approached he set up a howl and started for the bluffs. The snow was so deep, though, that he made little progress and was lost to sight at every jump. We concluded it was a wolf, and, as I had a good, green club, we naturally felt he was given over into our hands. So, burying the jug in the snow, we started after the beast. I wish you might have seen us; we pushed on and on, snow waist deep; wolf would take a spurt of a quarter or half a mile, then stop; when we thought, "Now, old fellow, we've got you sure," and begin to reckon on how much we should get for his hide at Rock River and how we should have one good dinner anyway. We had no money except the twenty cents to pay for the whiskey. So we pushed on and on, and always when hope had reached the highest point the old fellow would let out a yelp and be off again. So it went for hours, and with wind, courage and hope nearly gone we could see that the wolf was in about the same fix; so 'twas a fair race between two naughty boys and a naughty wolf. Finally, when we could scarcely set one foot before the other, we struggled close enough so that the wolf turned and sat a moment showing his long, white teeth, when with club raised I fetched him one pat where the bottle got the cork, and after a lively tussle we massacred him, swung him by cutting a hole through his gambrels onto my club; then raising the club to our shoulders we started back, Indian file, over the way we had come. Oh! that was a tough, tough job, and we nearly gave it up, but at last reached the jug and the highway, limp and worn out, with some seven miles to walk before we returned to camp. So we buried Mister Wolf in the snow, started with the jug, got it filled, and got back to camp by night or a little after. What became of the wolf I don't remember, only that we got his skin.

At the time of this big snow, one early morning I saw, while lying in bed, a fine deer, not twenty feet from our door. We had bunks on the side of the wall, and I was in an upper berth. One window pane let into the wall was our window. We had an old squirrel rifle, and I jumped in the door and fired—a bad case of buck fever. The deer ran off, but only a few bounds at a time until he turned his head to look. I grabbed an old butcher knife and ran out, bridled a mule and started after him, bare-headed and in my shirt sleeves. The deer cut for the bluffs, running and stopping as the wolf had done, so I made sure I'd get him, but the mule had different ideas. I argued the case with the point of the butcher knife and made good headway for a while. My hopes were lurid, for the deer was losing ground, when all at once the mule seemed to reach a conclusion and came to a halt. I tried my best to convince him and with energetic entreaty encourage him to go forward, but without avail, and so returned to camp nearly frozen to death and covered with blood, for in prodding the mule my hand slipped from the handle to the blade of the knife. I thawed out and took the jibes of the choppers and my coffee in humility. They told me that if I had caught up with the deer and dismounted from my mule the deer would surely have killed me, but I never believed it, and don't know. Certain it is that if I had caught him I should have given him a fair chance.

Here Billy and I set trot lines[3] and caught great cat fish. We would attach a small cord to the main line and then tie it to any overhanging bough, fastening a small bell to the bough, and when a big cat swallowed the hook he rang the bell to let us know, and we took him off. When the water came up over the flat and a sharp freeze followed, we went on the ice with axes and clubs and caught buffaloes—plenty of them—they were a big, course sort of carp.

Well, those days are gone. Billy went into the army, and died. I'm not sure what regiment but think the Sixty-fifth O.V.I.;[4] while most of the wood and hay started to London by way of New Orleans and the Gulf stream. The story of our lives out there your Dad can tell much better than I. During the time Will and I were together you came, and I think crowded us out into the cold world. Whether you selected Ohio or concluded to be born in Iowa I have forgotten—maybe you remember? If you do, set it down here.[5] What we ever went to Iowa for, and what good we did while there, puzzles me yet. We were in all sorts of business, even kept tavern for a short time. I think I should have been at school and your Dad in the law office of Bassett & Kent at Toledo. This is the best hindsight opinion I can give. After being in the West perhaps two years I went home, and soon after I got there Hartzell Shafer,[6] a nephew of your grand-father, who had opened a little store at Beloit, came one day to our old home and said: "Uncle Fred, I have bought the station at Smithfield (now Beloit) and am trying to keep store there, but have no capital. If you will lend me your name until I can get on my feet, I shall be glad to have you"—with much more of the same sort. Your Grandfather, who believed in almost everybody, said: "Go ahead." At this point commences a story which brought misery to us all for more than thirty years. Most of the matters connected with it are clear to my mind yet, but I cannot think of any good that can come from setting them down, except to make a connection between this and my soldier life. I shall tell you that the store ran about three years, when Shafer came up one day and said: "Uncle Fred, we will have to make an assignment." It was done, and later, when your Grand-father began to realize what it meant, the Assignment was lifted, the creditors secured, Uncle John,[7] his oldest brother, coming to his rescue. Our old home and all our lands were sold. Your Father came home overland with a pair of mules and a lot of cattle, your Grandfather sending for him, I think, to help in saving part of the wreck. You and your Mother came by rail, and set up house-keeping in Uncle Jake Sheets' house. Soon afterwards the store was traded for a hundred acres of land, and we all moved into a house there was on it. Your Father went to Canton and took charge of the "Stark County Republican," and from this time on you all know the history of the family as well as I do.

I staid home, being a man now, and worked hard to help get a start for another home which we might call our own, and during the few years we were together there I learned to love your Grandfather with a perfect love. Our great misfortune showed the man in a new light—scales fell from my eyes. While he lived he impressed deeply into my mind this: "A good name is rather to be chosen than great riches"; and to that end have I labored steadily.

In concluding this, the story of my boyhood, let me look back a little. Today is February 1st, 1897. When I was born there were no railroads west of the Allegheny mountains, no telegraph, no thresher, no binder or mower, or any of the labor-saving devices we have now. We knew nothing of electricity, except the power of it in riving great trees to flinders.[8]

When young folks were married they sent round invitations to their friends by word of mouth. When they died the whole countryside turned out to see them buried. Real friendliness was the rule. People loved their relatives and, whether they came by ones or twos or by the wagonload, they were always welcome, never saying "by your leave" or "is it convenient?"—for it was always convenient to treat one's uncles, aunts or cousins to the best.

People all held their own neighborhood in the highest esteem. One couldn't expect much from the Georgetown, Berlin or Deerfield folk, for they hadn't the intellectual advantages we had, so we loved our own neighbors better than the rest of the world, and much time was spent visiting. Every farmer's house was a little factory, where each member had something to do. The minister was the man of education and was greatly respected on that account as well as for his sacred office. The smith, the miller, the carpenter and the wagon-maker were all busy members of the community, and the lawyers were unfortunate professionals, but doctors held a high place in our esteem, though they worked hard for it.

Out of our family nine first-cousins went to the war, John E. Mac-Gowan and his brothers Eli and Jonas, and of the Hartzell boys there were Adam, Seth, Josh, Jim, Jess and myself.[9] Of my mates from the old red schoolhouse seventeen went. In the whole party were two colonels, one major, one ass't surgeon, one lieutenant and one captain.

The question often comes to my mind if the times of my boyhood were not better than these later times? It seems to me that then each man counted for something, stood for a purpose, had an individuality. In these later days of trusts and monster corporations the man stands for much less than the machine. If the machine is out of order, it claims the attention and solicitude of the best minds of the age, but if man, the noblest work of the great Creator, is out of order, his place is easily filled, and he can go die or mend himself.[10]

In the days that were, if a neighbor fell sick, all considered it both a duty and a pleasure to offer sympathy and aid. Now it is different. Certain it is that the days of the old tin lanthorn, the flint and steel, the flintlock gun, the card, distaff, little and big spinning wheels, candle stick and snuffers, reaping hook and grain cradle, crane, ash hopper, out-oven, soap kettle and all the oldtimey, familiar and useful, everyday things are gone forever, buried in the same grave with the oldtime customs of hearty good-will and neighborly friendship.

Soon after we commenced our new life here the ominous forebodings of war were making themselves heard. We of the North paid little attention to them, not conceiving such a thing as war to be possible, but you will find all that in the history of our country, much better told than I can tell it. It is sufficient for this narrative to say that I was ready to go at the first call, but I loved and pitied my parents, and knew my place was to stay by them as long as I could; anyway, people said the three months' fellows would finish it, so I remained at home, all the while chaffing as I mowed and hoed and held the plow, and Bull Run, Donaldson and Shiloh were fought. Then came a loud call for three hundred thousand, and one hot, harvest day I hung my grain cradle on a little sugar tree in the wheat field as two young fellows came along the dusty road with fife and drum, jumped the fence, followed them to town and enlisted. The company was not assigned, and not full. I came home at night, told your Grandfather and Grandmother. Your Grandfather said very solemnly: "Son, the last twenty years I have been praying to God to let the oppressed go free; after the darkness light will come; go, my son."

So I went, helped recruit the company to overflowing. That company joined the 115th O.V.I., hung around Cincinnati for a year, then went to Nashville and Murfreesboro, and remained as guards to the Nashville and Chattanooga Railroad to the close of the war. The company I joined assembled at Canfield, then our County town. We were immediately ordered to Cleveland, so drove over to Youngstown one night, and in the morning were ready to embark. While waiting, many fathers, mothers and sweethearts of the boys gathered about to say good-bye. Such weeping one doesn't often see, and having once seen doesn't want to see again. No one clasped me in a last fond embrace, and yet somehow the tap got turned and the water was on, and I retired to the privacy of an old tie pile and sat down, resting my head in my hands, while great beads of brine traveled down my nose, wetting the gravel all about; in fact, I took a good cry, what for I don't know, except that I always had a fondness for good company. Some of the girls went with us up to Cleveland, where we soon arrived; then marched up through the city, the girls with us, to the barracks, and, as that was no place for them, the last good-byes were said, the very last by many, for they never "looked in loving eyes again." The next day we were put in line and ordered to elect officers, and almost as quickly as I can write it I was Second Lieutenant of Company "H," O.V.I.[11] How it came about I never can tell, as we never had a chance to talk it over, and it was all done in a whirl, for the duties of a Second Lieutenant I had as little idea as your Jamie. However, the regiment was immediately ordered to embark for Cincinnati, for Kirby Smith[12] had broken through the Cumberland mountains in Big Creek Gap, and was moving towards Cincinnati, leaving Generals Morgan, Baird[13] and others at Cumberland Gap, quite in the rear. Bragg[14] had broken into Kentucky with a great army, and it looked as though our own Ohio was to be the seat of war. At Cincinnati we were well fed and lay on the sidewalks and in the market house all night. All soldiers who had the money bought pistols and revolvers. As we were going to kill people it was thought the right thing to be prepared to kill as many as a half dozen when we got to the place. We took a train of stock cars the next day for Lexington, Kentucky. Along the road we all got to trying our pistols, so at the first step the Adjutant came and took them all away, except those held by the officers, so I scored one for the Second Lieutenant. There were bushels of them, and the men all swore and said the Colonel[15] didn't want to put down the rebellion, etc., but just now I must say that the taking of those pistols was one of the wise things, if not the wisest, our Colonel ever did. The service would have received no harm if he had taken them all. A pistol is useful perhaps to an assassin or thief, but I cannot conceive an honest man or an infantry soldier needing one. It soon became a useless burden, and in six weeks what was left of the regiment could wander over a battle field where pistols might be had by the cart load for picking them up, but no man thought it worth while. The only occasion I remember of an officer putting his pistol to use, was when our First Lieutenant, after the battle of Perryville, used his to shoot himself through the hand, and, as he had retired in the face of the enemy, his resignation was immediately required and cheerfully given. So the pistol benefited us to the extent of ridding us of a great coward early in our history.

We went to camp in Lexington on the farm of Henry Clay,[16] remained there a few days, got our arms and equipments and formed a few dress parades. Here the men, poor fellows, receiving their allotment of clothing, took the whole outfit—underclothing, overcoats, blankets—the sun blazing and the mercury frying in the thermometer. In four days we started to support General Nelson at Richmond, a distance of about twenty-five miles. We could hear the cannon pounding away and knew the fight was on. As we pushed forward, sun hot, men thirsty, officers all the time crying "close up, close up, close up, men," knapsacks heavy, our cavalry flying to the rear in squads of three or five or more, swearing and saying "you're marching right into the mouth of hell!" sweat pouring from the poor fellows' faces and cutting the thick, brown dust away in streaks. Ah, me! it was awful and we scarcely a week from the farm and school and shop at home. We were too late, however. Kirby Smith gave our fellows a dressing before we reached the battle ground. Then we cursed our luck and said we expected we'd never get a chance at them. Next day we started on the weary return march to Lexington, from there to Louisville, Kentucky, via Paris, Versailles and Frankfort, with the hurrying stimulus of a victorious rebel army in the rear. No words of mine can picture the horrible misery of those days; truly a "hell march" it was without parallel in history. When you think of our utter greenness and ignorance of the ways of a soldier and his life, you can see some reason for what I say.

Scarcely ten men in our regiment knew how to "right, face." The way was strewn with clothing, and our line of march blue with overcoats thrown away. Ox and mule teams were pressed into service from the farmers, the sick and worn out were permitted to ride the vehicles, with men both riding and hanging on. Night and day we kept on the move, halting now and then for a few minutes' rest, when we would just drop in our tracks, asleep almost before we touched the ground, all too soon to stagger up at the cry of "fall in, men, fall in." Often we formed in line of battle[17] across the road until all had passed, then take up our wretched way again, half asleep and the other half dead, with mounted officers cursing and goading us on and on, until finally we arrived at Louisville, about a hundred miles from Lexington.

A Second Lieutenant with the other company officers present, you must know, is a sort of useless appendage. The only justification for him is as an extra, as the extra wheel is carried by light artillery, as extra ropes and chains on ship board in case of breakage, or as a farmer carried bits of string or nails in vest pocket in case of accident to harness or thill.[18] So when the Captain is knocked out and the First Lieutenant retires, the Second, if he is around, which he generally is—like the spotted dog under the pole—walks to the front and takes command, thereafter being of use. Such accidents did happen, when I saw that an extra linch pin the tool box was not bad business. Then if your Second Lieutenant is a bright fellow, he is a sort of anchor to windward. On this march, though I had no knowledge of any use to which I could be put, I went in on my own hook, carried knapsacks and guns, did everything and anything I could to keep up as much cheerfulness and courage as possible. "Water, water, water," was the incessant cry, so I would take a dozen canteens, get away from the line of march, as all wells on the line were drunk dry before we came up, find a well and fill them. About the last day I found a big sorrel mule and loaded him with overcoats and blankets until only his ears were to be seen, and got the load to camp in charge of the boys. The upshot of it was that Company "H" had a hundred and one officers and men to answer at roll call the first morning at Louisville, the full complement, and Company "H" was the only company in the regiment that could make the boast, some coming in as many as forty short. General Terrell,[19] a regular army officer, managed the retreat, and, though we all thought him hard and cruel, he no doubt did what he deemed the best.

Here we lay doing camp picket duty and drill for about two weeks and I began to get acquainted with my company and its officers for, with the exception of a few of our home boys, I had never seen their faces until we met at Canfield. Our Captain, Robert Wilson,[20] of Poland, in the County of Mahoning, was an old Mexican soldier, a fine man, though slow to act and with very little knowledge of his duties. Our Orderly Sergeant was a bright, chipper stub of nineteen year old boy, with a fair knowledge of his duties and quite competent as a scholar. At present he is a member of the Pennsylvania Senate—Frank Mansfield.[21] He and I slept under the same blanket for two years. Our boys would average in age about twenty-one, though many were mere boys of sixteen to eighteen, and looked quite unfit for the service, but the result proved the reverse to be true. Here we held a grand review which lasted all day, weather hot, and men marching and counter marching from morning until night. During the day while we were standing at attention near the Galt House, General Jeff C. Davis[22] shot and killed General Nelson the landing of the steps of that hotel.

The first of October we started south after General Bragg, who had taken a back track, and marched eight days seeking that ever object of our ambitions—a fight.

At Louisville we had been assigned to the 33rd Brigade, which was made of the 123rd and 80th Illinois, 101st Indiana and 105th O.V.I., and received a new field battery. Volunteers were asked from our regiment, ten men from each company and two commissioned officers. The men responded promptly, and I was the first officer to answer the call. The reply I received was: "Lieutenant, go back to your Company, you're too damned good a marcher to leave my regiment," so the vision of a horse and saddle vanished in anguish; I returned to my duty.

On the fourth or fifth day out of Louisville we ran out of rations and foraged corn-meal. You can well imagine, my boy, that it was quite a little in a short month from your Grandmother's table to hard bread, beans, raw fat pork and black coffee, and now cornmeal alone and cook it yourself. However we managed I don't know, but we did. On the night of the 7th I did a mean thing; I think the very meanest in my life. After we went into camp Orderly and I started out across country to forage, and soon came to a plantation deserted by all save the slaves. Ducks were plenty and I bought three. I must tell you that in Cleveland the boys found a lot of advertisements of a Cleveland book bindery, printed on green paper and very like five dollar greenbacks in appearance. I had one and gave it for three ducks and two dollars—good dollars on the State of Ohio—in exchange. We both thought that was good business and very smart to cheat a poor old darkey so. We hurried back to camp, skinned the ducks, and soon had them boiling in a camp kettle; but they were tough, and while we slept one was stolen, and never until last fall did know what became of that duck, when John Nesbit, Postmaster at Poland, now gray-headed and nearly blind, told me he was the guilty fellow. Next morning Frank and I each stowed a duck in our haversack and were sure of nourishment for one day at least. At noon, as the regiment lay in the woods to rest and we tussled with our tough ducks, perhaps a dozen guns of the enemy opened up, and the balls came over us shrieking and howling: "Where is you? Where is you?" Then our boys took up the tune in sheer wantonness of mockery, and said, "We'll show you where is we"; and more other folly than you can think of. The Captain looked grave and said words like these: "I may not have another opportunity, and I want to tell you that you don't know what this means. I do. This is a holy cause, be men, keep your country's flag in sight and stay by it like men." Hardly had he finished the only sentiment I ever heard him utter, when the ringing, earnest cry of our Colonel reached us—"Attention, battalion"—to be repeated by every officer in the regiment, and this accompanied by the long roll and double quick march sent us all off tearing over hill and dale, through brush and timber, until the command, "Halt, front!" came quick, short and sharp; then "About, face!"; and, when that was executed, what a sight was there, my countrymen. We were on the side of a hill; our fine, new battery on a crest some five hundred feet in front of our line. Two rods in our rear was a double rail fence, or two fences, from two to four feet apart and running parallel to our line—called a "Devil's Lane."

As we stood, faced by our rear rank, we could see our battery in action and almost captured, dead horses lying all about and a furious struggle going on right among the guns, the bullets whistling all about us. My place in action should have been behind the rear of the Company, but here I was, and, as the fire leaped from our entire line, I found myself between "the devil and the deep sea." The last I saw of our brave, old Captain, he stood some two feet in front of the right of the Company, drew his sabre and, pointing it at the oncoming line of the enemy, cried: "Give them a volley there, boys!" How I got to my place I cannot tell, only that I did get there. The rebels poured steadily over the brow of the hill in open order, firing right in our faces as they came. Then came the order to fix bayonets and charge, which we did in good order.

In coming to a halt from the double quick the files had been too close for the free use of our arms, but now the thinning of the ranks by deaths and wounds left more freedom of movement, so when we started on the charge at double quick we made good our contention and soon had the Johnnies on the go. But as we pressed on over the brow of the hill we saw lying in the long grass another line of butternuts.[23] This line rose up, when the Colonel shouted: "105th Ohio, retreat!" And then it became too horrible to tell about, 'twas each man for himself, and I think we made fairish time too, but in crossing this fence many of our men were killed and fell between, most of our regiment was gone, but right here behind this lane was quite a handful of our fellows. Where I got over were twenty or more, and here we held our ground and made a good fight. I got a gun and banged away, but the bullets were coming like hail against the old fences, when finally an Orderly came on the run with an order from the Colonel to get out of there, and we got. As we left, the Johnnies began to pour over the fences, but many a one staid to keep company with his late foes. And now the bullets were coming like angry bees, so I got an oak tree behind my back and in line with the firing, turned on the juice and ran true, turning neither to the right nor left. I had very important business that lay right in front of me. It had to be done and I was doing it. My first run of a hundred yards took me to the foot of the slope, and upon the opposite slope was a field of standing corn. As I entered the corn a glimpse over my shoulder showed the gentlemen in gray swarming down the slope in a deliberate way, firing as they came, and a few of our lads making the best time possible, some entering the corn and some scooting down the dry bed of a break in the ravine. As I passed up through the corn, the bullets rattling through the blades like driving hail and cutting the loose earth about my feet, I came upon a line of blue coats lying flat and perfectly quiet—General Starkweather's[24] brigade, mostly Wisconsin troops, I think. This was our true line of battle upon which we should have been placed, only that some one had blundered. Soon the lads in gray came up through the corn, firing steadily as they came. I didn't like to step over Starkweather's men, and as they were not in action, as I walked along in front looking for an opening, I noticed what fine men they were, though evidently new and untried like ourselves. But the moment soon came for the test, and then, with front rank kneeling and rear rank standing, they delivered such a deadly blast down that slope as covered it with dead and checked and cowed the living. The oncoming wave was checked, and the corn was cut, and the heart was cut out of the fight on that part of the line at least. Oh! if we could have gone into the fight at the right place I might tell you a different story.

Passing in the rear of the line to the left I fell in with a few of our fellows, but we all felt sad and said little. As we passed out of the corn a great sight met our eyes. We were now on the extreme left of our line of battle, and a fine battery of six guns was stationed and in action at this point. The gray overlapped the blue here, not very far, but were trying to curl around the flank in the shape of a reaping hook. Some of our guns were directed straight to the front, but the left-half battery was gradually turned to suit the conditions. The gray lines advanced in good style, mounted officers in the rear waving swords, men, grim and gray, charging into the fiery furnace, gunners running, leaping and yelling and ramming home the deadly charges, guns jumping and bellowing, shot tearing and hurtling. The gray lads quailed and, as the gaps in their line increased, sought cover. At each discharge the gunners would yell: "Well done, Margaret"—"Betsy"— "Polly"—as the case might be, and run to caress and pat the gun as if it were a living thing. I found afterwards that it was common among the batteries for the boys to give their guns pet names.

That was a sight I wish you might have seen, then you would understand how utterly impossible it is for one to picture it in truth and fidelity. I think I wasn't looking on this scene more than two minutes, but a glance made a picture, indelible while life lasts. The firing was now heavy away off to the right, and all along the line for that matter, but smoke so enveloped all that my view was limited. I had thrown away my gun when I left the "Devil's Lane," but guns lay loose everywhere and I picked up another. By this time about a dozen of my company were with me and, being as sheep without a shepherd, we fell back of a crest to our rear, going forward at intervals to fire. Back of this crest were many stragglers and wounded gathered around a great fresh spring and pool in the rocks, and this is what those gray lads who tried to turn our flank wanted. Soon shells and solid shot began to come screaming over us, a little lower until they had the range down fine. As the shells burst, each piece sang a different tune, all lacking in either sweetness or harmony. Here Brigadier-General Correll was killed.[25] His great, big, nice brigade had vanished, melted away. He had always hitherto been an artillery officer, and when the action commenced he forgot all about his Infantry and rushed to the battle to fight it—so we were told. Anyway here he was mourning in a dazed, helpless manner, and here he was killed in my presence—his whole right breast shot away, ribs and all. Our assistant surgeon, Dr. Taft, placed him in a sitting position with his back to a big rock, then his face turned blue, and he joined the great pale army of the dead.

From this point we could see mounted officers, general officers and orderlies galloping here and there like the wind, some in fine dress uniforms and red sashes, with fine horses and equipments. Now and then a horse and rider came into view, but night soon closed the scene. Suddenly all the roar and rout of the tumult ceased, except at intervals the surly bellow of a great gun, until all was quiet save the moans and groans of the poor, luckless fellows we had left behind. There had been nothing gained on either side, except perhaps Bragg had gained time to save the trains of plunder he had gathered in Kentucky, but certainly it was costly plunder.

Here by the spring my little squad remained all night. We could see lanterns or lights of some kind moving all over the battle field. I was safe and sound without a scratch. I carried my blanket twisted in a rope over my left shoulder with the ends tied together with a string, falling under my right arm. On unrolling it I found a bullet had passed through it just where it rested on my shoulder, making twenty-one holes. But a miss is as good as a mile, and as there were thousands of blankets to be had for picking them up I made an exchange. I was dead tired, heartsick and homesick, hungry and discouraged, but soon smothered it all in sleep. In the morning we saw no organized troops, only ambulances and stretcher bearers everywhere caring for the wounded, so we started, some seventeen of us, to find some authority to take us in. Stragglers were here, there, everywhere, poor wounded being helped by comrades, crawling, crippling along, dead and dying all about. The dead had all be robbed, pockets cut or turned inside out, and every article of value, such as watches, rings, etc., gone. Often the dead clasped the gun in his hand with a last, dying grip. Pistols and small arms lay all about and an occasional stray, dismounted cannon.

We finally found the Colonel[26] sitting on a cracker box under a tree, with a hundred or more men and officers about him. He began immediately to question me, short and sharp, thus: "And where have you been, sir?" I told him some few things that came in my mind, with as much sweetness as I could dust into my speech, and he soon dropped his inquiries, with: "Oh! I see he's been there," and ordered me to take command of my Company. Our Captain had been killed and the First Lieutenant had not been seen in the engagement at all.[27] So here I was less than sixty days from the plow tail, destitute of any kind of a proper education or fitness, chucked, as it were, a square peg into a round hole. To shorten my story—stragglers kept coming in all day; Bragg was scurrying off; and a detail of four men from each Company was left me, with orders to bury the dead of our regiment and follow as soon as possible.

The troops moved on, and we were alone except for those who were left behind for a like purpose—the hospitals and their attendants, surgeons, stretcher bearers, etc. With shovels and stretchers we started for that part of the Devil's Lane where I had crossed. Ambulances were everywhere, gathering up their ghastly, groaning freight, twisting, turning and backing to avoid running over the dead wholly about in all sorts of shapes and places, often in groups of half a dozen, all blackened and swollen. Arrived at the lane we located a trench, and, while some dug, others bore the bodies and laid them on the margin. It was almost impossible to go to a proper depth, the ground being so dry and hard, so we concluded on two feet. It was very hard to identify even our own men, though we did the best we could, and as we laid the bodies in the trench, spread the limbs of each wide apart, resting the head of each on another, covering the whole with blankets, then with earth. Forty-two were in that trench, I think. It was a sad business, anyway. Around the battery were a good many, a dozen or more between the fences, some in the grass and weeds all over the hill. All down the slope were as many or more of the lads in gray.

Here where a few of us made this stand at the lane, Captain Canfield[28] fell by my side. After a bit he got up, pale as a ghost. A buckshot had hit him true in the center of the forehead at the hair line, plowed its way under the scalp to his crown and passed out. A stream of blood ran down his nose, there parted and trickled down in a little rill on either side. I said: "Captain, you're done for, get away if you can." "Not by a d. . .n sight," said he. Hathaway, his Orderly-Sergeant, was nearby, working away industriously, and the Captain reared out, "Hathaway, give 'em hell!" Hathaway turned his face for a second, and in a hurt voice replied: "Captain, ain't I givin' 'em hell?," and banged away again. Afterward I marched many a day and shared luck with the Captain; his was Company "E" and joined me on the left. Here too a little Dutch boy of my Company—Hernstein—got a tick with a buckshot about the ankle, from which he died. You see, according to the rights of it, I think the Captain should have died and the boy get well. Some folks stand a lot more shooting than others.

All this gives you but a faint glimpse of what one, green, young fellow saw where "death held a reception and he had been invited." My mind, as I write, is full of it, and what to tell, what to leave untold, is hard to decide. In this bootless fight about forty-five hundred men were lost to us, about as many as the whole Mexican War cost us. General Buell[29] was Chief of our forces, and Bragg was Chief of the other side. The battle on our side was fought mainly by new troops, while older troops lay near and would willingly have helped. A few days after I was told this by my old desk mate of the little red school house, Colonel Stratten[30] of the 19th O.V.I. He said: "Oh! we heard it all and were not three miles away; we knew you were catching it and would have been glad to come to your aid."

No two men would tell you the same tale about this or any other fight. In line of battle and the heat of an engagement one can't see much of the battle except what is in his immediate front. An infantry officer doing duty in the line knows nothing of the movements of the army he is with, not even of his own brigade or regiment. He is like a checker on the board; he goes where he is sent, and stays until he is moved or gobbled up.

We went into the battle of Perryville six hundred strong, and I think never had four hundred in line afterward, and never took more than three hundred and fifty into action. The regiment soon ran down to three hundred or three hundred and fifty, and stayed there to the end. So you see the casualties of the service in two short months—killed, wounded, discharged, and those who died of disease in hospital—amounted to more men than there were left. We never really courted a fight after this.

At Danville, Kentucky, we caught up with our regiment and were switched out of line to Munfordsville to guard a high bridge over Green

River on the line of the Lousiville & Nashville Railroad. Here we lay for a month or more. Bragg had established his headquarters at Murfreesboro, Tennessee, and Rosecrans[31] was made Chief of our army. Buell was never heard of again in army life.

We arrived at this place about the 1st of November, 1862, and remained nearly a month. Here was started a school for officers at the Colonel's quarters. He and our Lieutenant Colonel[32] had been officers in the 41st O.V.I. and had seen a year's service. A few of the other officers had been in the service, but the greater part were as green as I. Some came from schools—several from Oberlin and Hiram—and these had quite the advantage in the matter of education. Some were men of middle age or past, patriotic old fellows, but the service was too hard and exacting for them, and most all them resigned soon to go home, and nearly all of them went to early graves.

Well, the tactics from the books were hard for me to master until I could see a movement in squad, company or battalion drill, when all came clear to me, and my Company could make as good showing as any. The danger here was supposed to be a dash of cavalry to burn the bridge, so we practiced forming hollow squares, in which movement we became very efficient. This was to guard against surprise and resist cavalry. When formed, these hollow squares were very impressive to look at, with fixed bayonets, the front rank kneeling, the rear rank standing. At charge, bayonets presented a double line of glittering steel points faced outwards on all sides, with the officers and file closed in the center. This movement we learned to make at a moment's warning and with precision, and I want to tell you that we all felt that the bits of territory within these squares were in the Union, though we were in a hostile State, and that all manner of civil employments might have been carried on there in peace and quietness—even the assessor, tax gatherer, shoemaker or blacksmith might have followed each his calling in the utmost safety as against cavalry. Indeed, I would go far to see the like again. Truth, however, compels me to say that fraught though our service was with all kinds of peril, it was never in the least danger of having such squares broken, and I never saw an occasion requiring their formation except for practice. True it is that we had no fear of cavalry except the apprehension of being run over by our own "critter companies."[33]

Here I must go back a bit to our march on Richmond, where I told you we met the cavalry as we were plodding on our weary march. These fellows, with jingling spurs, sabres flying, carbines bumping, came crashing right through our ranks. One horse ran your Uncle down, knocked him helter-skelter and hurt him, and as he sat him down upon a log to rub his sore places he forged a choice lot of short, sharp weapons, fashioned in style like a reaping hook with a sickle tooth edge. As fast as they fell from the forge they were tested, labeled, packed in dozens, and laid carefully away in his mind to be used in guarding against cavalry. In truth, from that day forward our regiment had a most unreasoning hatred for the mounted arm of our service. We lost no opportunity to show our vengeful malice. Saddle flaps kept our regimental cobbler in shoe soles.

We had but one opportunity to meet the cavalry in gray, and that was the dandiest, jolliest, happiest racket we had, and I don't think that cavalry command ever committed such audacious foolishness again as that which led them into this scrape, but I will tell you of that in its proper place.

I want to tell you here of a visit made with my Orderly to our hospital after the Perryville fight. After burying the dead he and I hurried back across the battle field to an old church in the rear. I remember as we hastened along we found wounded men, in the last agonies, gasping for breath, and, without removing our canteens, drew the stoppers, dropped upon one knee, gave each a sup, and went on. The church was full of poor, mangled fellows. Surgeons were busy, and piles of naked and bloody limbs, hands, feet, legs and arms lay about the church. We shook hands with those who were equal to it, bade the poor fellows a sad good bye and lit out. Your Father visited that hospital some weeks after and can tell better than I what it looked like to him.

It was at this time too, while we were burying the dead, I unbuckled my sabre belt, took it off, and, leaning the sabre against the tree which had given me protection during the fight, took hold of a stretcher and helped. When we had finished my sabre was gone, stolen by some prowler. Just then a mounted Orderly of our Colonel's staff rode up, heard me explaining my views in words of which he caught the import, and, saying: "Oh! that's all right, I'll soon fix you out" was back in a trice with the old sabre I now have, the only thing I have left from the great Rebellion. The scabbard of this being of steel it must have belonged to a mounted officer, and its history would doubtless be of interest could we but know it. The scabbard of the infantry line officer's sabre in those days was always of leather tipped with brass, and as it usually got soaking wet two or three times a week, and shrunk when it dried, the brass tip came off and the point of the naked blade stuck out from one to four inches, looking like highwater pants on a country pumpkin roller.[34] So though I didn't wear a regulation sabre I liked it much better.

The days passed—tough too—weather cold and cheerless—and at all times of the night the long roll would beat, the regiment get into line double quick and be marched in line of battle through wet grass, weeds and tangled brush to God knows where, to wait and anticipate an attack in darkness, cold and gloom, only to be relieved at daylight. This sort of thing was kept up all the time we laid at Mumfordsville, about thirty days, and as it began to grow old, and we knew it was only for practice, I won't say but the men learned to grumble, and even swear some, though it might have been so.

Now the storm center seemed to be gathering again at the South. Great accounts of old Rosey's grand army at Nashville came to us through the newspapers, and there was a certain vague feeling among us that another might crisis was close at hand. The contentments of outlying troops[35] were being broken up and pushed forward for Nashville, and we soon received orders to prepare. I had orders as commandant of my Company to receipt for all my Company's property, which I did, for the full equipment of the Company as it stood at Lexington before a move was made—ninety-six guns with all their appurtenances, a like number of knapsacks and mess kettles, six Sibley tents,[36] etc. I think the whole value was some Twenty-one Thousand Dollars, and I actually had in the Company less than half of the men or equipments, but I was ordered to do it, and did so, neither knowing nor caring about the financial responsibility. We all enlisted to "put down the Rebellion," and I had no thought that good Uncle Sam would make me pay for a gun, a screw-driver or cone wrench, stanchion, belt plate or measly, old worn-out, ragged knapsack or canteen, when I was doing my best to serve him with all my life and strength; and I was right. The grand, old fellow is good and fair to his honest friends, and soon after the close of the war he passed a sweeping law and jumped accounts with all such heedless, careless fellows, else your Uncle had been sadly pinched. Had I known the ins and outs of the trade I could rightly have lost and dropped from my accounts a big load of stuff by reason of the battle of Perryville. Quarterly returns should have been made, but our way of campaigning left little time for book-keeping, if I had known how, which I didn't, and was too busy just then to take a term at commercial college.

Here we had the usual army rations, but we soon longed for a change, and I fear some fair-intentioned, well-brought-up, young fellows were overcome by temptation. Anyway we now and then had a bit of fresh pork and fowl with other knick-knacks which I had not noticed on the commissary bill of fare.

As we were about to start on our march it occurred to me that so far I had no dress or uniform except such as privates wore, and the only distinguishing mark I had was shoulder straps on my private's blouse and my sabre, it being impossible to obtain an officer's uniform; so I went to sutler and bought a pair of seven-league boots;[37] and when we started off, route step,[38] flag unfurled, band playing, horses prancing, and me in my knee boots, Oh! you should have seen me. I felt fit for anything. But, alack and alas, the "best laid schemes of mice and men" go bad and leave nothing to speak of but grief and pain. Pride goes before a fall the world over. I paid Sixteen Dollars for those boots and had a right to be proud of them. Captain Canfield of Company "E" was in rear of me, Captain Mason of Company "C"[39] next in front, so my new boots were duly admired, and I was prone to believe envied by all. I took special pains show the iron plates on the heels to Mason and Canfield. They congratulated me, but smiled doubtfully, as with a reservation, something back that I didn't sense. Both had been in the three months' service and knew one thing, maybe two. The line of march lay over an unused stone pike, very broken and washed out. Before noon my big boots began to be a burden, but there was no let up; the skin rubbed off my heels; my ankles were chafed and sore; every step was burning misery. By two P.M. I would have sold my interest in the world for a farthing and thrown in the boots. I marched bow-legged, cross legged, pigeon-toed, and tried every bias and slant to get any ease, while on and on we marched with steady tread. Oh! I never saw the sun lag so, but this too must have an end. The sun at last shut his glories in, and "Halt" never sounded so sweet. Before arms were stacked I lay prone and suffering, but the end was not yet, for soon came the Adjutant, with: "Lieutenant Hartzell for picket!" Words do well enough in their places, but here they are of no account whatever. I went out into the dark night and philosophized. The conclusion at which I arrived was this: Ignorance and pride make a tough school-master. Through weary life this lesson learn, that "man was made to mourn." In the morning, when the pickets were drawn in, I went to my company teamster, exchanged my seven-league boots for a pair of broad-bottomed, army brogans, and from that day to this—I have kept my feet out of high top leather boots. After this, though the marching was heavy, I was always equal to my duty, and we had all come to have an idea of the life and duties of soldiers.

Passing Glasgow we arrived at Gallatin, Tennessee, where our march was directed to Huntsville, a point on the Tennessee River where was a ford or bridge which was being guarded by two regiments to prevent the rebels crossing and getting into our rear to destroy our railroad, burn bridges, etc. These two regiments had been surprised and captured, and a force of rebel cavalry passed us in the rear. So we were started back, infantry after cavalry. In this rapid counter-march much grumbling was indulged in, many men gave out, and the ambulances were full of poor, suffering victims all the time. When the bugles sounded sick call in the morning, many a wornout, dejected, homesick chap responded.

This was in the Month of December,[40] cold, raw and cheerless. One day we waded Barren River which was covered with a thin sheet of ice. One of the officers tried to ford and found the water belly deep to his horse. The men stripped shoes, socks and trousers and carried them high and dry with their other accouterments, and so made the crossing. The Lieutenant-Colonel asked me to mount behind him, but I didn't, and I well recollect what a sight those men were as they came out of the water. From a well-defined line in the middle the lower halves of their bodies were dark blue.

Soon we passed through Glasgow again, and now, from hard service and want of good shoes, the men were marching with much suffering, and being on the line of railway, each passing train to the South was looked upon with longing and yearning eyes, hoping at each station to be invited to ride. Sometimes a few of the worst shod would be sent forward by rail, but very few. It was a case where many thought they were called but few chosen, and here I must tell you a little story.

Companies "A" and "C" were mostly Irish and Welsh miners and iron workers from Youngstown, Girard and Niles. During our last night away back at Lexington an Irishman of Company "A," Dennis McCanna, procured a canteen of whiskey. In the morning, before starting on our retreat to Louisville, he was placed upon camp guard, pending the "fall in." The sun was hot, so at the end of this beat he took off his canteen and laid it on the ground and deposited his knapsack and blankets on top. During the day, mid the heat and dust of the forced march, he thought to revive his drooping spirits by a sup from his canteen, but was greatly surprised and shocked on putting it to his mouth to find it contained nothing in the world but just plain water. Of course Dennis was troubled in his mind, but finally solved the mystery thus: Bob Hunter of the same Company was on the next beat and had exchanged canteens while Dennis' back was turned. When the water was thus made plain, Dennis said to himself: "Robert, I'll be even wid yez if it takes tin years or during the war." So now the day of vengeance had arrived, Bob's hour was to come. On the day before we arrived at Glasgow Dennis, by hook or crook, had secured a pair of new shoes, and just before the bugle sounded "Fall in" had found out that all ill shod were to get a ride, and, knowing that Bob Hunter's shoes were so bad as to fetch him luck, he hustled off to find Bob coming out a shanty with a full canteen. Immediately Dennis assumed the painful limp of a sad cripple, and as they met, in answer to Bob's: "What's the matter now, Dennis?" replied: "Oh! Bob, see me new shoes, me fate is a killin' me. How will ye thrade?" "I've got no money, Dinnis, but take a drink," handing him the canteen. "Take aff one ay your shoes, Bob, and let me thry it an." So Bob took off first one, then the other, and the trade was satisfactorily concluded, with a promise from Bob to pay the difference on the first pay day. Another drink sealed the bargain. Then the bugle sounded "Fall in," and as the regiment stood in line, fronting a train in which was an empty gondola, the Adjutant sang out: "All whose shoes are worn out step three paces to the front." Dennis stepped out, passed inspection, mounted the gondola, and, as he looked down at Bob in his new shoes, laid his thumb aside of his nose, wiggled his fingers and said: "Now, Bob, we've aven." So he rode to Nashville, while Hunter walked; and today, though his blessed old head is as white as snow, he tells this as his finest achievement in the great war. You see the railroad was pushed to its utmost carrying troops ordnance and all sorts of army supplies to the front.

CHAPTER TEN

⟨⚬⟩

[Battle of Stones River; Winter Campaign; Scouting; Illness; On the March]

Our Colonel[1] was ambitious and wanted promotion. Already he was in command of the brigade in place of General Terrill, killed at Perryville. We thought him willing to sacrifice every man he had to get a star.

I think it was here at Glasgow we received word which led us to believe there was great preparation making for the struggle that could not be put off much longer, and when we again started towards the South the Colonel took every mile out of us he could get each day. One day, when on the march, we had news of a great victory at Stone River.[2] Then the flag was given to the wind, we cheered ourselves hoarse, the band struck up, and the straggling, weary, sullen column took shape and step and pushed on, transformed in a moment to a happy, joking, jolly lot of boys who thought they saw visions of speedy peace and home and friends once more.

The battle of Stone River was fought on January 1st, 1863,[3] and we entered Nashville soon after. When we arrived, long lines of ambulances were still coming in from the field, bearing the wounded. We immediately started out to guard a great train of wagons loaded with supplies for the front. As we came upon the field the sights now made familiar were again before us. Of course this was a much greater engagement than Perryville, the lines more extended and more troops engaged, yet the scenes were practically the same. Long, low lines of protection—earth, rails, logs, anything to stop a bullet, were to be seen here and there—zig-zagging in every shape as the swaying, charging lines to make them in the lull of battle.

Field and post hospitals were crowded to overflowing. We were kept on the go all the time. Large supplies had to be brought up from Nashville, some thirty miles distant, and every train had a strong escort. I recollect once we arrived late and I remained overnight, so I went through as many hospitals as I could, to see if I could find anyone I knew. In one I found my boy crony and desk-mate, Colonel Stratton,[4] sadly wounded. In a private house I found three officers, two of my acquaintance, Captain James Mc-Cleery and Major Wolcott of the 41st,[5] and Captain Erwin[6] of the 19th. He was from Salineville and was shot entirely through the body. The ball passed through the lungs, and he could speak only in a whisper. Wolcott had a foot off and Mac was minus his right arm, with a ball through the fleshy part of the thighs. All three were in one room twelve or fifteen feet square, and were as jolly a party as one would often meet. The talk was as to how they would make a living when they got home. They thought to run a fish wagon, Erwin to drive, Wolcott to take in the money, and Jim McCleery to walk along side and shout "Fresh fish!" Erwin and McCleery died within a year,[7] and of Wolcott I have no further knowledge, but think he got well.

The winter of '62–'63 was a busy one for our little brigade, reduced now from the original four thousand to thirteen hundred, which figures tell the tale of hardship in more eloquent words than I can employ. The Confederate Army under General Bragg and our army under "Old Rosey" lay from fifty to seventy miles apart, Bragg with headquarters at Tullahoma and Rosey at Murfreesboro. Lines of outposts with foragers, scouts and small detachments, such as regiments, brigades, etc., patrolled the fronts and all the intervening territory. Each day brought something of interest, and the sound of the fife, drum and bugle was blended with and accented by the song of the bullet and crash of the shell. To the right, left or in front we had daily notice that we were in the presence of an ever-vigilant foe. Our little brigade camped near the front and was kept on the go continually, while the great army that had fought the battle of Stone River lay nursing its wounded and scouring its equipments for the struggle that was sure to come in the spring.

Often we'd steal out at night, with forty rounds of ammunition and four of five days' rations, march into the darkness, single file, over hills and rocks, through cedar brakes and old deadnings, by silent farm-houses, wade streams, wet, muddy and sleepy, like Indians on the war path, without notice. Even the cracking of a twig or rattling of the canteen against a bayonet was guarded against, while the darkness and silence, together with the utter ignorance of out mission or destination, was most oppressive. But the morning would find us alert, with a complete cordon drawn around some village, ready to close in on some noted guerrilla or partisan troop of the enemy; or perhaps some cotton factory or supplies were to be destroyed. Then patrol for days, or until supplies had to be replenished, or for any other cause we returned to camp.

What I remember of that winter's campaign would fill a book, and perhaps be of no interest to you. A company of Colonel Brownlow's east Tennessee cavalry[8] (Captain Blackburn's) always went along to act as guides, and generally a section of our brigade battery, Captain Harris, 10th Indiana,[9] so we could fight, or forage, or run, and have a shindy[10] almost any day at the drop of the hat.

Servants here became plenty, and there was some rivalry between the officers as to whose was the best. Captain Stambaugh,[11] who commanded Company "A," had one, "Nigger Ned," acknowledged the very best in the regiment, good cook, good forager, good anything. I had had poor success with mine, but finally got what appeared to be a good one, a fine looking boy, and immediately rigged him up in great style, new suit, shiny haversack, bought of the butler, great big, new, rubber blanket—looked like a movable quartermaster's supply store when I had him loaded.

Well, one morning we were off for a scout, the first for my new darky George, who the day before, while I was on picket duty, had gotten a chicken and cooked it and had it in the haversack, so I bade him load up. The regiment fell into line, darkies in the rear. Then in the pride of my heart I directed Dam Stambaugh's attention to my darky, and made a clumsy atttempt to cut a pigeon wing. We lit out, but along towards noon we ran against a snag. A long, low, cleared hill cut our line of march at right angle. Along its crest ran an old rail fence, and behind that fence were some gentlemen who seemed to want to hold an argument with us on some disputed points in politics which were prominently before the public at that time; but our Colonel had urgent business further south and would not stop for discussion. Our regiment being in the lead we formed in line of battle, and my Company was thrown as skirmishers, my green servant, without my knowledge, following in rear of the skirmish-line. As we approached the fence a weak fusillade was opened by the lads above, but as we were on the charge we soon took the fence, but the heavy cost of it fell on your Uncle. My George was gone, with all my Quartermaster and Company stores. Where he went, or how he went, no man ever knew,—only that he went. Music was new to him and he vanished, leaving me to eat much humble pie; and I reflect again that all pride, either of purse or property, is almost sure to have a fall.

After this I took a man from the ranks for my servant, a good fellow but a sly thief, who could never abide the stink of powder, could loot a sutler and scent anything fit to eat or drink, whether milk or applejack, within five miles of the line of march when the wind was right; considered his duty well done if he kept my wants supplied, and in this I sought no argument or quarrel with him. Moreover, he was a kind nurse, and, though he finished up by robbing me, I forgive him.

On one of these scouting expeditions, while advancing in column, we met a half dozen or more county wagons loaded with dressed poultry, smoked meats, and all kinds of goodies going to Bragg's army. The wagons moved to the side of the road, and as kind Providence had so arranged it that our regiment was in the lead that day, when the boys saw the manna which had dropped down in their pathway they fixed bayonet without orders, and each file as it passed ornamented the bayonet-points with chicken, turkey, ham or flat pieces of bacon, so that the wagons were soon empty and the drivers were grieved and sad; but the column swung its guns to right shoulder shift and kept steadily on, singing, "We'll hang Jeff Davis on a sour apple tree"; and again it was proved that "the best laid plans of mice and men gang aft agley, and leave us naught but grief or pain for promised joy."[12] So the drivers thought anyway, athough it was a very pleasant diversion for we'uns.

On the night of the 19th of March, 1863, while on a scout, our little brigade bivouacked, after a hard day's march, on the side of a wooded hill.[13] It was raining, and each man fixed bayonets, reversed his gun, jammed the bayonet into the ground and left it with the butt sticking up, then, rolled in his wool and rubber blanket, laid down just where he happened to halt, and dropped into such deep sleep as it is given only to a tired soldier to know.

In the morning, just as a little faint gilding of the horizon began to show in the East, picket firing began nearby, so there was no cause to shout "Fall in!," but in an instant every man was in his place, and we took up our line of march which led up hill by a dug road to level ground above. When the infantry marching in column had reached the top and made some progress on the level, we halted, and in a few minutes the old cedar fence was all aglow with fire, the men all busy making coffee in empty fruit cans with wire bails, hung in little, forked, green limbs cut with a pocket-knife anywhere by the wayside and stuck into the soft ground so as to overhang the fire. Some were toasting meat on the end of iron ramrods, or frying it in skillets made of half a canteen with a stiff piece of wire for the handle. Everything was steaming in a few minutes. Arms were stacked in the road. One section of the battery remained in the rear at the head of the dug road, and just as the boys were ready to gulp their hot coffee and the bacon was sizzling, those two, old parrots[14] went "Boom! Boom!" The scene which followed is too much for my old stub of a pencil, so I pass it by. I assure you no orders to fall in were required. In a moment out regiment was thrown into line of battle on the left of the road and the 101st Indiana on the right, while the two other regiments marched in column on the road, and thus we took up our march towards Murfreesboro some nine miles away. The two guns in our battery made haste to close up on our rear, and in a very short time the "critter companies" of the gentlemen in gray began to pour up the dug road and take line in our rear, overlapping our flanks far enough. A rocky hill crossed our line of march at right angles. A rail fence followed along the foot of it. As we reached the fence the gentlemen in gray were coming within easy range. Our regiment crossed and very placidly balanced their muskets, caliber 54, on that fence, and the wave of retreat was checked there, because a large number of the gentlemen in gray became suddenly fatigued and took a rest, excused from duty, in fact the war was over for them. We climbed and, in a hasty sort of leisure, prepared a reception,—for that fool cavalry was bound to hold one,—and, inasmuch as they were urgent, we thought to give them a warm welcome and a satisfactory time, which the same we did. The right wing of our regiment was held in reserve, a sort of flying squadron. The cavalry dismounted, brought up six field pieces and two howitzers, all in plain sight. The ball opened with a full chorus, and the reception lasted until about 3:30 PM.

This little fight was in plain sight of us all, was well fought; and in my mind is an unfaded photograph of it to this 12th day of February, 1897. After they had had just a little whiff of our style of arguing politics they saw the logic of it, and the whole line retired, left their critters somewhere out of sight, and returned in double line, searching to find or make a break in our line. They struck the 101st Indiana, great big, stout, slouchy fellows armed with Belgian rifles with muzzles like railroad tunnels and heavy sabre bayonets. Ah! if you could have heard those fellows giving their first hearty greeting to our would-be guests. Those big-throated, old rifles roared till they fairly made the rocks jingle with their welcome, gaps were made, and our little flying squadron was kept busy all day long. The big guns kept pounding away with all sorts of stuff. Most of the time we were lying behind any defence, such as logs, stumps and roots. A big rock was cheerful security, while a pebble the size of a tin cup, right against your crown as you lie flat, may stop a bullet or deflect a grape, and is not to be despised. I was lying close to the turnpike highway, and here, right in the center of the fight, stood one of our field pieces, commanded by Lieutenant Stackhouse.[15] My place was not more than a rod from where it stood, giving and receiving compliments all day long, getting so hot at times as to require a breathing spell to cool off. I wish I could give you a little glimpse of the way those fellows did act with that old gun, and of the Lieutenant who had charge of it; how the boys leaped and strained and rammed and swabbed, sighted and swore; how Stack was everywhere giving orders and timing fuses; and when the other side sought to press up to see the grape home and hear Stack's order to the gunners: "That's grape,[16] boys, sift it low, sift it low." Then how the boys would stoop with one hand on knee, the other shading the eyes, legs well spread like a baseball umpire, watching the effect of each shot; and then the language those fellows used that day was certainly shocking, such as no gentleman would use anywhere,— except perhaps right there. Captain Mason, Company "R"[17]—the rascal— with his back to a big rock, laughed at me shamefully because, when a bullet came near my ear with its vicious, little snip, or a splinter with its angry whiz, or a big fellow crying "Where is you? Where is you?" I had the politeness to stand aside, as much as to say "There's plenty of room for all of us and no crowding." A large, red oak tree grew out of the edge of the pike, and a headquarter's clerk, little Rice, who always staid in camp and complained of it, but was along on this scout to have an outing and some fun, took shelter behind this tree when the fight began. A twelve pound shot struck this tree in the center, some twelve feet or more from the ground, on the far side where Rice was crouched, tore out two great splinters, one above and the other below. The lower splinter fell outward from the shot hole and hung nearly to the ground, but Rice didn't wait for the splinter; he made off on all fours and never said "Good bye." Now here comes Uncle Dan,[18] claiming the honor of the victory of this battle of Milton. He had command of camp followers, pack mules, etc., and just at the critical moment, like the gillies at Bannockburn,[19] brought up his forces with such cheering and shouting as scared the enemy off, and peace and quiet reigned again.

There are always some fellows who gig back on account of the company, bad language or some other good reason; and you should have heard our Colonel that day, spurring his horse among them, pistol in hand, ordering them back to duty with the most "awdacious" language. Our surgeon, Charlie Fowler, came galloping up to me, right in the heat of it all, and said that he had heard I was killed or wounded, and set me down as a base deceiver, when 'twas the Captain of Company "H," 101st Indiana.

After the firing ceased and the enemy had retreated our Colonel with a number of mounted men rode over the field, while a lot of us tired fellows sat on a log by Stackhouse's gun near the pike, talking over the events of the day. The Colonel came riding back, much pleased and as he passed he dropped a blackened, bloody hand, which he held by the forefinger, into Stackhouse's lap, with "John Morgan sends his compliments."[20] You see this Morgan was the fellow whom we had followed up in Kentucky for a month or more in the early winter, and being made foot cavalry of made us feel sour and morose towards his "critter companies." We longed to exchange greetings with him, so when he came to our party we banged him around "skandalous."

The ground was rocky, and I hear the rattling spat of the grape yet as it struck the rocks and went whizzing off through the cedars. As our men lay on the ground their backs were green with cedar foliage cut by the hail of iron and lead. We had a few prisoners and had to hold them close to our line, as our foe was behind and before and all around, and oh! how they did whine and beg and cuss.

Before we left the field I walked a little way to the front and saw lying among the rebel dead a fine, young fellow, wearing a new, gray, frock coat with wide, silk velvet cuffs and collar of blue. He was dark featured, with mustache and long, curly, black hair, and very neat and tidy, but he had left father Abraham's house and wandered into a far country. Who[se] boy was he?

It was a grand, little scrap, just the chance at the cavalry we longed for. As Uncle Remus would say: "I don't think brer fox ever hankered atter cousin wild-cat atterwards . . ."[21]

About night we took up march again towards our old camp at Murfreesboro. There they had heard us pounding away and knew of our victory. So they came out, thousands of them, in fatigue dress, with torches and lights of all kinds. They formed in double line, and, as we marched between with banners flying, with music and the cheers of our comrades filling the night air, we stepped high, and I think I never before felt so big round nor so long up and down. We had hardly got off our traps when brave, old Joe Reynolds, our division commander, sent a lovely, little billet-doux which read: "The wine is on the table, time eight sharp." So we bustled off to headquarters and drank each other's health in the regulation bumpers and in the regulation stuff, and I can e'en a'most feel it biting yet. We thought we had done a good day's work and that the boys should have had an extra month's pay.

This was the last time out gallant Colonel ever led his brigade to duty, as he soon after died in camp. On this scouting many things of interest occurred daily. After this I was promoted to First Lieutenant;[22] in fact, my Company, on the field at Perryville, the day after the fight, made up a petition asking that I be made Captain; Vice-Captain Robert Wilson, killed; but this was not granted, as it would have been quite unmilitary to have jumped a Second over all the First Lieutenants, so a nephew of the Lieutenant-Colonel, Tuttle by name, was promoted; but we never saw him afterward, and I remained with the Company and got the business experience, while he had the plum, but I'm glad of it.

About this time my Orderly was promoted to Second Lieutenant,[23] and I fell sick, so he wore my old coat-straps and sabre while I lay in a tent and burned up with a fever. The regiment soon moved to a better camp ground, right near to our general field hospital, a great city of fresh, white-walled tents. I lay in the end tent to the left in the front row, and I remember as the days grew warmer how the flies pestered me, forming in squadrons round my eyes, nose and mouth. For a while I would languidly pass my hand over my face, so driving them off for a moment, but after a time I grew indifferent and left them alone. Ambulances with the dead, with music and guard with reversed arms, were daily and hourly passing, passing in solemn monotony. Some of my comrades died in my tent, while the surgeons plied their gruesome task before my eyes. To tell you more particularly of it would be neither pleasant nor profitable. A goodish bit of time passed of which I have no recollection, when one day a half dozen or more of my Company were standing by my cot and one of them said: "Lieutenant, do you know me?" I named him, and so on—all the lot— then they said: "Oh! he's all right," and went out. Colonel Tolles,[24] who was now our Colonel, came one day, talked so nice and kind, and asked me what I would like to eat. I said, "Onions;" and it wasn't long till he came back with a little onion about as large as a hickory nut. In a few days he got me out to pitch quoits, and, with the pegs some fifteen feet apart, I couldn't send mine more than three or four feet beyond my toes.

Charlie Fowler, our surgeon, made fun of my legs and said, if I had another one behind, the same size, I'd made a splendid music rack for our Dutch brigade bandmaster. In truth, at the knee they were larger than any other place. You could almost span them with one hand. Well, anyway I kept out on the bone-yard, though by a close shave, as I weighed only ninety-six pounds. How many poor boys passed from this city of tents to that city whose maker and builder is God, I shouldn't dare to guess. Fathers and mothers and friends from the homes far away came in troops to see and either mark the graves or carry away all that was mortal of their boys.

Murdock, the great elocutionist,[25] had a son in the artillery who was killed. He came after the body, and while with us gave readings from the Bible. Going from one division to another, taking a stump or cracker box for his stand, he would read a chapter, then go on, and soon had half the army at his heels. I heard him read the third chapter of St. John, and it did seem that I never had heard it before. Such an ovation of silent admiration few men have ever had.

While in the old camp here General Garfield and your Uncle, Colonel John E. MacGowan,[26] came to see me, and together we ate a soldier's dinner.

Now came June 24th, the day the great forward movement was to begin, and I in the hospital. Charlie Fowler came to give me a ticket to report at post hospital in town, so I donned my traps and, when this brigade was in line, took my place with my Company. My Second Lieutenant having been made Quartermaster of the division ambulance corps I was again left alone with the Company. When the surgeon saw me in the ranks he said: "If you will go, take these," giving me a handful of powders, with instructions to take one whenever I felt bad; so I soon took them all and got so drunk I reeled all over the road, till my big man, Jerry Whetstone,[27] put his powerful arm under mine, then I got on finely.

We were now Second Brigade, Third Division, Fourteenth Army Corps, and I tell you it was glorious to see that old army corps as each division took up the line of march, artillery all in place, everything spick and span, banners floating in the bright sunshine, drums and fifes, with bugles and brass bands everywhere, soldiers marching with swinging, easy step, bayonets bright and glinting, horses champing[28] and rearing, or dashing here and there with officers of all grades looking their very best; couriers in hot haste, with dispatches in belt, like bees darting straight for the hive. Ah! this was the grand pageantry of war, this was power on exhibition. I never saw its equal but once, and that was in Washington—the Grand Review[29]—at the close of the war, and almost in a day after this great anaconda of war, which had dragged its length over so many weary miles, leaving a broad trail of blood and ruin behind it, dissolved, melted away like snow before a summer sun, never, I hope, to be seen again in this blessed land.

Well, we pushed on south this day, making a good march. We struck roasting ears and blackberries. Between these and Doctor Fowler's medicine the diet was improving, and Richard was soon himself again. There was a heavy swell of war music to our right all day long, and in the evening we ran into a big hornet's nest at Hoover's Gap. As our division passed General Reynolds[30] each Company commander was beckoned to his side, when he leaned low and whispered, very mildly and confidential-like, into his ear: "Lieutenant, tell your men to aim low, aim low, wing 'em, wing 'em. It takes two able soldiers to carry off a wounded man." So with this pleasant confidence in our ears we dashed in and made short work. Darkness was just falling and rain coming down like suds.

We bivouacked in line just below the crest of the hill on which we had the scrap. My first file big men, Whetstone and Silver,[31] got some cedar boughs to lay on the loose stones for a bed, and said: "Now, we'll take the Lieutenant between us or he'll be washed down hill." We had one, big, rubber blanket which covered us all three, head and heels. I could hear the water rushing down between the stones beneath us as the rain fell all night long. Nearby lay seven deceased men in gray, and my old Jerry over and anon bawled orders to those to fall in, with such vaiations as came to his mind. With the morning we were ready for action. There was an open space in the timber, and, while we were preparing for the day's work, our Major,[32] with one or two other officers who had field-glasses, stepped to this opening to take a survey, but speedily retired. The sharp[33] had the range and kept that space open. We pushed on in line of battle nearly all day. Sometime during this day we came upon two big guns on a hill in our front, which were flinging very objectionable matter at us. Our order was to charge; I was weak and felt cowardly; my legs would gladly have sneaked off, but the rest of me was too proud to agree, as it was open daylight; when much to my relief, the gentlemen on the other side withdrew.

On we went in column for days and days; rain all the time and mud, mud, mud. All the glitter was guns. Mud, misery, and the music of minnie balls took its place. Finally we lined up one day near Tullahoma, where we felt sure of finding the enemy in great force and having a big fight.[34] I was on the skirmish line which advanced, wading the water half leg deep. Night fell, and the skirmishers were to remain as picket guards, so I fumbled around and got two old rails, and resting an end of each on a log out of the water had an inclined plane for a resting-place. Not being relieved we were on duty all night. By daylight our cook came wading out to us with hot coffee and bean soup, and as we could drink both we were soon refreshed and ready for business. We were then pushed forward and soon came to and passed through the Village of Tullahoma. Just beyond was a city of tents, each one being slashed and cut as the cavalry of the rebels had charged and sabred the empty tents. Here we found much tobacco and other supplies and, most valuable of all, many dutch ovens. My cook got one and immediately we commenced a very high style of living, for now a glorious summer was upon us; berries, peaches, and all kinds of fruits were plenty. For flour, crackers could be banged up fine; sugar we had; while condensed milk, pickled pigs feet, etc., could be had from the sutlers; and, oh! the good stuff that came out of our dutch oven. I was soon fatter than I had been lean a month before.

We pushed on with a little exchange greeting by the big guns almost every day, with occasionally a matinee. One such was at Elk River, where the gentlemen in gray made a claim that we had come just about far enough and any proper respect for their feelings would lead us to retire to our home and quit pestering them. Very shortly the arguments on both sides became serious, and Pappy Thomas (General George H.),[35] our corps commander, held that they were all wrong on that side, that his business engagements called him somewhat farther south, and that affairs were pressing; so his logic prevailed, and soon the noisy debate ceased. Our opponents saw the sense of it and departed, while we crossed and soon reached the mountains which had been in our view for many days. By dint of pulling and tugging, pushing and yelling, we arrived at the top of one called "University Heights." The top was a level plateau of some three or four miles, park-like in appearance, beautiful in every respect. No matter which way one looked the scenery was grand, while the situation was almost inaccessible, so that but little guard duty was necessary. We quickly laid out and built a city with a court, judges, mayor, police, etc., and were soon established with many conveniences. Here we wrote and received many letters and reveled in good things. The clouds were for the most part below us, so while we lay stretched at ease in the cool shade of trees on the edge of a cliff we could see rain clouds scurrying across the valley below, the trains, as they wound in and out of woods and tunnels, peeping through here and there as they followed the torturous iron rail, of this south land of mountains and valley.

I think we had a new division commander assigned us here, Colonel Edward King, an educated soldier, and some changes were made in the brigade. Our last rag of a knapsack we had left behind us, so we marched very light. That means that each man carried one-half of a wool blanket, a small rubber one, and half of a shelter tent—a piece of light, cotton canvas, say four by six foot—so arranged as to be quickly joined to its mate and in a few minutes put up as shelter from sun or rain, the whole weighing perhaps six pounds. Our cooking outfit was nothing to speak of,—half a canteen and a few mess kettles for cooking beans was all,—so that at the sound of long roll or marching orders our city vanished like a hurrying cloud before the wind. The walls and roofs and all the appurtenances belonging to the city, with its legal and police machinery, which stood in the morning early,—a busy, humming hive of humanity,—long before the morning sun had lifted midway in the heavens, was miles away, and the rugged hills would never again echo with the cheery, rattling din of bugle, fife, and drum which regulated the duties of the day; and the thousand twinkling lights of night, all were gone—our city had vanished. How many we builded,—some to stand for an hour, some a night, others a week or more,—but, no matter when or where the order came, we built with the same care and after the same manner and form as to streets, parades and general utility, so that quite a degree of comfort soon prevailed.

Cooking was most simple and easy, when we had things to cook. Candles were part of our rations, and a bayonet stuck in the ground served well for a [candle holder].[36] Leaves and cedar boughs furnished beds; and, though we were but yearlings, we were up to all the ways of a veteran and were well hardened by the Bessemer process.[37]

Now we go down to the valley again, easing down the wagons and artillery with ropes, and away through a fine, fertile country. Sequatchie valley was to me then and is now a remembrance of beauty and peace.

Our boys had grown a bit loose in their view of property rights and held to a theory like this: That such landscape as we had passed through was in and part of the Union, and they being laborers in the Union vineyard were earning a right to the fruits thereof, so helped themselves freely to whatever fell in the way. To this some of our leading gentlemen strongly objected, either because of their great learning or their less pressing needs. Strict orders were issued against "pilfering," I believe they called it. Company officers were to search out the miscreants and see that they were punished as a court martial might direct, or, failing in this, their own pay and perquisites were to be stopped until all was paid unto the uttermost farthing; but these orders proved unavailing and were growing dry, and, generally speaking, the eyes of the company officers were so blinded with dust that little could be seen beyond marching fast. General Turchin,[38] whose brigade, and a good one it was, was in our division, seemed blind or sleepy on every occasion when our late orders should have held him wide awake. His men all loved him, and, if his column was marching by, our boys never forsook labor even in peach orchard or potato field. Our Colonel King was a terror to evil-doers, so in the rear of our brigade we usually had a heavy tail of culprits taken in the very act. At the close of the day's march those were sent to their own command under guard and with a list of proper charges, there to be punished as the law directed. About this time we camped near Jasper, a pretty, little town in the valley. I was sent in with my Company as provost guard. Soon a batch of prisoners came to me with this instruction: "Take these men to General Turchin, give him my compliments and say these men were found violating order so and so." On arriving in front of the General's tent I lined up my men and, taking off my cap, delivered the message, when the old Dutchman smilingly said: "Dot was righd, Lieutenant, you are exgused." I lingered in retirement a bit to see the outcome of it, and soon heard the hand clap and shout which told that the punishment was remitted or deferred.

A few miles from Jasper was the Tennessee River, a mighty stream, and here at last, hedged about by nature's grandeur, our troops were to cross on a pontoon bridge at Shell Mound, a little, brick station on the south side of the River, belonging to the Nashville and Chattanooga Railroad. Delay occurred; gentlemen in gray over the river objected; council was called. There are certain small insects, without horn or bone yet persistent hangers-on, which seize any location on a soldier's body, hold it, and set about forming domestic relations and raising large families, infect his scanty clothing, and eventually become a great nuisance, trenching upon his constitutional rights to life and the pursuit of happiness; in short, after the first few settlements have been made the soldier's peace has fled; so when the question came up as to whether we should dislodge the enemy in gray across the river or the enemy in gray on our side of the river, we at once turned our attention to the enemy nearest at hand. Had you been there on that hot August day of 1863 you would have seen an unique sight. Hundreds, perhaps thousands of soldiers sitting or standing in all sorts of postures, each earnestly and industriously engaged with straining eyes, peering and peeping, gazing and searching with prudent solicitude over his body and clothing, and in turn each scratching his fellow's back. Literally we all said: "Now, if you'll scratch my back, I'll scratch your'n"; and we did it with hearty good-will and comradeship and many jests and gibes. The hours wore on, and the slaughter never ceased until the going down of the sun, and many graybacks[39] perished that day. However, this was neither the first nor the last battle we had with this social, little enemy. He was like the poor of all times—"ever present with us"—and jiggers[40] too had to be reckoned with.

CHAPTER ELEVEN

◠

[Battle of Chickamauga; Snodgrass Hill]

SOON THE ANGRY disputants, with the lovely river flowing peacefully between, became vicious. Ugly compliments and the ping of the cruel minnies[1] and the rush and roar of the big shells were the rude chorus provided for our reception. Sharp-shooters found lodgment in the little, brick station and at ease plied their cruel trade. And now if you will look, you will see, through that great cloud of dust, foaming, champing, galloping horses spanned to great guns—six of them. See them whirl into line with the rush of a mighty tornado! See the flash, and the guns recoil like living things! Quick! now look at the brick station, and the rats deserting a sinking ship amid flying bricks and clouds of dust.

You mind that, my boy, that's our Harris.[2] See how he sits his horse, straight as a ramrod, solemn as an owl. He's happy now he knows his trade, and prides himself on doing good work. Poor fellow, he's camping on the other side now, but I'm sure he will never be contented there without some artillery practice.

The little controversy thus concluded, the other side retired with less grace than speed. Soon the pontoon bridge was laid, and with steady tread the column began to pour over it. The south bank of the beautiful river, with overhanging trees and wild grape vines, was covered with soldiers, the blue having taken the place of the gray, and hundreds of shouting, laughing swimmers were disporting themselves in its placid waters.

About this time we heard of the victories of Gettysburg and Vicksburg.[3] The scenes of rejoicing would be difficult to describe, but this is something of the vision I have of it: A tired, dusty, thirsty, cross, grumpy, growly column of troops crawling slowly along over miserable dirt roads, winding in and out, over and around hill and valley; buzzards hanging lazily in a burning sky; no noise save the clip of a bayonet against the side of a naked canteen or the dull rumble of the artillery; a courier, in hot haste, waving an envelope; field and staff officers at head of column halt; courier delivers his dispatch; and back like madmen, along the dragging line gray with dust and grime, fly the messengers shouting the great news. To tell you how wildly and foolishly those men behaved, tossing up their caps, shouting, flinging down their loads and kicking them, dancing jigs, is more than I can do, but it is a part of the story, so I do the best I can. A few days more and we'd be singing "home again, home again from a foreign shore"; "the boys would run, the men would shout, the ladies they would all turn out, for Johnny's marching home."[4] But the proud and mighty Mars loved battle's wild commotion and demanded his tithes in blood and scars. The end was not yet, but a long way off, and led many a poor fellow through the valley of the shadow of death.

But here comes our battery; see what a long train it is, more than a hundred horses to only six guns, two Parrots and four Rodmans;[5] the latter are steel rifles, I think, and the Parrots smooth bare brass. Here is the first one on the bridge; see how the bridge sinks under its weight, forming an inverted arch; the horses strain at the traces, and the gun seems to be climbing a steep hill all the time; the bridge swings and sways and seems to be shackly and unsafe, and certainly is a makeshift, but a good one, and like the bray of the mule, the grayback, the sutler, and driver's shout, is ever with us and indispensable.

Here is the little, brick station. See it is pierced with many shot holes, both front and rear walls, and the floor is littered with broken bricks and mortar. It looks badly used; but I see you look in vain for the bodies of the slain; and now learn this lesson: In war as in peace it isn't always the fellow who makes the most noise that is most to be feared. These big guns have their uses, not the least of which is to make a racket and kick up a dust to scare people and make confusion. They speak a fearful language, and on occasion can do very wicked work, so that no army is at all equipped without them; and the little stuff they handle, such as case-grape and little pokes of minnie balls, which are gathered where much target practice is indulged in by the infantry, are very deadly at close range; but the hasty, little minnie from the rifles of the ranks sings the death-dealing song. It may be a far-off call in a fine key, or nearby in a dry whistle, but all the same it's looking for you and will get you too, if you don't watch out.

But now comes news of the evacuation of Chattanooga, and away we go over mountain and valley until we reach Lookout valley, which we follow for several days to the southward.[6] One of these days, while on the march, I was on advance guard, with General Turchin and staff riding in my rear, when I saw a lot of soldiers loaded with plunder approaching the column. I expected that on sight of a general officer and his staff they would be discreet, but not so; they knew Turchin. Our famous orders on pilfering permitted buying and all fair trade, so these men came boldly to the roadside in advance of us, dropped their purchases, and as the corners of the shelter tents fell apart they revealed good things, with peaches and sweet potatoes in abundance; and again I lingered to hear what the General would say. As he came up he turned his horse's head, halted, took a good look at the plunder, and smilingly remarked: "Dem ish fine sweed bodatoes, poys. Paid haf a toller for dem, huh?"—and rode on.

Here we camped one night on a thrifty plantation whose owner asked a guard and got one. The boys commenced to buy things, and he was ready to sell, but refused greenbacks as pay. In this he displayed neither prudence nor forethought, and very soon had opportunity to chew the bitter cud of repentance, for, when General Reynolds received the word, the guard was dismissed, and the last state of that man was worse than the first. He had a large bee-yard, and to see about a hundred of our lads snatch each a scap[7] and toss it on his shoulder, open end to the rear, with a mob of other lads following hard after, eager to divide the spoils, the bees striking for their altars and their fires, was a sight to cause some levity, and as long as any actors in the scene live the remembrance of it will not fade.

Along the raw slopes of Lookout was a seam of coal in plain view and about four feet thick. Here were now, though unfinished, iron works, the first I had ever seen, and my friend Stambaugh[8] gave me some bits of information in regard to iron making which were quite new to me. We passed a little town called Trenton and halted at Steven's Gap, where we were to cross to the east side of Lookout. We looked for a depression or opening or something answering to a gap, but found only a rough, crooked trail. However, the crossing had to be made, and we made it, after night too. A long rope was made fast to each big gun, stretching away in front of the teams. This was seized by thirty or more men, and away we went. The course of the road was zigzag, and we tacked like a ship trying to make headway against the wind. A couple of musicians were stationed at each sharp turn, with horn or drum or fife and a torch or two for light.[9] Each of these points afforded us a sharp pull, requiring both wind and muscle, so the musicians and teamsters furnished the wind, and we boys, together with the horses and mules, furnished the muscle. When a gun or loaded team was on the swing of the turn or pinch, the boys straining on the long ropes, then the drums beat, the horns tooted, a ringing cheer went up which rent the air of Georgia and made the rocky ribs of old Lookout rattle. Oh! Willie, I have the picture made with an exposure of three hours or more, so it's well burnt in. I'd like to have you see it as I did. Next day as we lay near the head of the gap the surly roar of the cannon came drifting over the mountains at prolonged intervals, and we all knew that the giants were close to the arena and a grand struggle for mastery would soon be on.

Eighty rounds of ammunition were issued to each man, and other ominous signs increased our apprehensions, so that all frivolity and foolishness was laid aside, and each man went about his duties with a quiet sort of intensity that told of a state of mind both solemn and earnest. We soon took our way across the plateau and dropped down the east wall to the base. Old Lookout, his side flecked with the gently shifting shadows of the clouds as they sailed athwart the sky, wearing the same placid air of serenity as ever, stood now at our backs. Here the mails reached us and I received a letter from your Aunt Lucy with an invitation to her wedding.

We were now in MacLemore's Cove, near Pond Spring, a circular, pot-shaped pool of cool, limpid water, covering perhaps a half acre and receiving its supply from the bottom, with an outlet which thrust a heavy contribution into Chickamauga Creek nearby; a few rods of green turf; then a shelving, rocky rim sparsely covered with ragged, stunted trees. Here our brigade halted two or three days, awaiting events, and occasionally a company or regiment would make an excursion to the front. Cannons were booming off toward Ringgold, telling us that the dogs of war were beginning to scent blood,—the mælstrom was at hand. The picture of the men sitting around that pool, scattered about on nature's rocky benches, with slackened waist belts, writing letters, sending many last messages to loved ones at home, groups of mounted officers here and there with field glasses, anxious to peer through the unfathomed mysteries of the next day or hour, all earnest and intent, with almost severe expression,— is another of the indelibly penciled pictures that hang on the wall of my memory. All were longing for movement, though solemnly awaiting the mighty contest which was to decide who should hold Chattanooga. Failure on our part to achieve this would mean defeat and the almost certain annihilation of our splendid army. The stake was a heavy one, and we were none of us ignorant of the value of it to our side if we won, or the disaster and disgrace should defeat come to us. Those were anxious days for us, and I stand almost dumb in trying to give you the faintest conception of the events of the next forty-eight hours, in fact, my boy, it is not in human power to do it.[10]

On the evening of the 18th day of September, 1863, while we were in the position I have just described, an Orderly came in hot haste, bearing a message from our division commander, and just as the shadows of old Lookout began to darken the cove our troop began its march eastward. Colonel Perkins of our 105th received an order to detail two of his largest companies to guard the division ammunition train consisting of fifteen or twenty wagons. My Company ("H") and Company "C" being the largest were detailed for that duty and marched in the rear of the division while the other troops hastened forward, and soon the burning fences on either side of the road plainly indicated the tortuous line of march, by their glowing light. The roads were crowded with troops. Frequent, unavoidable halts were made all the night through, the soldiers lingered by the roadside to toast pork—in army parlance, "sow belly"—or make a can of coffee.[11]

My train was put in order of march with the two companies taking intervals on either side from front to rear. I took station in front. Mrs. Turchin, who was her husband's constant companion throughout the entire war, was riding a horse just in advance of the lead team and leading another at her side. I marched all night at her bridle rein and until we arrived opposite the General's brigade in the rear of our line of battle, when she left me.

The glowing beds of coals on each side of the road, from which fire in places had seized an old dry pine and mounted upward, the flame making a great flambeau, casting weird, uncanny shadows all around, the clicking of the bayonets and the rattling of the sabres of the mounted men, the steady marching of many thousand feet and the rumble of the wagons as they jolted over the stony road,—all made an indescribable scene, "grand, gloomy and peculiar"; and, although the distance is but four miles, when daylight dawned at last we were just passing Crawfish Springs, which is the outflow of an underground stream, as in Pond Spring, only the stream is heavier. Here we filled our canteens in passing, and around its margin were many other soldier boys doing the same thing. During the day many weary, wounded and dying sought its refreshing waters, for here we struck the right of our line where some fighting had been going on the day before; but we kept on toward the East on the Dry Valley road,—I think past the widow Glenn's house and in rear of our line. At one point near here we encountered a battery in action. It was fired by volley, and the recoil sent the guns clear off the road. Then by prodding up the mules we could pass a wagon or two between each discharge; and here, sitting on logs and stumps, we found the old 19th O. V. I., with Colonels Manderson, Nash, Stratton, Pete Lowbie, Cal Chamberlain, Dan Firestone and a lot of others, some of my mates from the little, old, red schoolhouse.[12] No better ever answered the long roll than were here waiting their turn at the fiery furnace. The smell of battle had already come to us and hung like a dark veil over our line of fighters in front of us, and between us and them a constant, ever-widening stream of poor, wounded fellows, running, limping, halting, hopping, crawling and falling; and the gods of war are grinning and gathering in their sheaves.

As we came opposite to our own regiment a smooth-faced, little fellow of Company "C," who had never been in battle, told some of his comrades that he had been cheated out of all the battles so far and now was going to make up for it. He started on a run for the front, and we never saw him again. But the great vortex seemed to be farther east. Our troops were hurrying to this point of fiercest contact, and from every direction could be seen regiments, brigades and divisions hurrying toward the grim holocaust. A number of fine, young officers, leading their men into that roaring, seething cauldron of war, passed me and were soon lost to sight in the smoke of the volcano, and I took such note of them as to remember distinctly to this day how they looked.

Soon came a staff officer to direct our line to a sheltered spot behind Snodgrass Hill. There I parked the train, and interest soon led us to the highest point. We passed a number of hospital tents filled with victims and surgeons busy at their ghastly work, though it was yet early in the day. From the height where we stood the sight that met our gaze was beyond the power of description, and although in peace no temptation could be held out that would induce anyone to stand for a moment in such a place, then there was a fascination that held us to the spot, though not for long.

It was a scene to make angels weep and devils grin to see the vast improvement here upon the homely commonplace of the black pit. Here spread out before me, yet much hidden by the smoke of battle, stood the bone and brawn of America—Americans against Americans—struggling, fighting, bleeding, dying—for an idea. As each flag falls in its turn, only to be seized and borne aloft by other sturdy victims, the trembling earth resounds with the continuous throbs of the giant flails as they rise and fall in a ceaseless tumult, amid torrents of lead and iron.

Compared with this battle the great Waterloo of the past, about which soldiers and historians have gloried and shed barrels of ink, was rather a moderate affair, and the Man of Destiny[13] would certainly have learned some new tricks in war had he been with us. His Austerlitz, Wagram and Marengo do not compare favorably with this battle. No one engagement since the world began equals it for stubborn endurance, and no one great engagement has equaled it in the percentage of loss. The sun slowly rolls his halting way across the sky, the minutes are freighted with the songs of death, while down below me there, shut out from sight and sense, save sound, the gladiators are tossing the gauntlet back and forth on sheets of deadly flame; and from the rising of the sun to its going down,—for two long days,—hundreds of black, wide-mouthed cannon waked the echoes and tossed the challenge back and forth from mountain side to mountain side. "Ben Hur! Ben Hur! Jove with us! Jove with us!"[14]

I might go on and tell of the splendid fighting around the Kelly and the Poe fields, the Brotherton house, and the final change of storm-center from the Kelly field to the hill upon which I stood; of the coming of Granger and Steedman[15] on the eve of the unholy Sabbath day; of the splendid and repeated charges of Longstreet and Kershaw and Govan, Buckner, Walthall, Hood, Hindman, Bate, Colquitt and many others;[16] of the stubborn defence of Thomas, Baird, VanCleve, Wood, VanderVeer, Turchin, Crittenden, Brannon, Reynolds, King and a host of others;[17] but an intelligent knowledge of the causes, the object, the military craft—the parry and thrust—would be necessary to a solution of the puzzle, which would require time and labor; and the longer I live, and the more I learn about it, the more I am interested in this great battle.

It is but fair to say that while (in my opinion) our friends in gray won the lawsuit (the battle field), we got the mule (Chattanooga). On the 21st we stood ready to receive battle, but they did not offer it, and we retired into our hastily prepared works, in Chattanooga, on the night of the 21st.

Our people, both North and South, are compiling the sacred history of this great fight in stone and iron upon the blood baptized ground where it was fought, and I hope you all may go there sometime to look at the monuments erected to heroic patriotism and holy fidelity to our country's flag.[18] You will see on the south margin of the Kelly field a shell monument, erected to the memory of our Brigade Commander (King) who fell there. Then following the line of monuments towards the east and south you will see one to the 105th O. V. I.; and in front of the Brotherton house, perhaps a quarter of a mile from it, you will find a plain, granite stone marked with the number 105 on it. It shows our high-water mark the first day. Take a look at Snodgrass hill with its many monuments. There I stood, and in the heel of the horseshoe which it forms was my wagon train.

In this fight were killed eight Brigade Commanders, four on each side—for us Lytle, Baldwin, Hieg and King—of the confederates, Deshler, Helm, Preston Smith and Colquitt. A shell monument on the line of battle marks the spot where each fell. Lytle was the "poet soldier," and Helm, though a rebel, was brother-in-law to Lincoln. His widow has been Post-mistress of Elizabethtown, Kentucky, until a few months, having been appointed by Grant.

On account of the death of our Brigade Commander there is no record or report of the doings of our brigade in this battle. The last thing I saw from the hill where I stood was our line off to the right, giving way and curving back to Snodgrass hill, finally breaking into a rout, a line of gray following with steady step, firing as they came.

To save my train now was the question, and the hurry of it and worry of it I shall not try to describe. To prevent the drivers cutting the traces of the mules and scurrying off was the great trouble, and there the bayonet played a part. While we were at this General Jeff C. Davis came along and said naughty things to me, having it that I should deploy my sixty or seventy men to stop the stampede of a brigade or division.[19] Finally, after saving my train, I did deploy my men, with orders from General Davis to use the bayonet; but a fly could hardly be expected to capture a wild bull—no more could we stop the rout, though the men were pretty determined, and the line would gather weight until it would break, then unload, fill and break again, so our efforts were futile. We thought at the time that our entire line of battle was gone and the fight lost, but the break was one of the fortunes of war; a gap had been left in our lines; the vigilant Johnnies had found it, sent in a wedge and widened it. Soon we gathered hope, the battle raged with renewed fury; prisoners came to us, some were Longstreet's men, just off the cars from the Potomac, and I do think they were as fine specimens of men as I ever saw—tall, clean-made fellows without an ounce of extra flesh. Oh! what wicked words they said, cursing their hard luck, for they were sure we were on the run, and expected the invaders would soon be driven from their native soil. I guarded them in the big, old railroad depot at Chattanooga until they were sent North to prison. Our men divided rations with them, and I soon could not help but love my enemies, who were certainly fine fellows.[20]

I have met some of them since, especially at the World's Fair,[21] where I fell in with some old, South Carolina Johnnies, and a couple of hours flew away in about five minutes.

Saturday night was cold, with heavy frost, and we all suffered greatly, but as we were behind the line of battle and covered by the hill a few twinkling fires appeared, but there were no rations save what we had carried in our haversacks from Pond Springs. I sat with my back to the big rock and feet at a bed of coals, and soon fell asleep.

The next morning was Sunday, and all was quiet. I never so hoped the Sabbath day would be respected. As the morning hours passed I felt the same thought was in everyone's mind, but about nine o'clock Hades broke loose again, more frightful this time. The storm seemed to center on the Kelly field until noon or a little later, when it began to wheel north towards Chattanooga; then Snodgrass hill became the center, and no more gallant fighting ever took place under the blue dome of Heaven than was carried on here until dark; but old "Pappy Thomas, the rock of Chickamauga," stood fast, and here ended the battle. Two prominent officers, Longstreet and Kershaw,[22] fresh from Gettysburg and the army of the Potomac, declared they never saw Federals fight so well, nor saw Confederates fight better.

When night fell "Pappy Thomas" was still in position, but during the night he withdrew his forces to Rossville and McFarlan Gaps, so covering Chattanooga and giving Rosecrans time to make everything safe there; then retired leisurely to his new stronghold. As I marched with the prisoners the first thing I saw was our flag on a long pole above Fort Negly—a fort built by Bragg—and a line of low breastworks entirely surrounding the place.[23] In a day or two Bragg's whole army was brought up to within two miles, and battle was ordered to be delivered on the 23rd. Wisely for the gray the attack was not made, but instead a close investment and siege was laid.

The losses in the battle of Chickamauga were on our side sixteen thousand, one hundred and seventy-six (16,176); for the Confederates seventeen thousand, eight hundred and four (17,804); estimated to be one man in three of all engaged. Longstreet lost 44%, Brannan 40%, Steedman 38%, VanderVeer 50%. Some regiments lost as high as 80%, and as many as twenty regiments on each side lost 50%. Bushrod Johnson's (rebel) division lost 44%; Bate's brigade, Stewart's division 52%. I take these figures from the record. The six hundred (600) at Balaklava lost 36%. The loss at Marengo and Austerlitz was 14%; Moscow 4%; Solferino 9%; Gravelotte and Sedan 12%; Waterloo 14%. At Perrysville, Murfreesboro, Gettysburg, Atlanta, Mission Ridge and many more of the battles of our Civil War the losses exceeded those of any other wars, and averages of killed and wounded on one side or the other were 30%, with the loss unaccounted for as high or higher than 40%.

Here are nearly thirty-four thousand (34,000) men dropped in one engagement. The forces engaged on our side numbered fifty-five thousand (55,000). Bragg's report a week after the fight was thirty-eight thousand (38,000) effectives and eighteen thousand (18,000) lost in battle, making fifty-six thousand (56,000); but General Lee, in a letter to Jeff Davis, placed Bragg's force at seventy-six thousand (76,000), and concludes by saying: "as large a number, I presume, as he can operate with." That was before Longstreet started, and his force was not in Lee's estimate. The fighting was all at close range, and the perpetual wonder of it all to me is that the losses were not much greater.

I guess there were as many as a hundred mule wagonloads of minnie balls shot away by each side, anyway lead rolled in a perpetual torrent for two days.

On our side there were one hundred and eighty-two (182) separate organizations of troops; one hundred and twenty-nine (129) regiments of infantry; eighteen (18) regiments of cavalry; thirty-five (35) batteries of artillery; three (3) regiments of mounted infantry and one (1) company of sharp-shooters. Bragg had two hundred and fifty-one (251) organizations; one hundred and thirty-eight (138) regiments of infantry; thirty-three (33) of cavalry, and forty-seven (47) batteries, with thirty-three (33) other separate battalions of both cavalry and infantry.

I give these large details as they are easily comprehended, and for them I am indebted to recent history. I know well that I have no right to expect you and those still younger, who set their names to my "Round Robin," will be interested in these figures, but they give some idea of the greatness of the conflict, and display the power of our Uncle Sam when he bares his muscle. Slavery was the cause of this war, and long enough before it began Henry Clay, the one great statesman of his day, used every endeavor to have gradual emancipation adopted at a cost of about Twenty-five Millions of dollars.[24] I venture to say that the cost of this one battle, near and remote is or will be more than four times that amount, to say nothing of loss of life and the inestimable amount of distress and misery of it.

CHAPTER TWELVE

❧

Camp Life; The Siege of Chattanooga

Now I HAVE come to the siege and will try to be brief. Come, we'll walk around a bit. You say the shells are flying and you are afraid. Well, true enough, they do make an ugly noise, but there isn't much danger, so come along, and when they come too close we can be courteous and just bow low or drop flat,—kiss the earth like the Mohammedans. Boom! See the dirt fly! Down we go, make yourself thin, see me, your nose takes a little room, turn your cheek so. That fellow came straight in line, struck the ground in front of the breastworks and ricocheted. "Well, that's bilious and I don't like it." Yes, but, Willie, there is little danger. You can soon get used to most anything, and there are a lot of interesting things to look at. This is war, and you can't see the like of it every day. Away up there on Lookout—see the smoke and hear the echoes rolling back and forth from Waldrons to Mission Ridge and back to Lookout, round and round, and before one thunderous echo dies away,—a smoke and flash and,—a fresh one starts on a little different key; and over there is our Moccasin Point battery, its nose up at an angle of forty-five degrees, trying to exchange compliments with its lofty neighbor. Now they are both at it. We have a full chorus. It's music fit for all the gods, and will be ringing in your ears for many a day. "Won't they kill one another before long!" I reckon there isn't much danger of that, but then, you know, shoemakers die and carpenters sometimes fall off buildings and get hurt, so a gun might burst, caisson explode, and some one get hurt, but most of them will live to a ripe old age unless they change their employment—the air is so good up there.

But now those fellows on Lookout are giving us some attention. We can hear the shells rushing and groaning through the air, bursting like great torpedoes, and the splinters go whizzing, each on his busy, buzzing, vicious, little errand. "Those fellows are dangerous, aren't they?" "No, not very, we will only make obeisance to the big fellows."

Now let's go down to the rifle pits—here are the soldiers, some sitting on the breastworks, a rubber blanket under them, playing cards. Now look away down there on Chattanooga creek—there is our swamp angel, and they have our range pretty close. See that puff of smoke, and hear the sentinel shout, "Low bridge!" See our euchre players slide into the pits, like turtles off a log in the swamp on a sunny day. As they go each man turns his hand down. Now back they come to the same places, pick up their cards, and go on again all in order. See, these men have their shelter tents pinned to the breastworks, and the bayonets through the eyelets on the opposite edge of each, and, with the butts of their guns against the front wall of the pit at the bottom, the gun forms both a brace and a stretcher, and one-half of each pup tent makes a very decent awning and shelter, from either sun or rain, for the men who sit on the bottom of the pit. This awning has a couple of men under it, sewing on buttons and mending their clothes. See, each man has a little "house-wife" or wallet; some are faced with silk and needle work, the gift of a far away sweet girl who is mourning and waiting for the war to cease, when her Johnny will come marching home. Each "house-wife" has a separate place for buttons, thread, needles, etc., and these fellows all know how to use them, and if they don't get the patches on straight they will not keep the wind and cold out.

Now here a little farther along are a few men, stripped to the waist. What are they doing that they are too deeply interested to look up? Just watch and see if you can't guess. You see we've been lying around on the old camp ground of the gentleman in gray, and they always leave some gray stragglers[1] behind who give us a ready welcome. But, like poor relations, sometimes they become annoying, so we try to shed them.

You will notice some of the boys are reading old newspapers. You see when the pickets are good and friendly they often meet half way and trade things, sometimes newspapers; and when we get a Charleston, Richmond or New Orleans paper we gather in groups to hear it read.[2]

These men who are sitting on the bottom of the pits never get up or look up when the swamp angel lets go, unless a ball or shell should fall near. A spent cannon ball as it goes spinning along the ground is always interesting and looks harmless and innocent, but you just leave them alone. It's tending to its business, you to yours. A soldier of any wit knows he can't stop a cannon ball. One of our boys tried it, and now he wears a stout hickory stump from the knee down and gets a pension. That same fellow got a little splinter off a shell in him just where it made him "ouch" when he sat down, and our Charlie Fowler said he would cut it out in a minute and wouldn't hurt him much either, but the fellow wouldn't let him, for he said it would get him more pension.

Now stand up here on the breastworks with me and look away off there where those two old chimneys are standing. There is our part of the picket line. Do you see a man's head just above the ground? "Yes, and there's another and another." Well, those are our "gopher holes"; just big enough for a man to stand in with all the earth piled to the front, just a one man rifle pit; and if you were go to go out there you would see on the bank of each hole a nice, little pile of cartridges. Sometimes those fellows out there are bad, and when they are bad they are very, very bad,—sometimes shoot at one another for an hour or two. It seems as though it was just for fun, but it sounds like a real battle. Then the long roll beats in camp, the men hurrying on their accouterments and leap into the rifle pits, the officers stand on the fort and look through their field glasses, and, in less time than I write it, the whole army is ready for business, every man rifle in hand, at half cock, and a pile of loose cartridges behind him ready to serve customers. Sometimes the Johnnies make a reconnaissance in force, and as they don't send us any notice of their intentions we have always to be on the watch. Sometimes a fog fills the valley and we can hardly see twenty feet; then we keep a specially sharp watch, for when the fog lifts there is almost always something on hand.

But we have soon enough for one day and must try to find something to eat. We aren't living very high now, and you will get two hard crackers tonight and some soup or mush made of grated corn. Eat it and don't whine. Hear the drums roll and bugles blow all over the camp, and away down the valley and from Mission Ridge and Lookout comes the same music from the rebel camps, blending in sleepy harmony. It tells us all, friend and foe alike, that the sun has gone down and night is upon us. All must be quiet in camp at night, and if you kick up any fuss here after "retreat" the Colonel will send the Sergeant-major down, who will say the Colonel sends his compliments and wants to know of Lieutenant Hartzell what all that racket's about in Company "H," and he wants it stopped immediately. So, if you don't want to go to the guard house, you'd better behave.

Now tie the tent door shut, stick that old bayonet in the ground, put a candle in it, and we'll have a light. Hello! here are visitors—Wallace (Company "I"), Mason (Company "C") and Tourgee (Company "G"). Uncle Dan Stambaugh, Company "A," got a clip through the elbow the other day and went home, and Captain Spaulding, Company "E," got a bad wound and will die.[3] This is the first time we've met since Chickamauga, and we talk and talk of the fight and the campaign and its consequences, and pretty soon tattoo and taps sound. Lights out now, and wrap up in that blanket and go to sleep.

Hurrah! morning's come. You hear the reveille,—drums, fifes and bugles near and far,—and the Orderly's call, "Fall in, fall in!" Run out now, and be quick. Did you ever hear such a babble of noise? The Orderlies don't waste any time but begin with A and run down to Z in a couple of breaths. See the sleepy lads, with tousled heads, rub their eyes as they get into line, some barefoot and some half dressed, and the Orderly rattles off two or three names for extra duty. Of course those boys were slow in getting out, or answered before they were in line, and those fellows will have to chop wood or dig stumps or do some other kind of work that a soldier doesn't like. These orderly Sergeants don't take any foolishness, and the boys can't play any tricks on them in the matter of roll call anyway.

Now the cooks start the fires and scurry off for water. All the hillside inside the town and the valley back of the town are covered with camps; all the men are busy, and here if you come to the front you can see squads of men marching out to relieve the pickets, and the relieved parties marching back, while here and there goes a whole regiment, which halts half way between the breastworks and the pickets. They are the grand reserve,[4] and there are other and smaller reserve posts half way between the grand reserve and the pickets. The picket guards are on duty twenty-four hours, and the men stand post two hours on, four hours off, for the entire twenty-four hours. The Sergeant takes a squad of eight or ten men out to the line, and the first man in the "gopher hole" steps out with his traps, and a new man takes his place, and so on till the whole line is relieved, then he comes marching back with the same number of men he took out. In front of the main picket line, say four or six rods, is a line of videttes, all posted and relieved the same way by the same Sergeant. No man on either reserve post is allowed to slacken a strap of his equipments during the twenty-four hours, rain or shine. Each one must be ready for action at the drop of a hat, and, right here and now, they understand that and are never caught napping.

When an attack is made the thin line of videttes open fire first. Maybe only one watchful fellow peering through the fog sees a ghostly line of phantoms moving up in silence. He lets fly, and in a second all the pickets have done the same; the little reserves deploy and rush forward to strengthen the main line; the videttes fall back to it; and all together they hold it until the grand reserve comes forward at double quick, and the battle begins. All over the camp you hear the drums reeling off the long roll; the line officers calling "Fall in, fall in"; field officers are mounting; and in much less time than I can tell you of it forty thousand (40,000) men are at the works, all watching the outcome of that one shot. Maybe it will turn out only a scare, or maybe the other fellows sent out a feeler to look a bit into our affairs. Sometimes it's a heavy attack and our line sways back, then out sails a brigade, bayonets fixed. They push the gray line back beyond the "gopher holes," and the affair is over for one morning, except the work of the stretcher men and the surgeons. The hornets go back to their nests and all is quiet again.

Do you see the long line of ambulances coming in from the south? They have been running steadily ever since the battle. Being a christian nation,—instead of killing the wounded enemy we give him back. In this case the gentleman in gray said to the gentleman in blue, "You may go get your wounded"; and this ambulance train has come loaded every day for eight or ten days, loaded with the harvest of war. You can see them here as they pass, each loaded with a burden of pain and grief, some poor fellows lying, others sitting bowed over.

Tomorrow we will go to see the hospital where these poor fellows are being taken, but our Charlie Fowler isn't there. Like a brave knight, when our line on the right swayed back over his division hospital, he told the other surgeons to skip and leave him with plenty of instruments, bandages and the like; he would stay and risk it, and he did, working like a Trojan for both friend and foe till they sent him a prisoner to Libby.[5] So now we shan't see him again for a long time, maybe never. Oh! Willie, if you young robins could hear *him* tell war stories once, you would never ask to hear them from anyone else.

Hello! here comes Dick, a poor, little, white boy whose Daddy has been killed. He was on the wrong side, I think, though we aren't all of one mind in this world, so we fight and kill one another; anyhow Dick is a nice, little chap of twelve years. He has on a poor, little suit of half-worn butternut; came straggling into camp and my command back yonder on the first day of the fight, looking so sad and scared that I called him to me and gave him something to eat from my haversack. He has stuck to me ever since and wants to carry my haversack or canteen all the time. His name is Dick Cobb.[6]

Come here, Dick. Who have you been bunking with? Oh! Company "H." Well, here is Willie, my nephew, come to visit me from way off ever so far, and now you two boys go up to my quarters. No, wait a minute, away up towards town there see the crowds of soldiers, let's go. And as we go this is what we see—ten, twenty thousand soldiers, and more, come running from every direction. They naturally form into a line up an avenue—the line is a mile long—and soldiers pressing up from the rear make the lines deep masses. Cheer on cheer wake the echoes. What is the cause of it? Just look up the avenue and, walking this way, you will see four or five ladies, dressed *so* nicely. They are from the North, our homes, and look like angels from Heaven.[7] The swift lightning has told them of the great battle, and they have left their homes to come and care for the wounded and soothe the dying, and maybe they all have brothers or lovers among the unfortunate. They are the first *right* ladies many of these soldiers have seen since they left home, and they look so good, no wonder the boys shout, "Look, look, they're from God's own country." Well, they will soon see another sight, and find work to do that will try their courage. God give them health and strength for it.

Now you boys run off; it will soon be "retreat" and the patrol might get you; stay in the quarters until I come; Jess, the cook, will find you a bite to eat; I'm on duty tonight; hand me out my sabre and overcoat, it's going to storm; the Orderly Sergeant will sleep in the tent with you. Good night.

Good morning! Do you hear the drums? They are wet with fog and don't roll out the full sound, but the bugles are all right. Now, Willie, when this fog lifts a little you're going to see some fun, a little game of war, or I'm mightily mistaken; so swallow your coffee and take your hard bread in your hand; we'll go down to Fort Negly.[8] Dick, you stay around camp. Here we are at the fort. See the piles of shells and hand grenades, and there are three cannon, field guns. The fort is star shaped and of earth, good and strong. The rebels made it but we've got it and are going to keep it. Now we'll get up on the parapet and watch the fog beginning to lift. Bang! There goes a shot out on the picket line, and now it is followed rapidly by others all along the line—half a mile or more. All the reserves fall to work, and the troops are in the trenches. Away beyond our line you can see the line of gray coming out of the fog. The men stop while they fire and load, and then advance. They're a strong skirmish line with two mounted officers close in the rear of either flank.[9] As the fire grows hot the center of the line sways back like a kite string in a stiff breeze when the kite is well up. The officers draw their sabres and gallop back and forth, threatening and urging men forward, trying to push up the center; and now to their rear comes a solid line of support, about a brigade front.

Now look about you. Here comes Turchin. See his men leap the works and strike the double quick till they reach our skirmishers and blend, deliver a volley and sail in. Hear the cheer. Ho! you're getting too hot. Well get down in the fort and peep out under the head log. First thing you know the big guns will open out, and then you'll get the size of it. In war we stay where we're put, we eat, we sleep, we rise up, we lie down, we go forward to the right or the left, all by orders, orders for everything. I'm not ordered out there and I'm not going any more than you are. Hi! See our fellows now. How they run over the gray skirmish line. Will the support stand the coal steel? No! See they break and turn. Now up go our caps, and from the blue line of soldiers on the breastworks goes cheer on cheer. The music of the brass bands and fife and drum greet our returning heroes, and the thunders of a hundred cannon close the matinee. Here is a wagon road running close by the fort and out to the south through a gap in the rifle pits. See the ambulances scurrying out to gather up the sheaves. Here comes Turchin with his prisoners. Lots of our boys jibe the poor fellows, but I don't like it, it's tough enough as it is.

Let's go now. I got a pint of beans from Captain Wright, our quartermaster,[10] last night, and we're going to have a good dinner of bean soup and crackers, so you see we aren't so badly off yet. I see you have an old canteen; just skin it, put it in the fire and let it melt apart; then you will have two nice plates that won't break, one for you and one for Dick. My whole table outfit consists of a tin plate, a fork and an old dirk knife. The tin plate I bring out only when I have company. Tomorrow will be Sunday and we'll go take a look at the hospitals. I don't know of any churches here but there may be some up town. So far as I have seen, chaplains are scarce in this army. I haven't attended a preaching service since we left Mumfordsville, Kentucky. We had a chaplain at the start, but I think he went home to die soon after. We have some good, religious men with us, but our way of living isn't conducive to deep spirituality. I can't join war and religion and make a good job of it. We've just got to wait until we whip these rebels, then go to church and be good ever afterwards.

Now I'm going over to the 9th Ohio. We are brigaded with them now. You see the big fight we had shrunk the regiments up so that now instead of four or five regiments to a brigade we have seven or eight. We were 2nd Brigade, 4th Division, 14th Corps, but to-day they put us in 2nd Brigade, 3rd Division, 14th Corps, with General VanderVeer[11] as our brigade commander, and we have now our old brigade,—75th, 87th and 101st Indiana, 2nd Minnesota, 9th, 35th and 105th Ohio. The 9th Ohio was Colonel Bob McCrook's, but is now Colonel Kammarling's[12]—all dutch from Cincinnati—and if there's a thing to eat in the whole army they've got it, so I shall try for a Sunday dinner.

You have noticed how the mules' hips stick out. Well, it's just the bones pushing out through the skin. They haven't had a decent feed since they left Trenton, Georgia, and a lot of them will die before long if things don't get better. We have a little corn, but, although there is always a guard placed over the horses and mules when they are fed, the soldiers steal the corn away and eat it themselves.

But we'll do our errand and then go home. I want to sleep to-night, for I'm for picket to-morrow night. You see when there is bad blood on the line we relieve the pickets after night. Do you see that flag up on Lookout go this way and that, up and down quick? Well, turn and look on Mission Ridge, there's another; those are signal stations, and they are talking all day long, back and forth, sounding orders mostly. They can look right down on us and see just what we are doing, what we have to eat, and so on. They have telescopes up there and can spy out about everything, and they think they have the "cinch" on us. One of these days there will be a big racket around here, and then that will be decided. The Johnnies have the railroad clear down to Stevenson, and Wheeler is north of the river raising Cain between here and Nashville. Our cracker line is broken up and it looks bad, but we hear Father Abraham is going to send help, so we will hold on.[13] It won't do to let go here; we're too near the heart of the rebellion, and must hold our clutch, or we'll never get these rebels thrashed out. Now we'll talk dutch to the 9th Ohio boys, and I will get a half dozen crackers and a piece of meat before we go back.

Do you see that far away up there to the left? That's Fort Wood. The rebels tried to shell it the other day, but were not successful. Here we are at camp, and cook has our bean soup and crackers and coffee ready. Don't they smell good? And now fall to, and as soon as we are through I'm going to turn in. Don't be frightened if you hear me snore, and go to bed at taps. Good night.

The reveille always appears to sound just as soon as we get good and sure-enough asleep, and the nights don't seem more than an hour long, and if the daylight didn't come pretty soon we would be sure the bugler had lost his almanac, but he hasn't, and we fall to our breakfast. "A short horse is soon curried"; and we are off to the hospitals. General Bragg built perhaps a dozen, rough, board houses, about twenty by thirty feet in size, and white-washed them. These are filled up first, then the churches, and last private houses.

Inspections come first though, and the Orderly says the Company is ready. You see it on the company parade ground, in line, open order, faced inward. Each soldier has all his belongings exposed upon the ground at his feet and in front of him, and I as company commander, like a custom house officer, look over each article to see that all is clean and in proper order, while the man stands erect with his gun at order; then, when that is finished, ramrods are drawn and dropped in the barrels of the pieces, and each man in his turn tosses his gun to me. I examine it and see that it is quite free from rust and dirt, and with a quick toss send the ramrod half way up the barrel. If it comes back to the breach with a clear jingle, the gun is accounted all right; if with a dull sound, the gun is dirty and must be cleaned.

The Sunday inspection in camp is both formal and rigid, and is never passed lightly over. The man and all his belongings must be clean. Some careless fellows are sent to the water, with an escort armed with corn-cobs, and given a good scrubbing. After that has occurred once or twice we have no more trouble. With all the wet and dust our Springfield rifles cost much labor to keep them bright, and Sunday morning in camp is a busy time. The men say there is a difference in the guns. Anyway it's true that some guns are always bright, and others show mark of great labor. I think maybe the secret of it is that in some haversacks you will always find a strip of bacon rind, and when it rains the soldier rubs his piece thoroughly with it, and then neither ruin nor rust affect it.

Now we are through, and here and there you can hear a church call, but we'll go to the hospital. Here we are; the whole building is one, great room. Notice how each, pitiful, anxious face turns to look at us, hoping to see some loved one, so now look bright and say all the clever things you can think of to the poor fellows. Here they lie, each on his little cot, pale, weary and helpless,—many short an arm or leg. Here a young fellow smiles as we come up. "Heighho, Morris, you'll never shear sheep for Uncle Fred[14] again." He laughs and says: "Yes, I will." His name is Morris Taylor and his home is on Quaker Hill, almost in sight of mine in Ohio, and we were boys together. He laid on the battle field eight days; the worms got into his wounds; and he says a rebel filled a canteen for him. One leg broken at the thigh, and the other shot through and through the flesh under the bone; the same ball did both. His poor limbs are bandaged from thigh to toe. Your Daddy sends a newspaper to me almost every week, and one of these with a Harper's Weekly I hand out to him. I brought them to him every week as long as we staid. Here and there on both sides are those who seem covered up so their faces cannot be seen. They have gone to sleep and no sound will awake them to glory again. The ambulances are doing all they can, but the harvest is too great, and they can't keep up with their work.

Here is Billy Tannehill of Benton, now of the 19th Ohio. He has a ball through the lower jaw, near the point; the bone on both sides splintered and carried away. He should die, but the stubborn little fellow will get well, though ever after he will diet on "spoon victuals." Note: He lives today, 1897, out of pure contrariness, so he can draw his Four Dollars per month and give a chance to college professors, holding down fatly endowed chairs, and smart office lawyers and politicians, to make figures and speeches and write pretty magazine articles showing the wickedness of such fellows as Billy hanging on so long, and his awful dishonesty in robbing the government.[15]

Here are men without arms and men without legs, some with half a hand or with one arm or one leg, and some all right except for a foot or a hand or an eye or an ear or a nose. Take a good look at them, for the greater part will die. You don't want to see any more. Well, we've only done one building, and there are many more. Remember this sight, and when you hear folks talk of war and a fight think of this sight and find a better way out if you can. Each day the hospitals are gaining more patients, and as soon as the rear is opened they will all be moved back north, or at least all who have strength for the journey. You can hear how many of them plead to go home, and see others turn their faces to the wall when they hear talk of home.

Do you see how fast the trees are disappearing? This ground was all covered with timber when we came, which was very fortunate. In two more weeks the timber inside the camp will all be gone, including the stumps. We must have fuel to cook with and head logs for the breastworks, and we are cutting wood across the river now. It takes a lot of stuff to provide for an army like this. Do you see that long string of carriages, wagons, carts, old buggies and poor people going out south past Fort Negly? They all look sad, except some of the young women, who look defiant. You see this is war too, and these are citizens who choose to go or are sent south among their friends. We are in a state of siege, and every mouthful these people eat shortens the time we can hold on, and so we drive them either north or south, as they choose to go. They all take such household goods as they can carry, and plod on with aching hearts to seek a place where they can live and be protected. There they go, old and young, women and children and babes, and soon the town will be populated by soldiers only, and I'm afraid the poor, sad, weeping people will see trouble enough. This town had before the war from three to five thousand inhabitants, now it has forty thousand.

This army is like a wedge or a heavy pole ax. The heavy end lies to the rear, guarding supplies, hospitals and railroads. The whole number doing such duty, from here to Louisville, Kentucky, is maybe three times as many as are here. We are the cutting edge, and they, guarding the rear, are the heavy end of the wedge. Sometimes the edge is driven against hard things, and nicks are broken out, just as we were broken the other day at Chicka-mauga; in fact, this cutting edge is full of nicks now, but we will soon grind them out again, and the cutting edge will be as sharp as ever.

You see no camp guards, and details are made each day only for picket, one sentinel at each regimental headquarters, one for wood, and one for work on the fortifications, so we are all busy most of the time. Now we'll go home and eat our good supper, then I'm off for picket. It's going to be a bad night, and I want my poncho. Everything will go all right here, and if the tent breaks there are more rubber blankets. I won't be in until to-morrow night. Take care of yourself, and be good. You and Dick can go and see Uncle Dan or Major Edwards[16] to-morrow. Keep out of folks' way, and, if they ask, tell them who you are and where you belong; that you have two uncles in the army fighting with guns, and a Daddy at home fighting bat-tles with a goose quill, and they all three know their trade. Good night.

Hello, boys! What you got to eat this evening? A skilletful of stewed hardtack! Well that's filling, and there's a heap of it, but it don't fool your Uncle. Why a couple of those hard biscuits, if you soak them long enough, would fill up this tent. But never mind, take my blanket out to the fire and hang it on a pole to steam awhile. It was nasty enough out on the picket line last night, stormed and spit snow all night. Our reserve was back of a big elm log, and the men fixed their shelter tents much as they did at the breastworks. We sat with our backs to the log, except one sentinel on the gun stacks to watch for alarms, or the great rounds, for they are liable to come any time of night. In relieving our men on post I went along. We could find the line and keep it, but the misery was to find the videttes, so we agreed on a signal. A sharp, quick whistle was the signal of relief, two of danger, and so on. That way we got on pretty well, only we missed one man entirely, and he had to stand two tricks. Often when the fog is thick I've been fooled by a tall weed, and at other times would get clear outside our line, and that isn't a real nice, happy fix to be in. Last night the men off duty would slacken their waist belts a bit as they sat under the shelter, and before it was fairly light the sentinel shouted, "Grand rounds, fall in!"; and the men fell in behind the stacks, cold, wet and stiff, and were fumbling with their waist belts, trying to tighten them, when General Sheridan saw our fix (he was grand rounds). He put spurs to his horse and came up with a dash and began to use very naughty language, which so upset my little, bedraggled squad that as fast as each got his strap tightened he grabbed his gun out of the stack. Of course the stack fell over, and so it went. Little Phil saw me standing like a stick, and my lads picking their guns off the ground over beyond. I waited patiently as I could, or had to, and when all were ready presented arms, and he acknowledged the salute. Now here was a pretty kettle of fish. I expected he would take away my old toad sticker,[17] send me to camp, and I'd be tried and used scandalous. But the bad things we are looking for hardly ever occur, and he and his staff rushed right off to bear down on our grand reserve, the 9th Ohio. The dutchmen were in about the same fix, and old Colonel Hammerling[18] lost his sword for a few days and had to tag around in undress uniform, though not for long and that's the reason I never liked Sheridan.

Well, as soon as daylight broke I could see the men were all in bad humor, and they began shooting; then the swamp angel opened out, and with one thing and another we had a busy day of it; but a lull during the afternoon gave me a chance to go down to Chattanooga creek, and I got up a parley. We soon struck a trade, and I gave an old, dog-eared deck of cards for this little sack of kinikinick tobacco[19] and this Richmond newspaper, and now I hear there's to be no more trading on the picket line, but I've heard the like of that before.

Sometimes when the fog begins to lift we lie flat down and look under it to see the Johnnies coming, first their feet, then from the knees, and so on up until their whole bodies are in sight. Oh! if this old valley could tell tales, what a lot of them it would have. I only wish I had a little sugar or some vinegar, or something to dust on this hill of fare, but here we're glad to eat what's set before us. Now listen to the jangle of the drums beating tattoo, and I'm sleepy.

Hello, boys, here's that blamed, old reveille again, and the Adjutant says I must take my Company and go across the river for wood. Well, this morning we have no breakfast, but you two little fellows pile on the wagons, and I'll try to pick you up something. Men, get your axes and fall in, and away we go, north through the main street of town, and as we go I meet Jacob Heaton of Salem, a middle-aged citizen. I shake hands and inquire what he does here, and I find he's running a government bakery for the hospitals, so I beg and coax and wheedle an order for one-half dozen or so of loaves, just for old acquaintance sake, and we all go on, and the world looks brighter. We cross the river on a pontoon which the rebels, two or three miles above, are constantly trying to break by throwing into the river logs, brush and trees, but we have a boom above which catches most of the stuff, and it furnishes us with good wood. But today we go straight out to Stringer's ridge and get our wagons loaded. Do you see that high peak? Colonel Wilder of our mounted infantry[21] got a gun up there when we first came down here, and tossed the first shell into Chattanooga. Crittenden of the first corps[22] lay along the ridge and built thousands of fires at night, while we of the 14th corps were crossing at Bridgeport, Stevenson and Shell Mound. Then Bragg got scared and left.

Now we go back. Do you see that train of wagons coming? Well, they do get a few up on the north side of the river from Stevenson, with supplies, but it's dangerous business. They say the roads are lined with dead mules, as the mountains are filled with scouts and bush-whackers,[23] but every wagon load helps. Now, come, and we'll go over the camps to see what we can find. Here we come to Opdyk's old regiment, the 125th Ohio.[24] It is now commanded by Colonel Joe Bruff; he is from Damascus, about four miles from our Ohio home. We go into his tent and find him lying on a bale of cotton. He got a little tick on the ribs the other day, and is a bit sore and grumpy. He shows us a wad of greenbacks which the ball struck and split through lengthwise, then it glanced and followed a rib round aways, then shot off some other way. "I say, Joe, have you anything to eat?" And he brings out a bottleful of medicine, and we need some and take it right away; then he reaches under his bed and pulls out a cracker box which has twelve crackers in it. We take three each, and his cook takes some water from a camp kettle, puts it in a couple of skillets and puts three broken crackers in each. Pretty soon they begin to swell and swell until we have enough and to spare. Then the cook brings in a little poke of brown sugar and three tin spoons, and we have a dinner fit for the king of the cannibal islands and are all filled up. Such good luck doesn't come every day. Now I must tell you that you'll have to go back home, for there's going to be a big racket around here soon, and your Mother would cry her eyes out if you were to get shot. Old Joe Hooker[25] has reached Stevenson, and I reckon we'll soon have plenty of rations; then we'll go at them. Soldiers are always hungry, and rations a plenty keeps them in good humor.

"Well, how am I going to get home?" That's so, and what am I to do with Dick, good-natured, patient, little Dick? Aren't you asleep yet? "No, tell me a little story." If I do, will you go to sleep? Well, here goes. One time, long ago, when the Fort Wayne Railroad was new to us, and they began to haul sheep and cattle to Philadelphia on it. Some of our people got to thinking it a safe thing to do, so your Grandfather engaged in the business, and I went with the sheep several trips. I rode in the caboose, and when the train stopped would go forward to look at the sheep and right anything that might be wrong. Often there would be a dozen drovers on the same train, then we'd take turn about in looking after the stock. If the train should start while we were forward we would scramble up and run over the tops of the cars to the caboose. One, cold, frosty morning near Downington, Pennsylvania, I was out, the train started, and I scrambled up and ran back. The cars were then a distance of perhaps four feet apart, with a platform between for the brakeman, with the large brake wheel in the end of the car and perhaps six or eight inches from the wall. I was making my way slowly back, the train was running fast and swaying from side to side, the tops were frosty and slippery, so I carefully measured my steps from car to car, and while standing at the end of one, ready to step to the next, a low, overhead bridge struck the back of my head; I fell, rolled off the end of the car, and was caught on the axle of the brake wheel, pinched in tight between the wheel and the end of the car. There I hung limp, like an old, empty sack. When the train came to a halt again some one found me, and I was carried back to the caboose and taken to Philadelphia. My companions took care of the sheep, sold them, and one of the men came home with me. From the time I was hurt until I was half way home I knew nothing. The doctors wanted to saw into my head, dig in with a cant hook and sort of straighten things out, but I thought my head had most enough rough usage and wouldn't let them. Now, go to sleep. Hard bed? Yes, but you've got to get used to that.

To-morrow our regiment is to muster for pay. We haven't been paid for three or four months, and yesterday cook got a tinful of rice, so we are going to have a fine feeding. I wish we had a pickled pig's foot and some vinegar to put on the rice. Hello! here goes your toot, a toot, toot. The drums are beating in volleys, and if you listen you can hear the same over in the rebel camp. The music tells we are all of one country. The airs their bands play are often the same as ours, and all their calls are the same, and given at the same minute reach down into the valley, blend in harmony with our own.

Here comes the paymaster with his strong box. He takes his station with a cracker box for a seat, and for a table has a board laid on two empty barrels. The companies are formed and paid from right to left, beginning with "A." Each company commander stands by the pay table to identify his men. The company is paid off quickly, and the regiment is soon finished.

After pay there are many gamblers on hand to get in their miserable work. In all kinds of out-of-the-way places you can see groups of soldiers, and if you crowd in you will find a rubber blanket spread on the ground, with soldiers sitting on it, piles of money all about and dice boxes rattling, or maybe cards, and many of the poor fellows are soon fleeced of all they have. Those gamblers are often soldiers themselves, at least they are dressed like soldiers. This gambling is all a violation of orders, and patrols are on the go all through the camps to gobble the gamblers up.

Often it happens, when pay comes in the midst of a campaign, that we cannot send money back home for days or weeks, and it is hard for those who wish to do so to keep it safely, so our good State of Ohio has provided a state agent who receives all moneys entrusted to his care, and in the name of the State agrees to carry it home and to send it to the proper persons, or keep it safely until called for. Here he is, Mr. Williams, I think, and now many of the men gather round him and is kept busy. Here I got several hundred dollars in bonds, the first I ever saw. They are for Fifty Dollars each and are called seven thirties. We all get them, and are therefore bloated bondholders. My first experience on the battle field, seeing all the dead robbed, pockets cut, and so on, made me resolve that the fellow who plundered your Uncle's pockets should feel kind of sick, so I always made some haste to get rid of my pile,—which has never been difficult. Some of our fellows had rather more than a speaking acquaintance with a game called poker, and before I really knew it I had run up a little debt of that kind—One Hundred and Fifty Dollars—to Uncle Dan, who has the face of a graven image, while mine always tells tales. One night luck turned with me and I reduced the debt to Nine Dollars, then lost a dollar, and paid up, and have never gambled since. "Isn't that wicked?" Well, yes,

I reckon it is, but then what is a fellow to do right here? No books, no papers, only the game of war, and you see already you can watch for the puff of smoke, wait for the roar, and watch or dodge the big balls, see the dirt fly, and the explosion or ricochet with interest or indifference according to the course they take, and the business gets old unless you are on the move.

Now over at the 9th Ohio, being all dutch and from Ohio, they most always have some fun, and I am sometimes invited. When at night all the officers gather into the Quartermaster's big tent, some twenty or more sitting in a half circle, then hot water, condensed milk, a little spirits are put into a pan the size of a wash bowl, and commencing at one end each takes a sup and passes the pan to his neighbor. Thus the evening slips away finally, for all are good singers and sociable. Well, one night I took Uncle Dan along, but as the program was so simple I didn't relate it to him. He happened to be the end man and very drouthy; the pan was given to him first, and his whole face was soon buried in it; he gave back the pan; no one said a word, and it was soon filled again and passed as usual. Do you know what happened then to the Captain of Company "A"? Well, I'll just tell you that all the tent pins and guy ropes in the army of the Cumberland seemed to be in a conspiracy against us as we wound our way homeward; and if he and I live to see a hundred years, and the leather on our faces doesn't get too hard and dry, I think it will wrinkle into some sort of smile every time we meet, and I am likely to be abused by him till the day of my death.

I expect you never saw so many black people before in your life. We'll get a lot of them on the company parade ground to see them pat juba[26] and dance and hear them sing. They can all do that, big and little, old and young. Here they come already. See this old, white-headed fellow set his right foot forward, bend his knee, half close his eyes, throw back his head and begin to pat and hum through his nose. Here they go by ones, twos and threes till half of them are dancing all keeping the most perfect time, while one of their number sings or chants, all joining in the refrain. That old fellow has picked cotton many a long day and patted juba for just such a crowd at night for lo these seventy or eighty years, longing for the year of jubilee[27] which now he thinks has come. These poor people follow our army like a dark cloud, and now they are going to make soldiers of the young fellows, at least that's what Lincoln says.[28]

Well, you may wish we had a roast goose for dinner but I don't, and I'll tell you why. Back last winter, when we were scouting around Murfreesboro and the ground was white with snow, I had to go on picket at night. When I had my instructions and countersign and was ready to start with my men, Charlie Fowler said it was too bad, for we had been marching hard all day, so he put off to his ambulance and came back with a little barrel in his arms. As each man passed he held out his tin, and Fowler poured a little spirits into it. Of course, coming from our Doctor, it had to be taken, so we put out into the dark more cheerful like. Our line for the night ran across a road, perhaps three-quarters of a mile from camp, and on one side of the road stood a farm house, and a log barn stood on the other side. Overhead the barn was filled with corn blades. Here we made our reserve post and built a fire in the empty horse stable, its flames almost reaching the corn blades. The first relief that came off post gathered a dozen geese, we skinned them, and, together with some ham and cabbage we found at the house, we set about having a feast. I thought I should like some goose, and soon had a goodish hunk on the end of a ramrod, sizzling and sputtering over the fire. As the outside would shrivel and shrink I would eat in to the raw part, then hold it over the fire some more, and pack on some cabbage; so I had in my stomach a layer of cabbage and a layer of goose, and there they should have been digested in comfort, which they were not, but instead sought exit by the movement we call "by inversion, right wheel," and I went out into the darkness and parted with both the goose and cabbage; and since them I am content that the Jews shall have all the geese.

Now let's look at our rice. The camp kettle is half full, and it's swelling yet. I tell you rice and crackers are the stuff in a siege. With another pint of rice we could feed the whole regiment.

The soldiers are washing. With our regular rations we get soap, but here we have none, so we take off our shirts, put them in a camp kettle and boil them. That makes them shrink, and, as the shirt collar can't get away from its place, the tail goes toward the collar, and soon there is a coldness between the shirt and trousers, and they are hardly on speaking terms; so our soldier poet sings:

> "Like a man without a wife,
> Like a ship without a sail,
> The most useless thing in life
> Is a shirt without a tail."[29]

The contractors who contracted to make the shirts, made them on the "contract" plan, and, as soon as the soldiers put them on, they keep up the contract until the whole shirt is contracted into collar and armholes. I hope Hooker will clear up the railroads soon, so that we can have some new ones.

There's something going on. See the signal flags and the stir around headquarters. Tomorrow we'll hear news, get our mail and boxes of goodies from home. Hear away off over Lookout the cannon and small arms. Hooker is on Sand mountain.

We've got sauerkraut for supper. There are two commissions here who care for the wounded, the Christian Commission and the Sanitary Commission, and for some reason there is bad feeling between them. Each sought to make the best showing by getting signers to a petition or recommendation, setting forth their excellent qualities; so they went from one high official to another, and when they came to General Turchin he said: "If I sign dose babor, how many parrels sauerkraut you gif my boys, huh?" One offered him three and the other five, and the five carried off the General's signature. The 11th Ohio is in Turchin's brigade, and Joe Pennock and a lot of our neighbor boys are in the 11th, so I went over on a visit, and here is the kraut.

Hello! here comes Jim Hartzell[30] and Sam Fisher from the 7th Ohio. Hooker is down below, and they got in some way; and here come Creighton and Crane,[31] Colonel and Lieutenant Colonel, to visit us. Our Colonel Perkins is at home; he was wounded at Chickamauga. Now we'll have a grand visit. Aren't they fine fellows, and well dressed? They say we don't know what fighting is down here, and they've just come to teach us a trick or two. As they bid us good bye some warning voice says: "Look out, boys, you may run against a snag." Jim says the 7th is in General Garry's[32] division. They had a bit of a scrap down below, and Garry's son, a Lieutenant of Knap's battery[33] of their brigade, was killed with a lot more, and Garry is vicious.

To-morrow you must start home. The boats are running to Stevenson, and you can get through all right. I'll do the best I can for Dick, and tell you about it later. The rebels are all about us now. You can hear them shout and cheer, and at night their fires twinkle both on the slopes and in the valley. Every sign is a warning of impending trouble. I will get you a pass and transportation to-night, and I wish I had something good for you to eat.

Tell you a last story? Well, this is the last. One night, about a year ago, back in Kentucky, my Captain, Bob Wilson,[34] and I were on picket together, and took our quarters in a fine old mansion that had been deserted, the same day, by all the white folks, and everything in it was spick and span,—pianos, fine table ware and beds. Darkies were all about, so we ordered a good supper and in the morning a good breakfast. The meals were served by darkies in good style,—hot bread, ham, coffee, cream, all good and on the finest table ware I had ever seen. That was the good meal I've had. Captain Wilson was killed two days after. Now I'm done. I like to tell stories about good things to eat. Here comes the order,—eighty rounds to the man, and be prepared to move out at daylight to-morrow. Now in the morning, when you see the army go into the rifle pits, you skip for the wharf. Good bye, take keer yourself.

CHAPTER THIRTEEN

⟨✦⟩

Mission Ridge; The Pursuit after the Battle; Ordered to Ohio—and Steals a Visit Home

You READ OF the battle above the clouds. I saw it, and it was a sight not to be forgotten. I could see the men and the smoking line as it advanced. All the zigzags made by rocks, brush, timber and other obstructions were plainly indicated by the smoke and the flashes from the guns. When our line advanced, it crawled slowly, slowly, and we cheered ourselves hoarse, and when it halted, which it often did, then our hearts would sink, and all would be quiet until the rolling echoes began again. The sounds of battle were above us and all about us. The next day we faced Mission Ridge[1] and lay in front and to the left of Orchard Knob, under fire all day; but the plunging shot did little harm, only kept us in the utmost misery imaginable and plowed up the ground, covering us with dirt. I got a chunk as big as a hickory nut in my mouth, which I thought had taken my whole face away, for an instant.

We had two lines of Johnnies in sight all day, one at the foot of the ridge and one at the top. Those on the top seemed to take great delight in waving their flags and guidons[2] at us in defiance. I don't know how it was, but we all seemed to raise up and start at one time, the colors taking the lead and flanks hanging back, just as you see a flock of wild geese flying. It was quite a distance to charge and get so near the ridge as to be safe from the bursting shells, which kept up the most spiteful music. I was next our colors when a piece of shell struck the staff about two feet from the butt

149

socket, cut it half off, splitting it, and cutting off one of the tassels. John Geddes,[3] the color bearer, jumped like a stag, and I thought he was down, but, no, he stuck to the colors and still led us. The low works at the foot of the ridge were well manned, but we jumped right over them. Two guns with bayonets fixed were lying down behind, but we never stopped to disarm them; and now we were all out of wind. The trees had been cut from the slope, falling down hill, and the branches topped off, so forming an abatis[4] over which we made slow progress. We just crowded over and under and through, and made headway slowly but surely. Where I went up there was a sort of log pen filled with earth and leveled off. On it were two field guns which were being worked industriously, but could not be depressed enough to do us much harm. We all began to cluster up against this log pen like a swarm of bees on a limb. All at once, without orders, we burst up over the logs onto the gun platform. I wish I could tell you what I saw there. It was hand to hand fighting, and the "devil take the hindmost." The gunners stood to their guns like heroes, and the musket butts were pitted against sweat sticks and rammers, and, as we yelled "surrender" and charged, there was tremendous swearing among the rebels and our own men. I remember one of my men bit his cartridge, called "surrender," and the ball stuck half way down the gun barrel; the other fellow was coming at him, and he flung down his musket, picked up a big rock, and let drive. We got only a whack or two at the infantry when they scooted down the far slope through the timber. The crest by this time was covered with our troops, all in disorder so far as I could see.

The big guns were in our hands, and two caissons and teams, about half the horses shot and the other half standing helpless by their mates. Such a scene of wild exultation. We had accomplished that which, for more than two months, we had looked upon as an impossibility. To attack and carry the fortified ridge had in nowise entered into our calculations; but here we were, and victory had sent our blood up to one hundred and forty or more; and when that is the case men do things that aren't put down in books on etiquette. Well, we raged around there a bit.

Just as the gloom of night was beginning to fall scattering shots began to come back at us, when, all at once, a blazing volley leaped out of the woods,—the Johnnies had turned on us. We were a mob, when the command of "lie down, lie down," rang out from our officers, we fell flat; then our fellows commenced to return the fire. Some of our men ran out to the broken guns and carriages and the dead and living horses that were stranded in our front, and used them for a breastwork against the enemy, though here they were in quite as much danger from friend as from foe, and for a little time the firing was furious. Here I lost a fine boy, Ashel Kirkbride, perhaps eighteen years old, a pleasant, happy-dispositioned lad, who had been with me every day from the beginning. He was shot through the stomach. The ball entered the waist belt, and he died sometime that night. Just before we charged the ridge he gave me a little stone Bible. At our camp on University Heights the boys took the mottled marble corner-stone from what was intended to be the Southern University, broke it up, and by a little cascade that fell over the palisades which hem in the mountain like a mighty wall, they rubbed and ground, washed and polished the bits of stone into many, little, ornamental keepsakes, and this was one. In many ways this boy gave evidence of a presentiment of his death, and I could multiply such cases. Our Captain Wallace,[5] Company "I," told me last fall at Chattanooga of one of his men who, just before a charge at Chickamauga, persisted in giving him his watch and all his valuables, with careful directions as to what should be done with each. All argument failed to change his mind, and the next few minutes proved his fear correct. You may call it what you like.

And here I approach a subject with hesitation, and it is, how a fellow feels in action. Many have tried to tell; I think none have made it clear, neither shall I, for there are many phases of it, from the wretched agony of waiting under fire, to the galling torture and crushing, humiliating, agonizing disappointment of defeat. When everything is going with us the blood rises up, up, up, from 120 to 200, 400, 800. A feeling of ecstasy, born of the roar of battle and smell of burnt powder, takes hold of you, and each man feels invincible, and in such a state of mind danger and death have no terrors. This feeling, I think, bears no relation to anger, or fear, or any other petty condition of mind.

To return to the battle. We all fell flat there on the ridge, simply from force of habit—the habit of obedience—but there was no restraint could hold the men in their places. Some would leap up and fire, others fired kneeling. Had they been armed entirely with only sticks and stones and received the order to charge down the slope through the timber, they would have done so with the same promptness as if armed with Spencer rifles,[6] and I believe would have gone to certain death, to a man, without thought or protest. This I call the exultation or ecstasy of battle.[7]

Our Major and Lieutenant Colonel had both been wounded at Chickamauga. Our Colonel,[8] a lean, dyspeptic, old fellow, who courted death and always put himself in the way of it, though a martinet ordinarily, grew mild and gracious on the day of battle. When we charged the hill numbers of men gave out for want of wind. The Colonel rode his old, black horse, keeping abreast, and in gentle pity would reach down and take a gun from any lagging, panting fellow, until he had a bundle of muskets across his horse's withers he could scarce reach over; then he found a road someplace and brought them safely to the top. While we lay there flat he looked over us in a sort of motherly solicitude, and would roar out with all the wind he had: "Keep your heads down there, men, or you will be shot." He was only a few feet from where I lay, and I ventured to ask: "Colonel, hadn't you better lie down too?" "Lieutenant, when I want any advice from you I'll let you know," was his stiff reply.

Close by my side, touching me, lay a boy, banging away all the time. He had raised his head—we were both looking—when a ball struck him fair in the forehead, about an inch below the hair. He head fell and turned face toward me, and I noticed the ball had split the visor of his cap just where the cap and visor joined. I thought once of keeping the cap as a memento of the battle, and because it showed such a true shot. I remember often to have gotten things to keep as mementos, but the harvest of trophies, relics and mementos was too great. We all began from the first to gather curiosities of war, but the first specimens were soon dropped by the wayside and fresher ones took their places, and when all transportation was denied to companies and each man had his own burdens to bear, he made that burden light, and we would hardly have stopped to pick up anything less valuable than jewels. Grub, forty rounds, gun and blanket were enough, and all we could tote. The late owner of the cap was just a lad, not a member of my Company, and where he belonged I don't know, as there were six or seven regiments of us mixed up as we lay there.

The enemy soon disappeared; the half light of evening deepened into darkness; the old rebel fires were chunked up; and the awesomeness of the scene is not to be described,—the naked wood, the weird shadows, the dead and wounded, rider and horse, great and small arms of every description strewn here and there in perfect abandon. There were two of the greatest surprises ever known, one for us and one for our enemy. We were never expected to take the hill, and they never expected us to make the attempt; but here we were, and where were they? Of course we felt sure we could rout them, but by other means; and I venture to say that, when our success was achieved, any officer who could have claimed the honor of giving the command to make the charge which resulted so gloriously, would have been proud to proclaim it, but so far the evidence goes to show that the advance was ordered only to the foot of the ridge, and when General Grant saw the men take the lower works and keep right on he inquired very sternly who gave the order for advance, and, as the event seemed in grave doubt, no one claimed the honor, and I believe no one claims it yet; so the best explanation, I think, is that the men were working for Thirteen Dollars ($13.00) a month and wanted to get in a full day on this occasion.[9]

The wounded were gathered up and carried back to Chattanooga, and our tired fellows bivouacked for the night, as we were all used up, so we lay on the rough rocks with our feet to the fires. And there the fitful lights of our little chunk fires showed two horsemen, slowly picking their way through groups of weary fellows, and as, here and there, some attempt was made to get out of their way, a low, pleasant voice said kindly: "Lie still, boys, we will be careful not to hurt you, lie still. Had a good time to-day, didn't we? We got even with them. Lie still and take your rest." These were Generals Grant and Thomas. Soon came some ladies and gentlemen of the Christian Commission, carrying big wicker demijohns, searching for any wounded that might have been overlooked by the stretcher men. Then we all fell asleep, and after that I was only wakened once, when the fire crept too near, and I raised up and pulled the man next me, whose feet were burning, back a bit. He wore the gray, and his feet were burnt sadly, but he never knew it.[10]

The blare of trumpets, roll of drum and din of fife came, as usual, all too early, and as the sun drove the darkness away what a sight met our eyes. The valleys all about were filled with impenetrable fog, only here and there a mountain peak rose above it. Overhead was the bright sky, while at our feet, and on a level with our position, lay a dead, blank level of fog, over which, it appeared, the whole army might march to Lookout. To the east of us was Chickamauga station where the rebels had many military stores to which they set fire and then abandoned. An explosion like an earthquake occurred, and with it the fog raised high and higher and higher until it looked like an inverted giant funnel, then the apex parted and rolled gently back until all settled again to its proper level. I shall never forget that picture.

And now everything told of business. The commissary was on hand by daylight; we were filling our haversacks and cartridge boxes, and were soon off, some for the south and others for Knoxville. Our route was south after Bragg. It was Thanksgiving Day, and for two days we pushed on, frequently passing abandoned guns and caissons, small arms and all kinds of debris from an army in flight. Garry [Geary] with his division was in advance, and we a close second. Thousands of tramping feet rendered our route a continuous bed of thin mortar.

The second day there was occasional firing, at times rising to the dignity of a small battle, and towards evening, as we marched towards Ringgold, the fighting sounded furious, and our head of column just arrived in time to see the 7th Ohio and 28th Pennsylvania repulsed,—the Potomac boys had struck that snag. Bragg in trying to save his train in passing through a gap in Pidgeon Mountain had a line of his troops on the crest of it to check pursuit, and had made protection with a line of logs, stumps, etc. Garry threw his division into line and made a direct assault, thinking to repeat what we had done at Mission Ridge, and soon had time to repent the folly.

When our brigade was fully up it had grown too dark to make a movement, so we prepared a bivouac, for it was raining. Pretty soon Cousin Jim Hartzell of the 7th found me, and he was in an unhappy frame of mind. Some of our boys had found some sheep, the skins of which made us a good bed. Jim and I lay together, and, while the rain beat a steady tattoo on our rubber blankets, he gave me an account of their unhappy luck. He said Creighton and Crane[11] were killed, and all their field and line were either killed our wounded except for the Adjutant; told how they advanced up the hill nearly to the crest, their line growing thinner all the time, he and the Adjutant and several others well in front, when the whole advance was checked. His party stopped behind a big rock near the crest, where they remained trying to form some plan of escape, when Jim proposed that he should fire and that would draw the fire of the enemy in the lines above, and as soon as that occurred they should cut sticks and run, every man for himself. The plan succeeded, and he came straight to me. He told me that he got his man with the last shot, and described him to me, to the color of his eyes and hair. In the morning the rebs were soon gone, and we went up to the place and found it was even so. Creighton and Crane were killed in the valley, while mounted and following close in the rear of the line, and I am sure the distance was more than a mile. Good shooting for an old-fashioned musket.

The next day pursuit was abandoned, the dead and wounded gathered up and put in three box cars which, with an engine and tender, made the train. I was given a guard, and the train put in my charge for Chattanooga. As it was my first railroad ride since we took the field, some danger in it, and I being in command, I thought it would be just the thing to ride on the cow catcher, so I sat straddle of the nose of it. I should guess it was thirty miles from there to Chattanooga, and as the train started I felt that I was the right man in the right place. The track and roadbed were all out of repair, and one of our blue coats, a regular Abe Lincoln hireling, at the throttle. Soon the nose of the old cow catcher began a sort of uncertain lurching, weaving motion, swaying from side to side, as though at each lurch the engine contemplated leaving the irons and taking the mud on one side or the other. The wind blew a hurricane in my face, and the throttle man turned on the juice until we fairly flew, and I felt like a wounded bird in a cyclone, and wished that the wicked, northern mudsill[12] at the throttle might be stricken with palsy; but nothing of the kind happened, contrariwise. Trees, tunnels, bridges, in fact the whole landscape seemed all mixed up in a mad race for the rear, and I went dashing, jerking and swaying from side to side in my mad, crazy flight through space. The gimp[13] began to ooze out of me at every pore, and the only hope that sustained me was that we must halt at Chattanooga. So I reached low on either side, took a firm grip on the iron frame, leaned forward so as to split the wind with my poll, and clung like a hurt squirrel to a tree limb, and even Mother's old dinner horn never sounded half so sweet as the prolonged whistle with which we approached Chattanooga. And in such a manner I learned that the cow catcher was never intended as a seat for first-class passengers.

Ambulance and woolen overcoats were in waiting, and soon we were relieved, much to my satisfaction, and we went back to our old quarters. How everything was changed. Citizens again walked the streets, piles on piles of cracker boxes, barrels and boxes of pork meat were all about, stores were open, the old flag gave its folds to the breeze from Point Lookout, and, in truth, we soon realized we were here in the Union once more.

Forts and long lines of rifle pits were almost tenantless, and only reminded us that this man on the checker-board of war had reached the king row and was secure.

In a day or two the brigade, all tired out and bedraggled with mud, returned, and soon we were laying out new cities and towns, outside the old fortifications, when in a day or so we were in positions of comparative comfort, with scarcely any guard or picket duty, except the guarding of military stores; and occasional scouts and visits to friends or points of interest on the vast battle field near at hand, with the improvised amusements so common to the soldiers, made the next few months pass rapidly.

Many old regiments, whose terms of three years were up, were veteranized and given thirty days furlough. Many, both officers and man, received furloughs, so there was much coming and going, and we had word every day or two from home. Loyal, gray-headed citizens came in on horseback from far and near, and would stand in groups in the fort under the waving stars and stripes, and often I have seen the tears roll down their old cheeks as they looked up at the flag they had been taught to love and honor. Such scenes were common. The country people came in to trade pies and many wonderful kinds of cookery; and as all had to find entrance through the picket lines, the boys on duty lived high. The traders not being allowed to come in unless armed with a pass from some very high officer, which very few could get, so, at the points where the lines crossed the highways, each day a most motley, interesting throng of people—white and black, men and women, clad in homespun and in the most primitive fashion, with the greatest variety of vehicles and motive power—gathered to trade with the soldiers who came out from the camps, and business grew lively. Corn-bread, pies, tobacco and trinkets were the main articles of commerce. The bread was solid, and was divided into two classes by our boys and named dough gods and Tennessee sinkers. The pies were top crusted and only invit-ing as a change from our ever-monotonous army rations. Some held that the crusts were pegged on, and others that they were sewed,—anyway the business was flourishing and furnished much fun and variety.

On the night of January 1st, 1864, I was on picket near Fort Wood, and my station was at the point where the line crossed the highway leading to-wards Knoxville, and my duty was to examine all comers as to passes, or, being without, to judge them and their business, which if I thought impor-tant to send them under guard to headquarters, as spies were coming and going all the time. Some were frauds and some genuine. Any suspicious per-son we held under guard at the reserve till morning, when they were taken to headquarters for examination. It rained all day and towards night grew colder. The men on post began to chill and, to keep from freezing, com-menced to walk a beat. At first the footsteps went slush, slush, but soon it set in to freeze, and then the men began to trot, and soon, from near and far, their steady trot, trot, trot, sounded like the hoof beats of a squadron of cavalry on a rocky road. The troop were coming in from Knoxville where they had been sent to help Burnside. The sorry artillery horses, jaded nearly to death with dragging of guns and heavy caissons through the red clay mortar of the road, made a pitiable picture, and as the mud froze harder the poor beasts—do their best—could go no farther, so were un-tackled from their pieces and sent into camp, while the guns were left in the grip of the winter king. That was a terrible night, and the chill of it hangs in my bones yet. The boys in camp knew it too, and before daybreak came the cooks were steaming camp kettles of hot, black coffee and bean soup. Never messengers were hailed with greater joy, and I think I can taste and smell the coffee still. It's hard to know how this frost-bitten, old world looked to a fellow after he was on the outside of a great cup of hot coffee and a hatful of bean soup, unless you've been there.

By a natural selection[14] our companies had broken into messes of from six to ten men each, and each member of the mess was cook in turn, or, if all agreed, one man was made permanent cook, drew the rations for his mess, and was general caterer, and I must say was always loyal to it or any member of it. No matter where or how engaged he would find his way to them with such viands as he could provide; for this, they took all his tricks of duty about the camp, and even on the march, so that at all times he had his eyes open for the good of his mess.

The artillery came in the morning with digging and prying tools, dug and lifted the guns out of their frosty beds, and the teams had a great pull to get them in, as they carried more frozen mud than the weight of the guns. Near Fort Wood we had parked our artillery, guns of all sorts, sizes and calibres, all showing marks of rough usage, bruised and battered old trophies of many a hard fight and long rough campaign.

The defunct soldier in gray, whom I drew back from the fire over on Mission Ridge,—he had a bayonet thrust through and through,—had the same fashion of carrying his equipment that we had, a blanket over his shoulder and tied at the ends. As I drew him back a pair of new, white, wool socks fell from the folds of his blanket, and as he had no particular use for them in his condition, and my necessities were pressing in that matter, I stripped the holey, shapeless rags from my feet and encased them in the warm, new, hand-knitted socks, which seemed to be sent me by a kind Providence. This may seem shocking to you, but, as neither fine points of ethics or theology enter largely into the articles of war, my mind was not afflicted by the moral aspect of it at the time, and isn't now, so I leave you to decide the quality of the proceeding.

This winter was cold and stormy. We took occasional scouts to the south in the direction of Rome, Georgia, and finally took up our residence near Ringgold as a sort of advanced post. The time, three years, of the older troops was nearly out; the end of the war seemed still a great way off; and Uncle Sam hated to loose these sturdy fighters; rightly too, for anyone of them was worth a half dozen recruits, as they had been shot over now for three years, bronzed, smoke-tanned, weather-beaten fellows, trained in all the duties and arts of war. From two to four hundred of the fittest of each original thousand remained. 'Twould seem though that nothing would induce them to re-enlist, and so many of them thought at first.[15] Our Uncle Sam offered each man a thirty days' furlough and Four Hundred Dollars who would re-enlist. Look at those sturdy fellows as they stand round a smoky, sodden camp fire, this snowy, cheerless day, caps tied over their heads, overcoats and, in fact, all their clothes wet and steaming as they turn back and front to catch the heat, moving here and there to avoid the blinding, pungent smoke, coats singed brown, with now and then great and small holes in both coats and trousers where the sparks have fallen and burned as they lay by camp fires on the field, bivouac or picket. See the greasy, old haversacks and battered canteens, and back there the dreary, little, pup tents, three feet high and four or five feet wide, covered with snow, and a few pine boughs for a bed and a coarse, rough blanket for bedding, with nothing better to hope for in the future if they stay. Very few of those fellows have seen home since they enlisted three years ago. Not one in a dozen have slept in a bed, eaten off a table, or had a good, square meal of well-cooked, Christian food, often wanting even the plain, black coffee, hard bread or fat pork, a soldier's rations. Those men were school boys, mechanics, clerks, farmer lads, and all left homes of plenty. They have seen most of their comrades left by the wayside,— sick, wounded, dead,—and coming out of battle have looked and called in vain for comrades, partners, friends. And those men, soldiers, know full well that, should they turn their backs upon the service now and return to their homes, remunerative employment awaits them, and every comfort and luxury heart can wish, together with hearty greeting and love of fathers and all their kindred and sweethearts. See them turn and turn. The snow has turned to rain and all is slush and mud about the log heap. They are discussing the question: Will they go or stay? In two weeks their time is out and they will be free. No excitement, no confusion, the talk is low and earnest; no spick and span, plausible recruiting officer to make highly-colored talk. No, that would be useless. They know well what is before them in either case. Some demur and say truly they have done their share and will let others take a turn, but a few, stout-hearted fellows say that they enlisted to follow their country's flag and defend it against all enemies, and that, so long as any enemies remain, they must do their parts, so, without hesitation, they step up to a stump, sign the roll, are followed by others and still others, and the regiment will start home to-morrow as veterans. The rest will be good for them too, for they have been "faithful in tramping out the vintage where the grapes of wrath are stored, and have built watch-fires in many hundred circling camps." When they come back, and the spring opens, "they will loose the fateful lightning" and write the fiery gospel that will convince the opposition, and we shall have peace, "for they have sounded forth the trumpet that shall never call retreat."[16]

Oh, ho! my boy, if you could see one of these singed, battered, old regiments go through the manual of arms, and hear the butts of these old muskets strike the earth as one, with the thud of a trip-hammer, and bringing their three or four hundred bayonets down to a charge—one time and two motions,—barrel upwards, point level with the eye; you would understand the persuasiveness of the gospel they preach—tipped with burnished steel and backed by most penetrating argument of lead, caliber 54. If you could hear just a little, five minutes discourse from a brigade of these evangelists, you would never forget it, but tell it to your children's children as the most convincing preaching you ever heard.[17] You would be so full of it you could scarce wait for the benediction, and these preachers are all coming back, thirty or forty regiments of them; and next summer the mountains between here and Atlanta, that so far have held only silent gossip with the clouds and stars, will roll and echo with strange, unfamiliar shoutings and thunderings as the mighty torrent of war rushes on its fateful way, and every hour of every day will claim its tribute of blood.

The highest rank in our army is Major General, except by special account of Congress, which in the cases of Washington and Grant, and, I believe, also Sherman and Sheridan, made the grade of General. The intermediate of Lieutenant General I think not more than three or four officers ever held, and when they passed away the grades also passed.

Grant was now made General, with command of all the forces, and went to Washington to organize a last, crushing campaign. The old, depleted regiments are to be consolidated or recruited up. On account of our depleted condition no promotion or muster of officers is permitted. We all kick at consolidation, as every soldier has infinite pride in his own regiment, division and corps. So to-day I stand ready to prove by the most convincing argument that the old 14th corps was, without cavil or disparity, the best corps of fighters in the whole army, and that Pappy Thomas was without a peer in the round world as corps commander.

On February 1st, 1864, a call for two hundred thousand volunteers was made; on March 14th two hundred thousand; July 18th five hundred thousand; December 19th five hundred thousand; all for three years, and all in 1864; so you can see that there was work ahead, and every old regiment was looking forward with eagerness to full ranks and a full line and field.

At this time many regiments were short of company officers.[18] Companies were commanded by Sergeants with commissions in their pockets, and all wanted to be mustered into their proper grades. Many officers had been killed and disabled, many had resigned, and both the inefficient and unpopular had been gotten rid of in one way or another. An unpopular officer had a dreary time in our service. If the enlisted men disliked him, they had many ways to make him feel it. In truth, almost every company had in its ranks men carrying muskets who were quite the equals and often the superiors of their officers in fortune and ability and education, though, as a rule, I think the officers were appointed and promoted for good, military reasons. On duty, except in camp, after the first year, on the march, bivouac and picket, men and officers often, I think, as a rule, slept around the same camp fire, ate the same rations, often glad to fill their tin cups from the same company camp kettle, whether with coffee or bean soup. It had to be so from the nature of the service.

After the first six months, or after the battle of Milton, very few men were punished. They didn't need it. It was far easier to do duty with the main army, move when it moved, camp when it camped, and fight when it fought, than to do outpost or scouting duty, as we did before we joined the army at Murfreesboro. At any rate we felt more at ease after that. The main army must be well fed. As General Sherman said, "An army moves on its belly." Of course when the big army gives battle, if your regiment is in a very hot place, it is liable to be annihilated, but the risks are not so great as on detached duty with a small force. The sense of security is much greater. The small force is always liable to surprise and capture or a bitter fight, and must be on the alert night and day, so guard duty is much lighter with the main army, where, except for a good, strong picket, comparatively little guard duty is required. I think after leaving Murfreesboro we never posted a camp guard. The Orderly of each company every day made details of men in regular order. A detail, no matter what the service, counted a trick, and the name of the soldier performing the trick went to the foot of the list, and he did no more tricks until his name came up in regular order. The Adjutant of the regiment kept just such a roster or list of the line officers, and the same order prevailed with them as to duty.

So on the 14th of February, 1864, my name was uppermost, and I was called by the Adjutant to headquarters and handed an order by Major General Thomas to proceed at once to Columbus, Ohio, and, together with four guards, report to Colonel Burbank, commanding draft rendezvous, to take in charge and forward to our regiment all recruits belonging to it, Quartermaster's department to furnish transportation.[19] If a thunder clap had fallen from a clear sky, or old St. Nick clapped his big claw on me, I should have been less surprised.

To go back to God's country again, where ladies and gentlemen lived and wore store clothes, and where there were fat cattle and big, red barns; to sit down at a table where there were custard pies, sweet cake, bursting links of brown sausage, clean knives and forks and spoons and linen, with onions, soup and egg pudding; to eat all I wanted, sleep as long as I pleased, see the pretty girls, and, who knew, maybe get home. Ah! it was too good to be true. And then come back with two or three hundred recruits, and fill up the old regiment, and get another bar.[20] Ah me! what visions and visions. I felt that swelling of the heart I ne'er shall feel again. I had never made application for leave of absence, and had expected none, so the pleasure was the greater, and the line gathered about me with many congratulations on my good luck. Each wanted so many men for his company; Wilcox wanted so many, and Braden, Stambaugh, Wallace, Crowell, Cummings;[21] every one of them must have so many, and would put up with no fewer. As we interpreted the order, I had nothing to do, and was armed with the power to do it. The boys expected me to go to the barracks at Columbus and order out the full complement of men asked for, and fifty or a hundred to make up for leakage, and return.

When Pappy Thomas said, "Go at once," it didn't mean to run around a dozen regiments and shake hands and say good-bye, and just have a little bit of a good time before starting; but it was right, face, march, and that's what we did. We left everything except our arms, my old sabre, the muskets, with blankets, haversacks and canteens. Those times, with orders and military transportation, we didn't wait for any particular trains. Pullmans, there were none; and but few old day coaches for passengers. Such roads as existed in the South were run entirely for the army, to feed and clothe it, transport all sorts of military supplies. Cannon, mules and horses, beef cattle and commissary supplies filled the bodies of all the cars, and soldiers rode on the tops. Armed guards patrolled all the roads south of Cincinnati and Louisville. Citizens of either North or South must give weighty reasons and pass severe official scrutiny to travel by any route; but a big fellow like your Uncle, armed with an order from Pap Thomas, was fit for anything, and could take passage on the first thing on wheels, which he did. The "Good-byes" were short, and the messages mostly related to eating and drinking. If my stomach had had the capacity of a freight car—which it hadn't—it wouldn't have held half the orders.

As the cars going North were, for the most part, empty, except sick and wounded soldiers going to hospitals in the rear, or furloughed men and officers going home, we soon found an empty box car, made our beds, secured our arms, and set in for a most luxurious time, with no drums and bugles to tell of fall in or reveille, taps or retreat. To just eat and sleep all we wanted was too good to talk about, so we set in to sleep, but would stick to our haversacks till we reached Cincinnati, and if, per adventure, there was enough there, would take a snack, just to take off the wire edge a little, and then go on to Columbus and have a dinner. We had a delightful trip, for there were thirty or forty officers, with their little guards, all on the same errand,—one from the 9th (Bob McCook's), one from the 35th (Brinton's), old regiments, both of our brigade and both with homes in Cincinnati, over the Rhine. First we stripped sufficient boarding off the cars for ventilation, then as we passed each landmark of our old trail each man had some interesting or funny incident to relate, which had occurred here or there, while a stray canteen in the party stimulated digestion and gave a lofty tone to the spirits of our party.

Guerrillas were continually tapping the lines, stealing information from the wires, and tearing up the tracks, capturing trains of supplies, and then retiring to their homes as loyal citizens. But I am of opinion that if any of those fellows had bothered our train they would have found themselves in the wrong pew, both men and officers being well armed, for on leaving we had resumed our guns, mostly colts and remingtons revolvers.[22] Anyway we were haunted by no fears and sped on our way rejoicing. We had heard of the draft riots at home,[23] and all looked forward to taking a hand in quelling them, in much the spirit of the school boy going to his first circus.

I should tell you that, from the beginning to the end, the army at the front was filled with news, rumors of victory, defeat, movements of the enemy, our own anticipated movements, etc., all clothed in mystery, but verified by some close friend of the General, or Governor, or President, or some truthful spy or Union man come to camp, or honest prisoner. All this kind of news, though much speculated on and discussed pro and con, was soon called "grape-vine telegraph," then simply "grape-vine."

When news came of the resistance to drafts, the Governors of the loyal States were to call a regiment or two of the old troops from the field to quell the riots, and each regiment was quite sure it was the fittest and favorite regiment of the State, or some of its officers were near or far-off relations of the Governor. Every Ohio regiment had it bad, and was to be on in a few days. The "grape-vine" fairly outdid itself, and that was a condition of things when we left. Yes, sir, we had lots of fun with the "grape-vine."

From Nashville to Louisville we had one, old day-coach, and, of course, this was too gorgeous to talk about, with cushioned seats and all. We went whirling back in twenty-four hours over a distance which had required nearly that many months to cover, with the army contesting almost every mile of it; but it was a jolly trip for us old web-feet, that being the classical name for the infantry in the western army, while in the eastern they were called doughboys.

On arriving at Cincinnati we marched to Glassner's Hall, "over the Rhine," where we unsaddled our appetites and turned them out to grass. During the night we got up a conspiracy. This was Wednesday night. All officers and men were to scoot for home, and report at Columbus on the Monday following; so I called my guard, opened the motion, and bound it with a solemn oath. It passed unanimously, and whoever failed to answer Monday morning was to be punished as a court-martial might direct. Well, so we all cut. My girl was at Ashland taking music lessons, and she had to be seen first.[24]

Between Calion[25] and Crestline my car jumped the track, a number of people were killed and injured; among the killed was a white-haired, old gentleman, a Mr. Dewitt of Cleveland. My shoulder was bruised so that I couldn't raise my left hand, had to carry it in a sling for a few days, but the right arm was in good order and served me faithfully. Here was a fine kettle of fish, though. I was way past my destination, absent without leave, a deserter,—fine way for a soldier to be killed or crippled. However there was a balm in Gilead, in Ashland, I mean, and I never did so much wish the war was over. Next day I cut for home, got to Beloit way after night, saw a light in Uncle Jake Sheets' window and rapped. The old fellow was alone, and asked me what I should like to eat. I told him "sauerkraut." He said that he wasn't feeling very well and I struck the thing he wanted, so we went down cellar, heaping full, put some lard or some sort of grease on it, gave it a good cooking, and the medicine seemed good for both of us. We slept together. He was a big, fat, old man, and carried the bed covers like the ridge pole of a tent so they didn't touch me, and I couldn't sleep in that kind of bed anyway, so crawled out on the floor and slept the sleep of the just.

The next morning I went home, and to try to tell you all would only reveal the poverty of words, so after the rough of our joy was scraped off a little I went all round the place, saw the sheep and cows, patted the horses, dogs and cats, looked down the cellar and well, drank the cream and left the milk, carried corn to the pigs, climbed on the straw stack and into the hay mow, pinched and tickled your Grandmother just to hear her laugh once more, and I never see your Granddad act so like a school boy. Rosy, Bob and Isa[27] were all there and looked so big. Your Uncle Jess[28] had gone the year before for a dashing cavalryman, and was somewhere in the South with General Burbridge. At family worship your Grandfather prayed the only right prayer I'd heard since I left home, and at last I realized I was in God's country. Hours never before galloped away at such a giddy pace. Your Grandfather and I went to Benton and raced around to shake hands and say "How do you do" and "Good-bye." Old Uncle John promised to take my little Dick Cobb if I could get him home. I took a hurried, joyful look at everything and everybody, came home, and next day, before starting, your Grandmother wanted to load me down with blanket and shoes and towels and taffy and salve and ointment and, in fact, everything her tender, mother love could think of; and I don't know what to do, but finally sat down and told her the story of how I had seen thousands of boys part sorrowfully, one by one, with just such things—albums, looking-glasses, shoe and clothes brushes, bibles and hymn books—anything and everything that added an extra ounce to his load. All that a right soldier cared about was his rough blanket, canteen and well-filled haversack. With these alone he was best off. She looked sorry and sad, and we said our good-byes. Then I was off for Canton, and of that visit you should remember something, for you brought me a pitcher of beer from Balzer's. You were quite a chunk of a boy and tagged at my heels all the time.

> NOTE: I do remember that visit. Uncle was very happy, and so were we all. I remember, among other things, while sitting with him and Father at Oberly's, Father said: "Well, Cal, when are you going to marry?" And he, gay deceiver, just from Ashland, replied, laughing: "When I can find a woman like Mary"; and I was old enough then to appreciate the compliment to my Mother. And I remember too that at that sitting Uncle Cal ate what seemed to me an enormous quantity of cheese and rye bread.

Well, we all got to Columbus in time, and I put in my order to Major John W. Skiles, an old, one-armed soldier of the 23rd Ohio, who commanded at Todd barracks, which was the draft rendezvous of the State. Here all returning, enlisted men came, whether from sick leave or furlough; it was a sort of mixed bureau of information. They had news of the whereabouts of all troops, what department each organization was in, gave transportation and safe conduct to all straggling, wayfaring, impecunious soldiers. There all drafted men, substitutes and recruits reported; and all soldiers, whether from east or west, coming or going, could find here what information they required, and be assisted to their commands. Todd barracks was the biggest, busiest, best-patronized hotel I ever saw, thousands upon thousands coming and going every day, and the new levies beginning to pour in from every direction, while the whole town was busy buying and selling substitutes. The draft was apportioned to the counties. Townships and wards failing to furnish their quotas pooled a purse, or bonded and raised the money, and sent a committee to Columbus, Cincinnati or Cleveland, which committee hunted up a trader and made a bargain for so many men at such a price.[29] The trader furnished the men and, when they were sworn in and mustered, got his money. Prices began low and ran from one to two, four, six, eight hundred, a thousand and two thousand dollars before the war closed.

CHAPTER FOURTEEN

꿍

End of the War

My dear Wilbur and
all you dear signers of my "Round Robin":—

A full year has passed away since my last attempt to please you, and
now I put my pen to paper with great diffidence, for I have read in clear,
bold type all that I have set down up to this date, and, for the most part,
my thoughts upon my part of the work are not flattering to myself, but I
am looking backward through the scenes of a busy life and the mists of
near two score years upon a time when duty called every man to defend
our country's flag, and the tragedies of a gigantic war for national existence
was the every-day theme upon every tongue.

> "Dunkel Wolken sehe Ich hengen
> Zwischen mir und seller zeit."[1]

The next morning after reporting at Todd barracks, Ohio's draft rendezvous (Todd barracks was near the Union Depot, and near or upon the
spot where the Columbus Buggy Works now stand), I, with a number of
officers on a like duty and from the same department, Army of the Cumberland, was handed an order from the Secretary of War[2] detaching us and
our guards and placing us on duty at the draft rendezvous of our State, and

I was ordered to report for duty immediately to Major John W. Skiles, Commandant of the barracks, with side arms and equipped as for field duty. I had taken the opportunity of the day before to uniform myself in the height of military fashion. Had you seen me then, with new hat, gold cord and tassels, new coat and trousers, with shoulder straps to match, new, shiny haversack, and all becorded and bestrapped in high art, you would at once disagree with the old pessimist who sang "The glories of this mortal state are shadows, not substantial things";[3] but for all that, the gloomy old fellow was right.

Well, I reported without the slightest idea of what my duty was to be. I found a line of recruits, drafted men and substitutes drawn up in the barrack yard in front of Major Skiles' office; and when I presented myself the Adjutant of the barracks handed me a set of rolls containing the names of the men, together with their accounts, and a special order directing me to take command of this detachment and proceed at once to the army of the Cumberland and deliver them to the different commands to which they were assigned.

These commands represented all arms of the service, as artillery, infantry, cavalry, engineers, etc., also different brigades and divisions, but all within the same army. I was called to a private office and given money in Five Hundred Dollar packages, and the amount was so great that I was quite dumbfounded, as previous to this I had never had in my possession or entrusted to my care more than a few hundred dollars at any one time. The money of the substitutes had been taken from them as they arrived at the barracks. They were taken to a private room and thoroughly searched by an old cavalry Sergeant, whose duty it was and who held that post until the war ended. The amount so taken was placed opposite the name of the substitute on the roll, and was to be paid him on his arrival at the command to which he was assigned, otherwise the officer in charge was to return it to the commanding officer at the draft rendezvous, though of all this money matter our written orders said not a word. Of course this was a scheme of the officers to secure the sure delivery of the substitute and to prevent bounty jumping, though I never knew that this scheme of our Major had any backing in civil or military law, and to the best of my knowledge it was not practiced in any other part of the country.[4]

To tell you how pleased I was to see this line of fresh men, which I supposed was for my own regiment, how the sight of it and the thoughts of the pleasure it would give to my companions in the line, as well as the old boys who lugged the forty rounds, and my disappointment when I found my mistake and received my orders and private instructions, would be of no use, and anyway a soldier's only duty is to obey orders. My orders read that I was to take the most direct route, and, when the duty was accomplished, return to these headquarters and make full report of the trip, as per Article so and so, Revised Army Regulations. These reports were to include everything of interest by the way, stops, starts, mishaps, sickness, desertions, and anything and everything in the heavens above and the earth beneath, and just here, my dear kinfolk they put your Uncle in a hole, for I never could bring myself to the level of trifling detail, and, although my old copy book often told me that the pen was mightier than the sword, I didn't enlist to handle the mightier weapon, and was more familiar with the rusty old blade, and with it made enough blunders. I tried to make a few reports, but Lieutenant Frame, Post-Adjutant, declared he couldn't make out whether it was an essay on agriculture or a sermon, and, as he was a good fellow and shed ink gracefully, I made my reports to him verbally. I had a guard of eight or ten men given me for this service. Being assured that I must return and remain in this service until relieved by competent authority, I resumed my old fatigue dress, except my fine hat, and would have been the hat better off had I left it also, but I was set on making some show and stuck to it.

I took passage on the first train going South, and with my command filled two coaches. At each car door I had a man with a musket and fixed bayonet, and none were allowed to leave the car without a pass from me, and when I tell you that at every station men and women were passing up bad whiskey and strong waters of all sorts through the windows, and at all the stops and changes of cars or boats a mob of human-carrion crows[5] followed my little command and kept up their annoying traffic, and hustled the column at every opportunity as it passed to give the bounty jumpers the opportunity they sought, you will see there was need of vigilance and that my lines had not fallen in pleasant places. I made my way through Cincinnati and Louisville without loss, and when I had my command aboard the train for Nashville I felt much relieved, for I was now in territory where all legal and most other matters were argued over the point of the bayonet.

We were on a heavy train. The first two cars were box freight, the next two were filled with my command, and several others in the rear were filled with men and officers returning to their commands from sick leave, furloughs, etc. There were also sutlers, citizens, men, women and children returning to their homes now uncovered by our advancing armies. We sped off South without incident. Towards evening two of my men jumped through the car windows while the train was running at fair speed; the place was open timber and descending ground; I saw them go, and my guards fired at them; I grabbed the bell rope, and the train came to a stand-still; and then came the military conductor, who was a very great man, much greater than your Uncle, and, when he found out from me what the trouble was, in vehement language he flung out a few scraps of informa-tion as to his place and my place, his duty and my duty, and much other information for my future guidance.

You will find among the first articles of war in the old blue book of that day that upon the luxury of profane words there was laid a pretty heavy tax, each swear graded according to rank, something like this, one cuss for a private Twenty or Thirty Cents, the same indulgence by an officer One Dollar; and I have often thought that had this article been enforced with strictness the war might have paid its running expenses and left a surplus for pensions.

Oh! the military conductor, a mighty man was he. The signal was given to go on, and our confab came to end. I lost two men, but that was noth-ing. Up to this time, soldiers were cheap and could be had for the asking, but mules cost the Government One Hundred Dollars or more, so in camp and on the march you would often hear this puzzling question: "What is the difference between a government mule and a government soldier?"— and many voices shouted many answers, but all gave the government mule first place. But now had come a time when the tables were turned, and, though we always heard the mule when he lifted up his voice in song, with gratitude and delight, as he toiled into camp with his great loads of sup-plies, the mule had now come to occupy second place, and the govern-ment soldier was coming to be much more valuable.

Just between the gloaming and the night we drew up in front of a little way station named Cave City, some few miles from Mammoth Cave. Here all who could leave the cars pressed into shanties where meals were to be had. I secured some hot biscuits and a cigar, and went back to the car and threw two seats apart, so that four of us, with the addition of our haver-sacks, made a good supper, and I lit my cigar. Night had fallen, no lights of any kind were allowed on the train, and we were rushing forward through the dark. I had fixed myself for a comfortable night's sleep, and maybe an inch or more of my cigar had burned away when, as I was hold-ing the glowing end against the window, we heard a great racket ahead, and in half a second our car was bumping along the ties. It left the track, swayed, and then fell on its side down an embankment. Unpleasant to be cheated out of a good smoke and the stub of a ten cent cigar.

I found myself on the undermost side of the car, and quite the undermost fellow. The first thing I remember was that I was hard pressed, or pressed hard, by a noisy, wiggling, groaning, unclassified mixture of our national defenders. There was considerable shouting and spattering of musketry of an inoffensive sort outside. I felt something sort of soft and warm on my face and forehead; my arms were useless by reason of the weight above, and I reasoned at first that I was entirely killed by the top of my head being busted and my brains working down over my face. As the weight grew less I got one arm loose, and with that hand made a careful exploration of my garret and dormer windows, which proved the upper story to be without serious damage, and when at last the pressure was further relieved I found it wasn't me at all but the fellow next above, who laid partly on me, and the damage of him leaked and overran its boundaries and strolled over my upper story at will; but I never held any ill will against him on that account, he couldn't help it, neither could I.

The men were escaping through the upper broken windows, and I made my way after them without delay. The car was well-nigh empty when I made my escape from it, and when I stood upon the top of it this is what I saw by the light of some torches in the hands of men in gray. Our locomotive, two box cars and my two soldier cars lay upon the side of an embankment. The locomotive was roaring, groaning, and sobbing in a fearful way with the escaping steam. It would soon die or explode. The place seemed to be a cup or dip, but it proved to be the head of a gorge, cut across and hemmed in by the railroad embankment, surrounded by trees coming to the verge of the depression. The cup itself was nearly bare of trees and contained maybe two acres; the embankment was ten or twelve feet high. The boys in gray thought to try a little game of pleasantry on the boys in blue, and they did it in fine style by removing a rail from the track with such complete skill as to spill us into this cup. Good enough for them, but not so charming for us. The cup was the shape of a horseshoe with the heel towards the track, and the show occurred about midway between the heel calks, the whole train being enclosed. The cars in rear of my soldier cars remained on the track. Right opposite me, and where the toe of the shoe came, stood a line of gray soldiers, say from twenty-five to fifty, fully armed, just in the edge of the timber. Others were running around the rim of the cup shouting "Surrender, surrender," and calling naughty names. Others were running around the cars which remained on the track, shouting and piloting the passengers and massing them on the edge of the timber. The night was dark, but the few torches made the plan of it plain. What firing had been done was only to add to the confusion. I suspect my boys who had gotten out were in the shelter of my two derailed cars. That is the way it looked to me and just as I remember it, though, of course, I had no shorthand reporter to take it down.

Well, when I had assembled two or three of my scattered wits, I jumped down from my perch, run along the two cars, shouting to my boys to cross the track and get behind the embankment, and in a minute we were all there who could get there. We had, I should say, about eight muskets and a few heavy pistols. Telling the unarmed men to lie close to the embankment we, who had arms, lay down and commenced firing over the rails, and we pegged away, with the effect that the line in our front took to the trees, while a man or two, whom I took to be officers, came down through the timber shouting "Surrender." We shouted back in a fragmentary way our views on the matter, and they disappeared. The cars now began to burn, shedding a bright light upon the whole scene. Soon came the military conductor down the center of the track, followed by a man in gray, of loud voice and much authority, who shouted to cease firing as we were shooting our own people—which I hold was a black lie—and that he (the military conductor) had surrendered the whole train. I dropped back in a little shelter of the bushes, unstrapped my sabre belt and pulled off my haversack, and made such quick concealment as I could.[6] I took off my watch and flung it as far as possible, rolled down my sock and thrust under the foot a wad of bills—I had drawn a month's pay in Louisville—reached with my right hand my left shoulder strap and with my left hand my right strap, tore them off, and fell into line with the men, ready for the next move. We were marched up near to the other prisoners, and all under guard were lined up, and the front rank ordered three or four paces to the front, which movement was attended by much wicked talk, as my poor fellows had no military training whatever, and where one went all went, like a flock of sheep. Finally our entertainers made the proper separation, and the front rank was about faced, so we stood facing inward, and, together with the soldiers who had been in the rear cars, we made a good haul for the Johnnies, and now with a strong guard all round us they put a half dozen or more men between the lines to prove us, as they said, and, beginning in regular order, they proceeded to relieve each man of such valuables as they could find. The man who prowled me found nothing, cast covetous eyes on my new hat, forgot the decalogue[7] and said: "Yank, that there hat of yores is shorely fine." I agreed with him and said it was all the hat I had. His reply was: "Oh! you shan't go bar'headed, you shall have a hat." Reaching for my hat with one hand and for his own with the other, with scant courtesy and less cleverness, he slapped a limp, white wool hat on my head and pulled it well down over my eyes, but through it all I felt comforted, for I knew that which he didn't know. While waiting in line I had time to think a little, and you who are sitting in the seats of the scornful remember that these things were happening in much less time than it takes me to set them down on paper.

The fire of the train, now grown to be a real pyrotechnic display, cast a great light over the whole scene. Right in my rear was a thick clump of blackberry bushes. The guards, I noticed, as they paced their beats only came to the edge of it and faced outward, back to back, and they were impatient, offering remarks and suggestions to those who were prowling us. My mind was soon made up, and I took the first opportunity to leap backward into the bushes, falling down, and I didn't wait to get up, but turned and ran off on my hands and knees until I came to a friendly tree, where I halted to catch fresh wind and search around for some ideas and collect a thought or two.

The light was grand, the fire was fast creeping up to the box cars, and the Johnnies were active. A great show, and not to be forgotten. All at once from the deep woods away in the rear came a thundering volley of musketry, and following in a moment came an awful explosion that shook the earth and scattered dirt and debris all about from the box cars, which had ammunition for their lading, and from a perfect glare of light we were in total darkness. The frantic shouts of our misguided brethren, as they commanded this or that to be done, and especially "fall in" and their buglers "boots and saddles,"[8] told that they were scampering for dear life; and as the fire soon began to blaze up in a feeble way I saw no more of the Johnnies. The clouds were gone, and the twinkling stars looked down on the wreckage. "A child might understand the De'il had business on his hand."[9]

It was only one of the little jokes of war, and something similar was happening every day of every year, but they counted for next to nothing in the great result, except to the victims. Well, I went to the crowd and found a lot of my old friends. Among them was Lieutenant-Colonel Jim Nash of the 19th O. V. I. He had been wounded, in fact, shot pretty full of holes, and was returning to his regiment with a stray finger of two on either hand and a limp in one leg offset by a hitch in the other, but he held he was a lucky fellow again, though he lost everything—overcoat, money and watch—but he was both saucy and jolly and immediately gave me several, left-handed compliments on my hat and unlaundried face, though with infinite pains I had swiped it off with handfuls of dried leaves and grass.

I shouted for my Sergeant, and we gathered up the command as best we could, marched them down the track to where it entered a cut, and then to the rising ground on one side, and made a little defense of logs and stumps and stones; called the roll, found twelve or fifteen men short, posted guards, and, with my Sergeant and ten or twelve men, I started to look for my plunder. The woods were dry and the fire from the train had caught in the leaves and trash on either side of the track. I soon found my haversack and sabre, but in the direction I had tossed my watch the ground had been completely burned over. We went back to camp. It was a bitter night for us all, but especially for me. I had briars in my hands, in my face, and in my heart. My men were gone, but a few men more or less didn't count, that was a matter for gossip at the front.

Quantrell, Champ Ferguson, and many other guerrilla chiefs,[10] with strong hands of daring, desperate, hardy, rough riders, were operating on all our long lines of communication, burning bridges, tearing up railroad track, gathering up and conscripting every man and boy who could bear arms for the Confederates, killing and driving out the Union people and destroying their property. The records of those dark deeds have never been published, and never will be. The most skillful and able Generals on our side had failed to capture the guerrillas, and they were the terror of the whole country. Along the entire line from Louisville to Chattanooga every bridge was covered by a fort and artillery, and stockades filled with soldiers were almost as common as mile-posts, and soldiers patrolled the whole line, at frequent intervals, night and day. The old fighters at the front made light of all this and said the boys who did the guarding at the rear had a soft snap, and called them feather-bed soldiers.

The telegraph would carry the news of our mishap to the "Courier Journal" at Louisville, almost our only newspaper in the army, and in an inch or two would all our misfortune be laid bare long before we could reach the front. This "Courier Journal" was much relied on in our army, as it told us where we were and who had been whipped in all our battles, what we were doing and what we were going to do, and what the enemy were doing and going to do, our Generals and all their plans. It was a great war newspaper and must have brought many sheckles to its owners.

Many, unhappy thoughts passed through my mind that night and kept me alert. I talked with my Sergeant, and we both agreed that to be killed in some notable battle, of which history should make some record, would be all right, but to be snuffed out in some such, trifling byplay would be humiliating and scandalous, and yet I had gotten off fairly well, and the loss was of small moment. Daylight came, and I determined to have a try for my watch, so I set off again with my Sergeant and a small squad and soon arrived at the place, deployed the squad, and I stood in front while upon hands and knees they searched and soon found the watch. Though it was glazed and black as tar, which I could not rub off, it was still ticking away, and the silk neck ribbon was burned, but a gold slide upon it, let-tered with the initials of the girl I left behind me, was found, and that, to-gether with my old sabre, is all I have left of the souvenirs of war.

As soon as possible I started my little detachment on the march South, following the railroad track. No trains were running, and we hoped to reach Bowling Green. We were completely stripped of supplies, as most of the troops had left everything in the cars, but the old guard brought out their guns and left them on the embankment when we surrendered, and so had them now. I halted, sat down on a tie pile, got out my little wad of money from its snug hiding place and divided it out among the men so as to buy supplies by the way. As I handed each man a bill he took my name with army and home address, and all seemed full of gratitude and would certainly pay me back the first pay day. I kept no record of their names and never heard of one of them again, so I think they all must be dead. I gave out a hundred and fifty dollars and reserved ten dollars for myself. We pushed on, a bedraggled, forlorn, straggling, little column, and arrived at Bowling Green without further accident, and there drew rations.

I was completely frazzled out, and I talked with the agent and operator. He said there would be no train along for some hours, and that I should go to his home and rest and be refreshed, to which I agreed. There I did wrong. His home was a typical, old southern home and quite a distance from the station, in an open wood, with an avenue to the road.

When we went in I came face to face with a Confederate soldier in uni-form, and was introduced to him by his brother, the agent. Just then I would have given all I ever dreamed of to be back with my little com-mand. This was no place to lose one's grip and show fear, but the agent soon put me on better footing by explaining that he was a "blue uniform man," while his brother was a Confederate, and had been for a long time sick, and had finally reached home to die or get well as the case might be.

The agent promised me that upon the first news of a train he would come or send a messenger in time, and left. I felt as though I was out of one trap and into another. I carefully unbuttoned the flap of my pistol holster while my rebel host was in the kitchen. One colored servant and the Johnny Reb was all in the household. They gave me a good meal, and we had some pleasant talk, avoiding irritating matters, and to my great joy a messenger came. My host brought me a pint bottle of medicine for my cough, first taking a dose himself. I offered him a dollar, which he refused, so I laid it on the table and bid him good-bye with a light heart. These two men were what the agent brother told me; they honestly held opposite views, one a reb and t'other a yank. The case could be duplicated all through the border States many times, but all the same I was glad to get out so luckily. Many a poor lad in blue got into the wrong pew in some such way, and never reported to his command again.

A freight train soon came thundering down from the North, and we piled on willy-nilly and arrived in Nashville without further incident. At Nashville had a wait and quartered my command in Zollikoffer barracks. Most soldiers of our department knew Zollikoffer barracks. They had an unsavory reputation. Zollikoffer was a man of wealth who had taken the wrong side of the question, and was killed at Mill Spring, Kentucky, in the early days of 1862 (the 2nd Minnesota and the 9th O. V. I. of our old brigade were in the engagement). Any way he left a large, unfinished business block on a main street of Nashville, which just served the rebels as barracks and prison, and then served the yanks as a sort of transfer barracks or human clearing-house for disorganized troops passing either way, and was very commodious, very dirty and occupied by swarms of the little tormentors which go to make a soldier's life miserable. The rascals hung in festoons from the seams of the naked floors above, and the soldiers held lighted candles along the populous cracks to give them a foretaste of what is in reserve for the wicked, traced their initials in black candle smoke, and cut and carved inspiring verse and prose all over the walls. Union men had been shot to death for standing in front of the windows while imprisoned therein, and just the history of that old barracks, with all the tales and legends connected with it, would satisfy you all with soldier yarns as long as you live. The men slept on the floor in their blankets, did their own cooking and other work. It was three or four stories high, and, as I recollect it, quite the most unhappy place inside the Union lines.

In due time we got off, and from here our ride was altogether on the tops of freight cars. The trains were heavily loaded with military supplies, ordinance, commissary and quartermaster stores, etc. When the engines ran out of fuel we took to the woods with axes and pickets out in every direction; but I can't dwell; we hastened on South slowly; and when we had a good stretch of clear track ahead the engineman shook us up good. The soldiers sat with feet dangling down the sides of the cars, and many of them, all tired out, would crawl up near the center and fall asleep, and, with the lurching, gradually slide down towards the falling-off place, so we had to keep pulling them up towards the center again. I roped myself fast to the running board with a piece of bell cord under my sabre belt, and so slept secure from all ills. The end of all journeys comes at last, and so did this. The camps about Ringgold, Georgia, finally came in sight, and we were all glad.

I distributed my detachment as per orders, paid off all those who answered to their names, took receipts for them, and struck for my old brigade, which I found nearly where I left it, and it seemed like getting home again. Of course they had all the news, and, for all the good-natured jokes and jibes I received, I felt glad to be back. There is something mighty hearty about soldiering which can't be put on paper.

Wit and wisdom were a fine blend with us that night. My little Dick was there too. I had just passed through a short term of normal school, and I wanted nothing better than to stay with my own company and regiment. Other easier places there were in plenty, but I was satisfied, and my late experience led me to think that the duty to which I had been assigned was fraught with the greatest danger, hardship and responsibility, without adequate return in honor, promotion, or profit of any kind, and I hoped now that I was back with my regiment there could be a way found by which I could be returned to my old duties, but in this I was soon undeceived. When Secretary Stanton laid his finger on either private or Major-General, the man was fast sure enough; and I, being without influence, had to make the best of it, so I assembled my guard and, with little Dick Cobb, made ready to start on my return trip, resolved to keep trying.

I noticed that our army was brightening up, and that the brigade and divisions were forming now camps out to the front, always inclining farther to the South. This was about the first of March, 1864. In reporting some men to a battery far to the front I found the guns deployed near to the picket lines, though housed under heavy canvas, were ready for action at any moment, and the old, familiar thunder was heard at intervals, echoing back and forth, telling that our Uncly Billy and Pappy Thomas and Howard, with Logan and McPherson, would soon be putting in the sickle to reap the harvest of war.[11]

I made my way back to Columbus without any unusual incident, but in a far different frame of mind than on my former trip north, and on my arrival at Columbus made report and turned in what money I had left. I think on this trip I had Eight or Ten Thousand Dollars, and brought back Two or Three Thousand. My receipts were all right, and I was ordered to report next morning. The account of my little mishap had been received and much elaborated and ornamented by my brother officers, and the things that they did, and the things they said for my especial benefit, entertainment and diversion, would be unwise to record in these days.

From this on until the close of the war recruits, substitutes and drafted men from all parts came pouring into rendezvous in an ever increasing stream, and the duty of forwarding them to the front was arduous and unceasing, with ever increasing responsibility. Each officer, on leaving his command at the front, was accompanied by a Sergeant and four good men, and these, of course, were a part of our permanent party,—in all some forty officers and one hundred and sixty good, reliable men.

There was a regiment, the 88th O. V. I., enlisted for guard duty in the State, and they did all the guard duty at the rendezvous, Johnson's Island[12] and other points, with the help of the invalid corps men, leaving us the duty of conducting all detachments to the front, and giving the men freedom to rest undisturbed who were returning from their duties at the front. The guard had a room of their own at the barracks. When the duty grew too heavy, old soldiers home on furlough were picked up as they were returning and added to our permanent party.

For one reason or another the number of officers grew less and less as time went by, and the front was continually moving farther and farther South, and frightful gaps daily occurring in the fighting line. Sherman and Grant were calling for men. Father Abraham called for volunteers, and the calls were responded to by the states. When the appeals failed, then draft followed draft. There was no rest for the soles of my feet. I would no sooner return from Atlanta or New Orleans than I would be ordered to Newburn, Hilton Head, Blair's Landing or Savannah,—any place and every place where armies were,—and this would often be the way of it. I would be ordered, say, to Cairo, Memphis or camp of distribution at Alexandria, Virginia, there to turn over my command to some officer. Arriving would find camp filled to overflowing, and maybe no one to receive my command. Then some officer in command at the post would tack on more—all the men I could handle—and give me further orders, so that when I left Columbus I had no time set for return, and no light was kept in the window for me.

On all these trips I carried enough money in my haversack to buy a steamboat or a small railroad, and frequently when I was ordered past my original destination, I was given more money as well as men, and with my sack already full, to make more room, I would take it by the lugs, like pulling on a boot, and set my foot on the stuff and crowd it down to make room. Of the large amounts of money I handled I never lost a dollar, though on every trip I lost men, and I got full receipts for all, and had a big surplus of money to knock down if I chose.

My duties carried me to armies engaged in action, and I often found the regiment I sought marching, sometimes in battle line and at others in active engagement; and as I approached a moving column, and came up with the regiment I wanted, I halloed to the commanding officer and said: "I have so many recruits for you." He, or some other officer designated by him, reined out of column, threw his leg over his pommel,—I handed up the roll containing the names,—and he, without verification, receipted the whole roll. I would sit down on a log or rock, call the names, and as each stepped up I gave him the amount due him; and, so, many times I have wandered through the great army of Grant, from regiment to battery, all day long, streams of bayonets flowing in one general direction, like the steady flow of a mighty river, to the rhythmical tap of the drum. Aye, boys, it was mighty. I was a young fellow then, but the recollection of it kind of stiffens my gray hair and makes me hanker to see the like once more. You see there is a lot of bull dog in most fellows when the moon is in the right sign. This little jingle explains it.

> "If the country gits ter fightin',
> Says the feller on my knee,
> Would you go to be a sojer
> Like they say yer used ter be?
> (I was all erlong with Jackson,
> And I faced the fight with Lee)
> I think I would, I answers
> Ter the feller on my knee.
> Then my mind went back a minute
> To the days o' sixty-three,
> And I saw the bayonets bristle,
> Heard the thunder of the guns,
> I was mixed up in the fightin'
> 'Fore Sherman struck the sea.

I think I'd go, I answers
Ter the feller on my knee.
Would you go and leave my mama,
Would you kiss goodbye ter me,
An' go marchin' with the sojers?
Says the feller on my knee.
(An' I feel a tear drop trickle,
I'm as techy as can be)
I think I would, I answers
Ter the feller on my knee.
But I hope the war air over,
That we'll dwell upon the sod
Forever and forever
In the loving peace of God
But spose they went to fightin',
Would you go an' help 'em out? says he.
I'm shore I would, I answers
To the feller on my knee."

(Frank Stanton)[13]

The officers with whom I came in contact at the front, in either army, were uniformly obliging and hospitable, but this was not always the case with those stationed in the rear. They usually wanted to show much authority, and made, or tried to make, much vexatious delay with their red tape, but I soon fooled these punctilious gents, and was armed with papers, not to be disregarded, which read: "Guards and pickets pass the bearer, Lieutenant J. C. Hartzell, any place in my department." By practice I learned how to hustle my way through and get pretty much what I wanted.

I remember one day, having finished up, I was making my way towards some landing to get transportation from Grant's army to Washington. In the gloaming I lost my way, which was no hard thing to do, and, before I knew where I was, marched up to our front line of works before Petersburg. It was night, and we were worn out. The mortars from both sides were giving a benefit, a fine pyrotechnic display, and, as the opportunity might not come again soon, we thought we would stay and enjoy it, for it was an improving sight. So we spread our blankets down on the white sand and lay flat on our backs, about twenty of us. The trajectory of the shells was high above us, and the radius of the same from the rebel side was quite beyond where we lay, although often, when one burst right over us, we could hear the pieces flung whizzing away or go whining through the darkness, and occasionally a piece would plunk down in the sand near us. By the light of the burning fuses we could see that the outward and upward trajectory of the shells was much longer than the downward—so—

So with bellowing of the big-throated mortars and the occasional click of the trigger of a musket in the hands of an alert picket, the night passed off grand.

You never stood in line of battle and heard the quick command, "Commence firing"; and you never heard the snappy crackle of a thousand triggers, as, with thumb on hammer, the men flung the butts of their muskets to shoulder—ominous music. Well, you can't understand what I'm trying to tell you very well. It's only the fellow who has heard that crackle as it ran through the living line, and has staid until the curtain fell, who can understand it. Once heard, it is not easy to forget, but I don't recommend the music.

As we lay there in the sand we were in close vicinity to an old field battery, one that had been in action the day before, or at least a short time previous. The men were working with one of the guns. Soon some visiting boys came from another battery, and there was much talk. After awhile I turned on my side, dug my elbows in the sand, rested my head on my hand, and listened. The night section was the one under discussion, and they were telling of their mishaps in the late action. Old "Mary" had kicked out of her breeching beause they had fed her some double case, and the old man would have her head too low—out of her trunnions—and old "Betsy" had her cascabel knob knocked off, and now they were going to call her "Bob-tailed Betsy."[14] But sleep! blessing on the man who invented sleep.

In the morning we toasted our bacon and made our coffee with the battery boys, and were off. Some of those old, regular batteries had interesting histories which dated back to the Revolution. We finally found the landing and had to wait for a boat. During the night a cavalry command had come in, which had been sent south of Richmond to cut railroads. There had followed the command into camp a great body of slaves—men, women, children—carrying all their earthly possessions tied up in old bedding with ropes, straps and pieces or strips of bark. Poor, very poor and ragged all of them, but happy in their squalor, for now they were sure the day of jubilee had come, and so they organized a praise meeting in which the had Massa Linkum, God, and Gineral Grant badly mixed.

I went many trips down the coast and met with many adventures, always going by way of New York. Once in marching up Broadway at the head of column a man skipped as we were crossing Courtland Street; and, with a throng of people on the street, a big guard at my side faced about and brought his musket to his shoulder, but in the nick of time I struck it up with my old sabre, and the ball did no harm. I corralled my command on a grass plot at the battery and threw my guard around them, but the line was too thin. A great mob of the toughest of the tough was trying to break through, and had my guard been green soldiers my men would have been scattered like a covey of quail. I had sent a messenger to Bedloe's Island, where the troops were to be quartered, and I was never happier than when he returned with his boat and I had my men secure.

Colonel Merchant, a kindly old officer, eighty-three years old, commanded the post. We had to wait several days for a transport, and he gave us the use of a small tug or dispatch boat to use as we chose. Bob Heller[15] was doing his tricks, and Artemus Ward[16] was lecturing, and after one of the lectures we had an Ohio supper with him. Finally a big transport, the Arago (Captain Gadsden) drew up. Colonel Merchant added a lot of other troops to my command, and we were off for the South. We chased a schooner running the blockade with cotton; smallpox broke out, and rough weather set in, and a lot of things happened; but all things have an end; so did this trip.

Another time I went down, only we were on the Illinois, an old roller.[17] In the hold were a lot of pails like wooden sugar buckets. The men, a lot of western troops, made sport of them, and many queries and much smart talk passed. Old Wisconsin, Michigan, Iowa, Ohio and Missouri soldiers had been left here and there, and were going to join Sherman at Savannah. They all knew a big lot of things about soldiering, but had never made the acquaintance of the ocean or the tantrums of it; so the poor fellows had experiences they will never forget, for the sea, the sea, the beautiful sea, can cut up a lot of didoes,[18] when the sign is right, and turn a fellow inside out with neatness and dispatch. There were also a lot of officers on board, returning to their commands. Among them was Father Brailey, Chaplain of the 90th Illinois, a jolly Irishman and fine companion.

We bowled along in fine style, though the water was pretty lumpy, until we got to Hatteras. There, while we were sitting at table, things took on a new aspect. Finally the old boat turned tail to the storm, lying down first on one side, then turning over and lying down on the other, as she went squealing and hissing through the water, sometimes on her nose with her tail in the air and the flukes of her propeller saying "r r r r r u u t t" until she settled her hind end down and her flukes caught the water. Her entrails were shaken loose, and we all piled into our bunks. Father Brailey took the upper and I the lower berth. They were crossways of the boat, and, as the old boat heaved and groaned and rolled from side to side in her distress, we were half the time on our heads and the other half on our feet. The inwards of the ship, made up of tables, chairs, dishes, bottles, cutlery, and such like, rattled and banged back and forth, piling themselves against the state-room doors first on one side then on the other with equal favor and alacrity. At every roll Father Brailey roared, "Oh Lord, my God!" repeating the same with more vigor and voice as we proceeded, when it came into my head to say: "Father Brailey, would it not be better to go to the bottom at once and bring this matter to an end?" Then came at once: "Ah, no, my young friend, it is far more glorious to die upon the field where you body may be found." This winning answer rather tickled my unhappy vitals, and the tang of the sly cunning of it remains.

On this rough voyage we passed a small steamer towing a schooner loaded with cattle. As we drew ahead, first the steamer would be out of sight and then the schooner. We also passed the monitor "Monadnock,"[19] puffing and wallowing and battling her toilsome way through the rough seas. The poor fellows in our steerage were in a sad plight; few attempted to put the sap pails to their proper use, and most of the pails remained in their original packages.

We ran into Pocotaligo Bay on a lighter[20] laden with military supplies for Sherman's army. Sherman was on the lighter, and as we ran inland with the tide the heavy laden boat kept poking her nose into the mud and backing and going ahead in a sort of vague, aimless way. Uncle Billy grew impatient and paced the deck in a quick, impatient manner and demanded more steam. I had seen him before in action, when he had his quarters under an oak tee; and as one courier or staff officer after another came dashing up to him as he was pacing a beat with quick, nervous stride, he would bring his arm around with a swing and order: "Send in another charge, send in another charge"—all this near Sherman Heights, Tennessee, about the 25th of November, 1863. I have told this to various ones of my comrades, and they uniformly agree that I was lying. My dear, old comrade, Captain Dan Stambaugh of Company "A," accuses me of lying also in my story of Mission Ridge.[21] He says the regiment split, and his end, the three right companies, charged up with the other troops and captured sixteen or eighteen guns. This seems lavish in one who is so economical of words; and if I share the fate of those who trifle with the truth, he will have to take a full field battery off that statement, or I'm sure of a quiet, good fellow for company hereafter.

When we left the boat I marched for the moving army. I made many such trips to this department; sometimes we had guides and sometimes none; start right away from the coast, through the old plantation fields and thick woods, bivouac anyplace where night overtook us,—in old cotton fields which were thrown out of use perhaps a hundred years ago and had grown up with heavy pine timber, the furrows still plain to be seen, or sometimes in old family cemeteries, left to neglect, in the midst of the forests. We passed many families, old husband and wife with daughters and small children and trusty old colored servants. They were often in what had once been fine family carriages. The ladies were often almost helpless—from training—but refined in style and manner and dressed in rich clothing. The old servants were uniformly kind and polite to their former owners, and there seemed a close bond of sympathy and good feeling between what had been master and slave. The people were refugees and were fleeing their homes till the storm should pass. We were in South Carolina, and the smoke of burning plantation homes attested that the wrath of outraged loyalty had fallen on this hot-bed of treason. All these scenes were common and pitiful, but these people were foremost in leading the great Rebellion. Even their poets sang treason. I give you a specimen taken from the Charleston Mercury in 1861.

"Call on thy children of the hill,
　Wake swamp and river, coast and rill
　Rouse all thy strength and all thy skill,
　　　Carolina.

Cite wealth and science, trade and art,
　Touch with thy fire the cautious mart,
　And pour thee through the people's heart,
　　　Carolina.

'Till e'en the coward shall spurn his fears,
　And all thy fields and fens and meres[22]
　Shall bristle like thy palm with spears,
　　　Carolina.

Girt with such wiles to do and dare,
Armed in right and mailed prayer,[23]
Thou shalt not bow thee to despair,
    Carolina.

Fling down thy gauntlet to the Huns,[24]
And roar thy challenge from thy guns,
And leave the future to thy sons,
    Carolina."

                    (Henry Timrod)[25]

This seems pretty good stuff, and it was hot, but the likes of it kindled the flame that burned them to ashes. When Uncle Billy came up through their fields and fens and meres they surely wished they had not flung down their gauntlets, or else wished there weren't so many Huns.

One day we were marching through the timber and came to a place where black men were sawing up the body of a fine pine tree in lengths for shakes, and as they were cut off they were ended up, and the clean, white ends of the blocks looked inviting for seats, and as we were all tired I ordered a halt and sat down on a block, and I was the only one who took advantage of these prepared seats, the rest all lying around on the pine needles and sand. After a short rest and command to "Fall in," your Uncle tried to rise. An uncontrollable grin spread over the faces of the whole detachment, followed by roars of laughter. I seemed bound to that block by most intimate and powerful relations, the problem was whether to carry the block along with me or leave my trousers on the block. The situation was difficult, delicate, and perplexing, as well as a bit mortifying. The boys really did not want to be rude or disrespectful, and would try to re-strain themselves, only to break out in fresh and more uproarious volleys, and as laughing is contagious, and it is better to laugh than mourn, I made the best of it, and with ready help and some expert manipulation my re-lations with the pine block were at last severed, and I stood up a free man, though on a conspicuous part of my anatomy was an ineffaceable brand, fragrant of tar, turpentine and rosin, and, in truth, of the whole pine forest.

We made our way to the column. My men were mostly for the 32nd O. V. I. I turned them over and went directly to General Blair's headquarters,[26] where I was most hospitably cared for, and, at parting, was given an ambulance and driver for the return trip to the coast.

A number of times I was down the Mississippi, twice to New Orleans and several times to Natchez, Vicksburg, Cairo and Memphis. A thing which much facilitated my duties was the corps badge. My orders usually directed me to a certain department, army and corps. The divisions were first, red; second, white; third; blue. My corps badge (14th) was an acorn, so when I came to the blue acorn my old regiment wasn't far away. If my detach-ment was assigned to the first division, the red badge told me without fail. Many of the regiments had adopted names, like "Buck tails," "Roosters," "Tigers," and the like.

Cousin Jim,[27] of the 7th O. V. I., came to Columbus with three other, enlisted men and an officer, on the same errand as my own, and likewise permanently detached, and I always tried to have him with me. His regi-ment at Antietam, under General Tyler,[28] did some meritorious thing, and the General called them his roosters. In the army of the Potomac they served under Slocum.[29] With their corps badge they always wore a rooster cut from any bit of cloth and sewed to the blouse. Jim was with me on one trip to New Orleans, and besides our men we had a heavy load of army supplies. Guerrillas on the shore pestered us a good bit, so on either side of the boat a high barricade of bales of hay protected the men, and the pilot house was shingled with a heavy plating of boiler iron, and as they rarely flung anything heavier than an ounce of lead we were quite secure, though at times the boat would stop and we had to scramble up the bank and drive them off.

We stopped at Memphis and left a detachment at Fort Pickering. While on the march through the streets a long, red-haired courier, with dispatch and yellow envelope in belt, dashed by. It was Seth,[30] as typical a rough rider as you would wish to see, long sabre whanging his horse's ribs at every jump, pistol in belt, red curly hair tossing up and down, and legs like the arms of an octopus swinging easily. We recognized each other in passing, and he was soon back with his empty envelope, and dismounted and guided us to the fort. He belonged to the 2nd Iowa, and the regiment was there for a fresh mount. He was the same old boy, only better filled. His legs showed the same reluctance about going forward promptly, and the gaps in the seat of his reinforced trousers told of long hours of diligent sitting in the saddle, and for rough, sure work he looked ideal.

The boat whistle sounded the recall, and the straining hawser groaned and slipped on the snubbing post, and the shore end of the gang plank slowly crunched the gravel as it crawled toward the brink, while the men stood ready to cast loose, and the navies hurried aboard the last bundles of lading. We raked up old times, drank from the same canteen, and parted, and thirty-three years passed before we met again.

> "If thou dost bid thy friend farewell,
> But for one day the parting be
> Press thou his hand in thine
> How canst thou tell how far
> Fate or caprice may lead his steps
> Ere that to-morrow come?"[31]

Seth served through the war and remained in Texas for quite awhile after the war closed, and passed through many thrilling adventures.

Standing in Park Square, at Memphis, was at that time a statue of General Jackson.[32] Deeply engraved in the plinth were these words: "The Union, it must and shall be preserved." Some traitor had tried to deface the loyal expression, but had failed, and only succeeded in advertising his treason.

As we passed down the river the guerrillas became more pestiferous. They followed along the banks to give us volley after volley, so that our smoke-stacks were riddled like sieves, and the smoke finding vent through the little holes made a sight to be remembered. This unpleasant conduct on the part of the rebs was not continuous, and we often ranged over the boat for hours.

One day, on the bow of the boat, Cousin Jim and I were standing in conversation. He wore his rooster conspicuously, and upon my hat or uniform I wore three, neat figures in silverwork, 105, and a silver acorn. Generals Slocum and J. J. Reynolds stood at the forward end of the upper deck talking. The former was Jim's old chief, and the latter mine. As they were talking Slocum noticed the rooster and Reynolds saw my badge and figures, and the two Major-Generals came trotting down the companion-way steps and greeted us like two, happy schoolboys. They made inquiries about our regiments and were interested in every detail of our ways of life. Slocum afterwards commanded the left wing of Sherman's army from Savannah to the surrender, and my General Reynolds was to take command of New Orleans. General Reynolds cordially invited me to pay him a visit when I could, which I did, and of course I was pleased, and he seemed no less so. At Chickamauga our line was broken near the flank of his division, and the enemy was pouring through the gap. He asked my Colonel[33] to check them by a strong charge, so that he could have time to put his division in safe position. The regiment obeyed and accomplished all that was asked, and this, with other good conduct on the part of our regiment, led to a good feeling for us on the part of our division chief.

We made a stop at Vicksburg. The long lines of big guns on the river front and upon terraces were yet mounted. Below Vicksburg the annoyance of the guerrillas became at times insupportable, and our boat was brought around with her bow upstream and her nose to the bank, and the armed men under my command were ordered off to chase them away. As there was no place to make fast, and the bank was loose, steep, and ten or twelve feet high, the ascent and descent were the greatest peril we encountered. Our enemies broke for a low, thick fringe of brush and timber which lay back from the river brink a mile or so. We only had a chance to give a sputtering volley, and they were lost to sight. We made a stop at Memphis where I turned over a number of men to an officer of the 7th or 9th Pennsylvania, who signed my name to the receipt, which caused me to ask questions, and I found he was from our old brood nest in eastern Pennsylvania.

Natchez was then, and is yet in my recollection, the most beautiful place I ever saw; and it was in slavery days the home of the wealthy planters who lived here in the enjoyment of all the pleasures and luxuries of proud and exclusive wealth.

We reached the limit of our trip at New Orleans. The Father of Waters[34] was at that time patrolled by small, armed steamers to prevent depredations and the crossing of armed enemies.

We arrived in Columbus in due time. I was with Sherman's army during its Atlanta campaign, saw some of the fighting, saw old Kenesaw[35] when it was in a blaze of glory, Atlanta a day or so after it was evacuated, and remember the way it was protected by abatis, chevaux-de-frise[36] and other contrivances to beat yankee courage and ingenuity.

In all our work we took such opportunity for enjoyment as fell in our way. I recall that once, while waiting for a transport at Hilton Head, South Carolina, we were exploring an inlet from the sea, and as the tide went out we discovered oysters in great plenty. We made a great brush fire and laid them on to open them. One day we took an old boat and went out half a mile or more and got a load of oysters, but time and tide wait for no man, and we soon found ourselves stuck in the mud. We made a prolonge[37] of some old chain and cable, hitched ourselves to the boat and waded out, dragging the boat through mud waist deep.

I will tell you now of the work of the engineers and pioneers. The engineers were regularly organized regiments, enlisted as soldiers from the skilled workers, axe men, and mechanics of all kinds. While in the field they were exempt from all arduous camp and picket duty, but were drilled in all the duties and evolutions of regular troops, being put into action only in emergencies. Their duties were to lay pontoons and build both railroad and other bridges. This duty they did often in the face of an active fire, though, of course, sheltered as much as possible by our own fire. They had much hard and dangerous work, but our work was rarely delayed for want of a bridge, and their average losses were equal to that of the fighting regiments. Mechanics were often drawn from the fighting regiments to repair their losses. They were a gallant, hardy and useful arm of the service.

The pioneers were volunteers from other regiments, made into smaller commands. These commands, in case of bad roads, swamps, etc., marched in advance, making minor repairs in the route. Corduroy roads occupied much time and labor. The men carried axes besides the ordinary, military equipment. When necessity for their services had passed, the men often returned to their original regiments, to be called out again when needed.

The engineers also worked on fortifications much of the time. If there was anything the common soldier hated to do, it was to build fortifications, unless it was to burrow a hole with his tin plate to hold the skirmish line, and that work was done quickly and with good-will.

There were truces for burying the dead, in which a limited time was given.[38] During this time the men would leap from the ditches and fraternize pleasantly until the last moment, when they would return to their work of killing with the same good-will. In the summer of '64 several such occurred, one on the slope of Kenesaw, in which the officers could hardly separate the men when the time was up. My regiment was in it. This was to me one of the most curious features of our war—the readiness of the men to stop shooting each other, meet half way to trade and gossip. Two men on picket, who for days would be watching each opportunity for a good shot at one another, would agree to a parley, lay down their guns and meet half way, if out of sight of an officer, and I never heard of bad faith in such cases. It may be that your Uncle did at times commit such breaches of discipline when he was honing[39] for something with which to fill his briarwood pipe, but it's a long time back.[40]

I had in Company "H" a short, square Dutchman, Sam Wire by name, and the tall man of whom I have told you. One was five feet, two inches, and the other six feet, seven inches, and lean and bony. These two, Jerry and Sam, were great friends. One marched at the foot and the other at the head of the company. They were a never-failing source of fun for the whole army when they started through the camps. Jerry at such times wore the high-crowned, regulation hat, and Sam wore a little fatigue cap. They took their arms and marched to time, Sam having to stretch his legs wide apart to keep an even pace with his partner. These freaks they often took to the enjoyment of all beholders.

The invalid corps was established to give employment to men unfitted for active field service by reason of wounds, or disabled by any casualty of the service. They could still take the places of better men in the rear, do post duty, and guard stores, hospitals and depots of supplies. They were commanded by invalid officers. It was not long until all the cowards and shirks in the army were trying to get into this corps, and many of them succeeded; so with the men at the front it had different fragrant names, perhaps unjustly, but the names stuck and are sticking yet.

One night after a hard march we went into camp late, and long after night Jerry and Sam Wire came in with a fine, old, family carriage loaded with a half barrel of sorghum molasses, a lot of hams and some poultry, with a pair of oxen for motive power. That night many waistbands were severely taxed, and the next day our haversacks were bulging with boiled beef.

I could tell you of most trying days while guarding trains of wagons and assisting mules stuck with their loads, and such like. The most trying of all was to be left on picket when the army set out on a big march. One might not be missed or relieved until the command was miles away. One might say that ten or twenty loose-footed men would soon catch up, but that's a mistake. I know, for I've tried it, and a more trying, wearisome, vexatious experience seldom fell to the lot of the soldier.

A soldier in our army rarely knew the names of comrads outside his own company. Of the men of other companies he spoke as a Company "C" man or a Company "A" man. He knew the men of his own regiment by sight, but rarely by name. A regiment is known in its own brigade, but not often outside. A soldier's duty and place is with his own regiment, and as soon as he gets into any other brigade, division, or corps he is a stranger.[41] When he is left behind and begins to pull up on the column and inquires for his command, he is met with many wise sayings and much valuable advice. He plods on and on, hoping all the time to see some familiar face; maybe late at night comes dragging and straggling into camp, disgusted and tired out. Maybe he camps by the wayside and tries again next day, but if he isn't in by roll-call in the morning he goes on the morning report as absent without leave. After that occurs a couple of times he is reported as a deserter, and it's much easier to get his name on the record as a deserter than to get it off.

Roll-call comes regularly every morning at reveille and gives in a few minutes the condition of the army for the day as present for duty, sick, absent (with or without leave), deserted; and so in a very few minutes the Commander knows all about the condition of his army for that day, and exactly how many muskets he can take into action. In emergencies roll may be called at any hour, and often is called in the face of the enemy, as men leave the ranks for one excuse or another, and the only way to keep them well in hand is to call the roll. The most unhappy duty in the life of a soldier, to my mind, is the first roll-call after a heavy engagement. It is sombre and cheerless. The Orderly loses his vim, and the quick "Here, heres" are interspersed with silent gaps that are depressing for a time. A man who has stood in his place in such a roll-call does not forget it.

Sick call is another distressing sight, especially during a hard campaign. The doctors station themselves under a tent fly, or tree, or any place, and as the Orderlies hear the bugles wail out "Quinine, quinine, come and get your quinine," the poor, straggling unkept fellows come forward, each group with its company Orderly-Sergeant, a despairing lot. The surgeon is brusque, for here he outranks the Major-General, and his word is law. Some of the soldiers, of course, try to play sick to get a ride in the ambulance, and they may work the game once and deceive the man of pills and quinine, but the second he faces "Saw-bones" he is apt to get a dose that stimulates activity for twenty-four hours at least, and the memory of it is a reminder that your army surgeon is a bad man to fool with. You see there is much depending on the doctor, and a soft-hearted fellow would soon fill all the ambulances and the heavy guns with soldiers and their equipments.

At the outstart, with three surgeons, the chief ranked as Major and wore a gold leaf, and the others as Captain and First Lieutenant. The casualties of the service soon left the regiment with only one, and I must say for them that they were as hard-worked, useful, brave and faithful men as any whose names were upon the master-roll, never hesitating to do their duty and remaining at their posts in the most trying times. In case of our lines giving way and hospitals falling into the enemy's hands, they stuck to their posts, ministering to friend and foe, and frequently went to prison and endured all the hardships of the common soldier. They were generally as fearless, in action, in rescuing the wounded as the bravest.

I believe there were no anesthetics used in our army until the Atlanta campaign,—summer of 1864. I am not sure of this, but after the Kenesaw Mountain battle Dr. Charlie Fowler, our division surgeon, told me that, while superintending the operation during and after the engagement, the surgeons made sad work, and he spoke of one surgeon who complained that the stuff was no good, that he had already had three men die during amputation, and the man under his hand would be the fourth, when our Charlie raised the victim's tongue and let breath into his body; then the operating "Saw-bones" had no further trouble.

While on this duty in the rear of the armies I saw many sad and many glorious sights. One I shall not soon forget was the sight of a compact mass of men,—a brigade or a division,—in a sheltered place. When ordered to the front they deployed, unfolded like a huge fan, advanced in line of battle with mounted and dismounted officers, and file closers steadying the line as it swayed backward or forward, or by the conformation of the ground or other accident was broken and confused. Then, when the ob-struction was passed, to see the ragged gap close up, resume its smooth alignment, colors flying and arms at right shoulder shift, and to see the same line double-quick, the point of the flag staff drooping to an angle of forty-five degrees, arms at a trail and bodies bent forward, was glorious.[42]

In those days men of the North were not all loyal, and in all neighbor-hoods there were men who rejoiced when the news of defeat and disaster came; and when the loyal boys were away at the front, whenever it was safe to do so, these men wore, to advertise their treason, ornaments made by sawing butternuts in sections. These sections were fastened on the coat with a pin, and the wearer was known as a copperhead.[43] They had an order known as "Knights of the Golden Circle," who armed and drilled at night and in secluded places, in order that they might resist drafts and be ready to assist our enemies when the time should be ripe. Where they were strong, they made a frivolous show of defying the Government, but they always came to grief. By letters from home the boys at the front heard of these carryings-on, and each man, as he received his thirty days furlough, put himself on a special order to gather and bring back as many butternut trophies as possible, and, without more ado, he began work upon arrival at home, and when he returned to duty he brought his trophies with him, properly labeled and with a narrative of the capture attached to each, which never failed to highly interest his companions. Often the crop was too much for one to gather. He would hunt up some other comrade, invalid or furlough man, and, sticking well together, they would go to public meetings, sales, and the like, reap the harvest together and divide the spoil.

No man who ever saw a month's service at the front was ever known to falter in his loyalty to the men who remained.

The clothes worn by the southern soldiers were dyed with butternut, so the butternut came to be the designation of a rebel, and was worn as an emblem by those who desired the success of the Rebellion.

All young men did not go to the war, many had business abroad or in Canada, many were ailing and straightway sought the physician. On the farm joining ours on the west were five boys, and on the east were other five, most of them of suitable age. In our township were several such families who had no representative in the service, and nearly all are living to-day,—muck-rakers to whom any high colored strip of calico on a pole would have as much meaning as the old banner which means so much to those who suffered for it. To this day, when soldiers and patriotic citizens meet to do honor to their noble dead, these men follow their usual labors.

The war found our Government totally unprovided for its emergencies, and, when hospitals began to fill up after great battles, hospital supplies were wanting. Then came the women to the front; they organized societies,[44] brought their old linen, picked it into lint, made bandages, and so on. In this work your mothers were all engaged.

In pursuance of my duty I crossed the States of Illinois, Indiana, Ohio, Pennsylvania and New York many times with train loads of soldiers; and one of the usual sights was the gatherings of sorrowing friends, mourners,—sad groups they were,—waiting for the train. When it came, maybe one or more long, wooden boxes would be reverently carried to a waiting or other conveyance, or a poor fellow on crutches, with an off leg, or the stump of an arm, or bandaged like a mummy, telling of broken bones or lacerated flesh,—wreck for life in any event.

Ah, me, there's a wrinkly side to war, and my duties gave me a good look at both sides. I saw a ship discharging her load of Andersonville prisoners,[45] some dead, and all starved skeletons. At most of our regular stopping-places the patriotic ladies gathered on the platforms at the stations, with steaming coffee-pots and all kinds of goodies in pans, cans and jars. Of course we had to keep guard on the doors, for so many pretty girls outside and so many young soldiers inside, had they been permitted to commingle at will, my command would soon have been like a discharged rocket, nothing left but the stick. So at all these trying points I put on extra guards. Each soldier had his tin cup, and arms were passed out through the windows with cups and heads crowded between; pretty compliments flying back and forth, and love looked love in the eyes which spoke again, with quick betrothals and promises of what was to be when the war was over and Johnny came marching home. At all such halts I overlooked my trains from the outside and had also a few of the old guard on duty there, for the temptation often proved too great, and confinement and handcuffs awaited the poor fellows who fell. All these good things were without money and without price. In large cities where we had to disembark the trainmen sent word of our numbers, and night or day the good women always had a fine lunch for any number. They had a hall or spacious apartment at some convenient point, and we marched directly there, where everything was steaming hot. There were long tables and good food in plenty, all served by the prettiest, kindest and best girls in the world.

> "Ah, me! those joyous days are gone.
> I little dreamt till they were flown
> How fleeting were the hours;
> For lest we break the pleasing spell,
> Time bears for youth a muffled bell
> And hides his face in flowers."[46]

Pittsburgh is one of those places which I think will live in the memories of many a chap who wore the blue in our great war.

Often, even in the northern States, we had only box cars with board seats; but in all such cases we made windows without the aid of carpenters.

Many of the old soldiers who served, and had been discharged by reason of expiration of time, reenlisted or went as substitutes for big money. Others who had been discharged for disabilities returned to duty as recruits after convalescence. The bounty-jumper reduced his business to science; Canada furnished a big quota of these. The toughs of all the country took the substitute's big pay, deserted, went to another State, changed names, and repeated the operation. Dealers in this class of cattle grew wealthy, but the great heart of the nation was loyal to the core.

As Sherman's army came up through Virginia I went out to meet them and marched with my old company in the grand review.

I saw Father Abraham often in life and once after his death.

I rejoice that I was permitted to bear ever so humble a part in securing the unity of our great country, and to share a little in the sufferings of its noble sons. So far as I recollect I did a soldier's duty in obeying every order from proper authority. I received my Captain's commission about September 8, 1864, and made strenuous and repeated efforts to be returned to duty with my company, but this was refused by the highest authority, with the promise that my interests should not be jeopardized by my absence. At different times I was offered higher rank in new, short-termed regiments, and at the close of the war a Second Lieutenant's commission in the regular army, both of which I refused. To be a soldier without a soldier's business had no attractions for me.

My regiment was never in a general engagement after Mission Ridge, nor was Sherman's army, although there was contact at some point nearly every day, and much hard fighting all the way from Chattanooga until after the fall of Atlanta, and much loss of life.[47]

Now I ask you to take any opportunity that falls in your way to visit our National Cemeteries. There you will realize a little of the truth of the story I have been trying to tell you, and as you walk along their avenues and see the little, white, stone markers, think that for each of these the swift lightning carried the news of death and the broken home circle to some loyal heart in the far away North. Under these stones lie the boys of '61-'65, the boys of the little, red school-house, the boys who left home, "The orchard, the meadow, the deep tangled wildwood and every loved spot that their infancy knew,"[48] to do and die; and then you must highly resolve that their lives shall not have been given in vain.[49]

These cities of the dead are peopled with the lads who are deserving the crowns of laurel wrought with crimson berries, and these cities, with an undivided country, rich and vast beyond comprehension, are the treasures we leave in your safe keeping.

In my story of the war I have tried to show you, as well as I could, the life of the man with the musket,[50] for it fell to my lot to be almost his constant companion, often his messmate and bedfellow. From February 14, 1864, to June, 1865, I slept most of the time in old fields and forests, my head pillowed on a haversack crammed with money, which could have been his by any act of vile treachery; he stood a sentinel faithful to his trust. The bad element was very small comparatively.

The question of the duration of the war, with so much disparity in the size of the armies, I would explain in this way. An interior line reaching from the Potomac to the Rio Grande and a coast line of twice that length; a determined and well-equipped enemy, with a million men on the inside, who could concentrate and break through.

NOTE: Bragg and Kirby Smith in '62, Lee in '63, John Morgan's Ohio raid, and Hood when Sherman started to the sea, and all kinds of block-ade runners and privateers.[41]

We had our friends to care for behind us, and our enemies in front. They fronted North, South, East or West; and, wherever they were, we were obliged to meet them. For our enemies,—I must say they fought for what they considered right and true, and no men ever displayed more for-titude and bravery. This great war, unlike any other of modern times, called into its ranks, on both sides, the best and noblest men, from priest to profligate, statesmen to philosophers, to school boys, and was a fight to the finish.

These are the names, as far as I can recall, of those under whom I served:[51] General Nelson (killed by Jeff C. Davis at the Gault House, Louisville, Kentucky); General Jackson, who was our first brigade com-mander and was killed at Perryville, October 8, 1863; Don Carlos Buell; then old Rosey—our Colonel was A. S. Hall, and he served as brigade commander; then E. A. King, who fell at Chickamauga—General J. J. Reynolds for division commander; and General George H. Thomas, corps commander; afterwards General Vanderveer commanded our brigade; and at different times under General Sheridan, Baird and Jeff C. Davis, with Grant or Sherman for chief; and during the last year and more I took or-ders from officers in all departments,—now all gone to the sunset land but one or two.

My only souvenir of the war is my old sabre, which I prize most, because its rough, rusty scabbard, in all weathers, furnished a never-failing spot to scratch matches to light unnumbered pipes, the smoke of whose burning carried a little taste of quiet comfort to many a good fellow whose going out was heralded by no solemn tolling bell; and so I bid good-bye forever to my old comrades and to this poor story.

Dear Wilbur:—

I am glad to drop this. My mind has been full of it so long, and the only limit to writing would be the ink and paper supply. I have wandered in every direction, without stopping-place or system, so you will have to do the best you can with it, and the Lord have mercy on the patient readers, if there be any, while I give my vagrant mind a rest.

With love to you all,
Your Uncle,
J.C.H.

Dear Wilbur:—

You have called my attention to the fact that I failed to complete the story of little Dick Cobb, so I give it to you here in a few words.

When I came home the first time I told Uncle John about litte Dick, and the old fellow's heart melted. He asked me to send the boy to him, and promised to raise him, so on my first trip to my regiment (the time of the wreck) I brought the boy back to Columbus, as I have already told you, and left him with the old guard at the barracks, hoping to take him home and introduce him to Uncle John, but I was unable to do so, and Dick soon ingratiated himself with the guard and all of the haedquarters' officers, and was so happy that I had no uneasiness as to his welfare, and was always glad to receive his honest, happy, hearty greeting on my return.

One day when I came back, Dick was not on hand. I made inquiry for him, and learned that my faithful, little friend and companion, whom I found a wandering waif amid the thunder of the cannons and the smoke of battle was gone. He died of measles, and was buried by the soldiers with a soldier's honors. I have always felt guilty in this matter, as I should have forwarded him immediately to his destination. My recollection of him, though mournful, is of one of the pleasantest, cheerfulest, little comrades a man ever had.

And now you have the story of little Dick Cobb.

Notes

Chapter 1

1. *Note:* Genealogical information and military service dates are given in abbreviated form. In the parenthetical listing of ancestors, the surname "Hartzell" is assumed, except for the last listing. When reference to township is missing, it is Deerfield Township (Twp).

The author is John Calvin Hartzell (Frederick, John, George Henry, Conrad Hartzell), b. 27 Nov 1837 in Deerfield Twp, Portage Co, OH, and d. 25 Apr 1918 in Smith Twp, Mahoning Co, OH. He married Louise Ann Lowrie Thompson 16 Aug 1865. They had six children: Dr. Thomas B., b. Jun 1866 in Smith Twp, Mahoning Co, OH, d. 1951 Hennepin Co, Minneapolis; Mary, b. 24 Dec 1869 in Smith Twp, Mahoning Co, OH, d. 16 Aug 1957 in Los Angeles Co, CA—married F. E. Kenaston; Ruth W., b. 14 Jun 1885, lived in Minnesota; Lucy, b. 18 Jun 1874, d. 18 Jan 1968—married Emerson Bennett Fritchman; Bertha O., b. 12 Jun 1877; Frederick W, b. 30 May 1879, d. May 1900.

"The House of Seven Gables" is the name John Calvin Hartzell (hereafter abbreviated JCH) gives to the home where he grew up, reminding one of a more famous use of the name by the New England novelist Nathaniel Hawthorne, whose romance of that title is clouded with mystery, curses, and Puritanism. In contrast, JCH's home is open, congenial, and comfortable, yet is doomed by future financial mismanagement by JCH's father.

"My dear nephew" is Wilbur Johnson Hartzell (Josiah, Frederick, John, George Henry, Conrad Hartzell), b. 22 Nov 1856 in Davenport, Scott Co, IA, and d. 1928, probably in Medford, OR. Wilbur would have been forty years old when JCH began his memoirs in 1896. He married Ruth Rebecca Smith and they had three children: James Hugh, Mary Kezra, and Dorothy. She d. in 1900 in Medford, Jackson Co, OR. He married Florence Wright 20 Nov 1901 and they had two children, Wilbur Wright and Josephine Virginia, who typed JCH's autobiography, with carbon copies, in the 1940s.

"Round Robin request"—See figure 4 in the introduction for a reproduction of the round robin request and note 7 to the introduction for definitions of "round robin." A transcription of the family's request to JCH immediately precedes chapter 1.

2. "Your great-grandfather"—John Hartzell (George Henry, Conrad Hartzell), b. 1 Dec 1765 in Northampton Co, PA, and d. 5 Aug 1846. He married Dorothy

Kleinhans ca. 1792 in Northampton Co, PA, daughter of George Frederick Klein-hans and Elizabeth Oberly (Aberly). Dorothy was b. 21 Apr 1770 in Northampton Co, PA, and d. 21 Nov 1848. They had eleven children: John, Elizabeth, Jacob, Susan, Christina, Henry, Jonas, Mary, Frederick, Ann, and Sarah.

"Your grandfather"—Frederick Hartzell (John, George Henry, Conrad Hartzell), b. 3 Jul 1810 and d. 13 Nov 1868. He married Mary Ickes ca. 1832. She was b. 8 May 1811 and d. 30 Aug 1888. They had ten children: Josiah, Joshua, John Calvin, Lucy A., Thomas E., Jesse Miller, Isaiah, Martin, James Robert, Rosella.

"Your father"—Josiah Hartzell (Frederick, John, George Henry, Conrad Hartzell), b. 7 Sep 1833 and d. 11 Nov 1914 in Canton, Stark Co, OH. He married Mary K. Johnson 21 Feb 1856, b. 26 Oct 1833 in Stark Co, OH, and d. 16 Aug 1911 in Canton, Stark Co, OH. They had eight children: Wilbur Johnson (to whom the memoirs are addressed), Dora Virginia, Frederick S., Charles, Mary K., Josiah II, Grace, Ralph W.

3. "Your great-great-grandfather George"—George Henry Hartzell (Conrad Hartzell), b. 1 May 1739 in probably Philadelphia Co, PA, and d. 20 May 1813. He married Christina Nowlan 28 Feb 1764 in Northampton Co, PA, who d. 28 Apr 1823. They had the following children: John, George, Jacob, Elizabeth, Christina, Anna Maria, William Henry, Susan, Peter, Abraham, Daniel, Joseph.

"Uncle Billy Lazarus"—William Lazarus (Sarah Hartzell, John, George Henry, Conrad Hartzell), b. 1836 and d. 1863 in the Civil War. His mother Sarah was b. 1814 and d. ca. 1890. She married Joseph Lazarus, son of Frederick Lazarus and Christina Hartzell (George Henry, Conrad Hartzell), 9 Mar 1836.

"Peter, his son"—Peter Hartzell (George Henry, Conrad Hartzell), b. 1 Oct 1780 in Northampton Co, PA, and d. betw. 1840 and 1850 in Perry Twp, Stark Co, OH. He married Mary before 1812. She was b. 1786 in PA and d. 3 Mar 1869. They had five children: Levi, Mary, Caroline, William, Anna Elizabeth.

Thompson Craig—b. 9 Feb 1802 and d. 8 Apr 1858 in Berlin Twp, Mahoning Co, OH; married Catherine Hartzell (George, George Henry, Conrad Hartzell) ca. 1833. They had seven children: Sarah, Christina, Julia, William, John, Lucy Odella, Mary M. William Craig d. 1863 in the Civil War.

Jacob Sheets—b. 1795 in Taneytown, Fredericks Co, MD, and d. 4 Dec 1884. He married Elizabeth Hartzell (John, George Henry, Conrad Hartzell), b. 5 Jan 1794 in Northampton/Lehigh Co, PA, and d. 12 Nov 1874. They had eight children: Clarissa, Ann Eliza, Lucy, Linus, Alvah, John Christian, Sarah Margaretta, Mary J.

"David and Tobias Hartzell"—David Hartzell (Jacob, George Henry, Conrad Hartzell), b. 20 Oct 1809 and d. 29 Jul 1881; Tobias Hartzell (Jacob, George Henry, Conrad Hartzell), b. 21 Dec 1814 and d. 4 Jan 1899. Their parents were Jacob Hartzell and Magdalena Kleinhans, daughter of George Frederick Kleinhans and Elizabeth Oberly (Aberly).

"George Hartzell and Henry"—George Hartzell (George Henry, Conrad Hartzell), b. 1768 in Northampton Co, PA, and d. 14 Jul 1852; married Christina Dice ca. 1791. They had ten children: John, Joseph, Peter, Christina, Elizabeth, Susan, George, William, Abraham, Catherine. Henry Hartzell (John, George Henry, Conrad Hartzell), b. 10 May 1801 in Northampton/LeHigh Co, PA, and d. 6 Aug 1895, married Anna Sheets 6 Jan 1825. She was b. 1807 and d. Apr

1835. He married Jane Smart 28 Apr 1836. She was b. 1810 and d. 23 Oct 1844. He married Catharine B. Sullivan 19 Oct 1848. Henry and Anna had five children: Simon, Mary, Homer, Harriet, John L. Henry and Jane had five children: Eli, James, Anna H., Lucy, George S.

"Old Abram and Young Abe"—"Old Abram" is Abraham Hartzell (George Henry, Conrad Hartzell), b. 15 Jan 1785 in Northampton Co, PA, and d. 2 Feb 1864; married Sarah Smith 16 Sep 1812 in Columbiana Co, OH. She was b. 21 Aug 1793 in York Co, PA, and d. 1 May 1875. They had six children: James, Nancy, Simeon F., Caroline, Sarah, Joseph. "Young Abe" is Abraham Hartzell (George, George Henry, Conrad Hartzell), b. 1807 and d. either 27 Jan 1884 or 20 Jul 1884; married Margaret Clark, b. 1811 and d. 8 Jun 1880. He married Amanda French 4 Mar 1881. Abe had no children.

"Uncle Billy Hartzell"—William Henry Hartzell (George Henry, Conrad Hartzell), b. 16 Aug 1778 in Northampton Co, PA, and d. 1 Dec 1867 in Berlin Twp, Mahoning Co, OH; married Mary Hummell ca. 1805. She was b. Jun 1784 and d. 5 May 1849 in Berlin Twp, Mahoning Co, OH. They had nine children: Boyd, Sarah, William, John, George, Solomon, Sophia, Daniel, Lucinda.

"Uncles John and Sam Macgowan"—The spelling of the family name Mac-Gowan varies. John McGowan (Adam McGowan), b. 28 Nov 1806, probably in Mercer/Lawrence Co, PA, and d. 18 Feb 1865 in Orland Steuben Co, IN, married Charlotte Churchill before 1832. She was b. ca. 1809 and d. 1844 in Portage Co, OH. They had five children: Harriet, Rebecca, Charloman (Wycliff?), Miletus, Irenus. Orderly Sergeant Miletus and Second Lieutenant Irenus of the 29th Indiana Regiment fought at Shiloh, Stones River, and Chickamauga, each sustaining several wounds. Both were captured at Chickamauga and imprisoned at Andersonville. Miletus died of chronic diarrhea in 1863. The Orland, IN, American Legion Post is named after him. "Sam Macgowan" is Samuel McGowan (Adam McGowan), b. 2 Aug 1796 and d. 28 Jul 1860 in Orland, Steuben Co, IN; married Susan Hartzell (John, George Henry, Conrad Hartzell) 4 Jan 1821. She was b. 30 Jul 1797 in Northampton/Lehigh Co, PA, and d. 24 Nov 1864 in Orland, Steuben Co, IN. They had ten children: Josiah, George (editor Switzer's line), Elizabeth, Andrew, John Encil MacGowan, Dorothy, Richard Eli, Jonas Hartzell, Frederick, Mary Marie. George, John Encil, Richard Eli, and Jonas served in the Union army during the Civil War.

The primary sources for genealogical information are RootsWeb.com (under George Henry Hartzell Portage Co OH by Susan K. McMahan), and Ruth Cowart, "McGowan Family History," unpublished.

4. A fulling mill is "a mill in which cloth is fulled or milled by being beaten with wooden mallets, which are let fall upon it (or in modern use, by being pressed between rollers) and cleansed with soap or fuller's earth," which is "a hydrous silicate of alumina, used in cleansing cloth" (*Oxford English Dictionary* [OED]; definitions of terms not otherwise attributed are based on *Merriam-Webster's Collegiate Dictionary*, 10th ed., 2002).

5. "My grandfather" is John Hartzell. See note 2 to this chapter. "Jonas" is Jonas Hartzell (John, George Henry, Conrad Hartzell), b. 19 Oct 1803 in Northampton/Lehigh Co, PA, and d. 1 Aug 1884 in Davenport, Scott Co, IA. "Your grandfather"

is Frederick Hartzell. "His father and mother" are John Hartzell, d. 5 Aug 1846, and Dorothy Kleinhans Hartzell, d. 21 Nov 1848.

6. "My tow linen pantaloons"—Tow linen is a fabric of shorter, less desirable flax fibers. A gallus is a suspender for holding up trousers.

7. To gall means to make sore by chafing. The second "gall" refers to the bitterness of it all.

8. "Docked and nicked large" refers to the fleshy part of the tail—the short or shortened end of a notched tail.

9. Joshua was b. 17 Jun 1835 and d. 20 Sep 1837 in Smith Twp, Mahoning Co, OH. "Jess" is Jesse Miller, b. 21 Jan 1845 and d. 8 Feb 1937. Lucy A. was b. 2 Jul 1840 and d. 12 Mar 1922, probably in Canton, Stark Co, OH. "Tommy" is Thomas E., b. 25 Dec 1842 and d. 24 Sep 1844.

10. "Skutched and hackled" refers to the preparation of fibrous material for spinning. To skutch is to separate the woody fiber from flax or hemp by beating; to hackle is to dress flax or hemp with a hackle, whereby the fibers are split, straightened, and combed out, so as to be in condition for spinning.

11. "Your Jamie"—Wilbur's son James Hugh Hartzell (Wilbur Johnson, Josiah, Frederick, John, George Henry, Conrad Hartzell), b. 3 Jun 1885 in Smith, King Co, WA.

12. The hymn is better known by the first line "God of the Morning, at Whose Voice," text by Isaac Watts (1674–1748), music attributed to John Hatton (1710–93).

Chapter 2

1. "My uncle John" is John McGowan; see note 3 to chapter 1.

2. "Tho' lost to sight . . .": George Linley (1798–1865).

3. Solomon Hartzell (William Henry, George Henry, Conrad Hartzell), b. 13 Aug 1813 and d. 2 Nov 1897, married Caroline Loomis 6 Nov 1844. She was b. 9 Nov 1819 and d. 31 Oct 1898. They had five children: Chester N., Sophia, Stratton Leonard, Daniel H., and Emma M.

4. "John Barleycorn" is the personification of barley, especially as the grain from which malt liquor is made, and, by extension, the personification of alcoholic liquor.

5. "Bill, the oldest boy"—George had a son named William, but he was next to the eldest, not the eldest.

6. "Your cousin Seth" is Seth Hartzell (Jacob, John, George Henry, Conrad Hartzell), b. 22 Jul 1814.

7. The two quotations are from poems by John Greenleaf Whittier (1807–92), "Barbara Frietchie" (line 6), and James Whitcomb Riley (1849–1916), "When the frost is on the punkin."

8. "Prentice" is the archaic form of apprentice (OED).

9. A still-house is "a building in which distillation is carried on, a distillery" (OED).

10. A flutter-wheel is "a water-wheel of moderate diameter placed at the bottom of a chute so as to receive the impact of the head of water in the chute and penstock" (OED).

11. A shite poke is a small green heron.

12. A spile is a spout inserted in a tree to draw off sap.

13. The quoted phrases are based on three lines from "Tam O'Shanter" by Robert Burns (1759–96): "The minutes wing'd their way wi' pleasure: / Kings may be blest, but Tam was glorious / O'er a' the ills o'life victorious!"

14. Warren Clark was raised by Uncle Abe and Peggy Clark Hartzell, who were childless.

15. The quotation is adapted from Robert Burns's "John Anderson, My Jo": "And monie a canty day, John, / We've had wi' ane anither."

16. Flotsam is floating wreckage of a ship or its cargo, hence a floating population; jetsam is cargo or equipment thrown overboard to lighten a ship's load in time of distress.

Chapter 3

1. Gigging is spearing or fishing with a gig, which can be either a pronged spear for catching fish or a line with hooks that is drawn through a school of fish. From JCH's description of his youthful gigging expeditions, evidently he and his friends gigged with pronged spears.

2. A riffle is a rapid or broken water in a stream.

3. A carding dam is "a machine for combing or cleaning wool or cotton, in which a large cylinder set with cards works in communion with smaller cylinders and a hollow shell similarly set with cards" (OED).

4. A withe is a tough, flexible twig suitable for binding things together.

5. A water dog is a large salamander or mud puppy.

6. The couplet is an adaptation of the opening lines of "Rock Me to Sleep" (1860), by Elizabeth Akers Allen (1832–1911): "Backward, turn backward, O Time, in your flight, / Make me a child again just for to-night!"

7. "Ground itch" is athlete's foot.

8. A flax-brake consists of "two pieces of timber with teeth made in them to bruise flax stalks (flax comb)" (OED).

9. A paling is a fence made of pales or pickets, hence a paling gate is a fence gate.

10. Lovage is one of several aromatic perennial herbs of the carrot family, sometimes cultivated as a domestic remedy or flavoring.

11. The poetry quotation is an adaptation of lines 42–45 from Robert Burns's "The Inventory":

> Till, faith! wee Davock's grown sae gleg,
> Tho' scarcely langer than your leg,
> He'll screed you aff Effectual Calling,
> As fast as ony in the dwalling.

12. JCH here discusses Presbyterian theology, based on John Calvin's teachings.

13. The quotation is from Robert Burns's "The Cotter's Saturday Night."

14. The story of Joseph's coat of many colors is found in Genesis 37–40.

15. The poetry quotation is from Robert Burns's "Tam O'Shanter," lines 59–62.

16. Hebrews 12:11.

Chapter 4

1. JCH jokes here that, as Presbyterians, they believed that only sheep are immersed totally in baptism!

2. Kit, a set of tools used by a workman, in this case refers to tools for shearing sheep.

3. The quotation is from a popular song, "Home Again," by Marshall S. Pike, published by E. H. Wade in Boston in 1850 in a piano arrangement by J. P. Ordway. The text of the chorus is as follows:

> Home again, home again,　　.
> 　　From a foreign shore,
> And oh! it fills my soul with joy,
> 　　To greet my friends once more.

Evidently well known in the second half of the nineteenth century, the song is also quoted by William Dean Howells in *Their Wedding Journey* (1871, chap. 10) and by Mark Twain in *Life on the Mississippi* (1883, chap. 48).

4. This is an echo of Lincoln's Gettysburg Address, pointing to the North's determination to preserve the union.

5. "Schnitts and knep"—According to *Dictionary of American Regional English*, edited by Frederic G. Cassidy and Joan Houston Hall (Cambridge, MA: Harvard University Press, 1991), knep is of Germanic origin (gnepp—dumplings): chiefly Pennsylvania dumplings, often served with schnitz, "made of dried apples, fat parts, and dough dumplings, cooked together." Ham, fish, or poultry could be included.

6. Grain cradles are "made of a frame of wood with a row of long curved teeth projecting above and parallel to a scythe for laying grain in bunches as it is cut" (*Random House Dictionary of the English Language*, College Edition, ed. Laurence Urdung).

7. To butt cut means to split a log in half.

8. In this echo of "The Star-Spangled Banner," the author discusses the sort of hearty food that nourishes men so that they can safely guard the flag. Underlying this passage is the important role of flags, including the national flag and regimental colors, in maintaining morale and unity.

9. The author uses military terms to describe everyday events and scenery; here, he imagines videttes (or vedettes), mounted guards in advance of the pickets, watching over the old sugar camp.

10. A cucumber is a tree of the American magnolia class with fruit that resembles small cucumbers.

11. JCH pokes fun at his nephew's father, Josiah, showing perhaps some envy of his elder brother's book learning.

12. "Deacon John" is John Craig (Catherine Hartzell, George, George Henry, Conrad Hartzell), b. Oct 1843 in Berlin Twp, Trimbell/Mahoning Co, OH, and d. 8 Feb 1920 in North Benton, Mahoning Co, OH.

"Your great-great-great-granddaddy" would be Conrad Hartzell, who came to America 6 Dec 1738. More likely JCH means George Henry Hartzell (1739–1813).

"Old uncle Fred Lazarus" is Frederick Lazarus, b. ca. 1797 in Northampton Co, PA, and d. 17 Aug 1850.

13. "Jake Sheets" is Jacob Sheets, b. 1795 in Taneytown, Frederick Co, MD, and d. 4 Dec 1884.

14. "Your grand-aunt Betsy" is Elizabeth Hartzell Sheets (John Hartzell, George Henry, Conrad Hartzell), b. 5 Jan 1794 in Northampton/Lehigh Co, PA, and d. 12 Nov 1874.

15. "The General" is Ulysses Simpson Grant (1822–85), who became commander of the Union army and went on to become president of the United States. Jesse Grant married Hannah Simpson in June 1821, and Ulysses S. Grant was b. 27 Apr 1822 in Point Pleasant, Clermont Co, OH.

16. "Jake Winans, his grandson" is Jacob S. Winans (Ann Eliza Sheets, Elizabeth Hartzell, John, George Henry, Conrad Hartzell) b. 1838 in Melton Twp, Mahoning Co, OH. His father is Isaac Winans, b. 3 Jul 1811 in Melton Twp, Mahoning Co, OH, and d. 3 Dec 1877 in New Brighton, Beaver Co, PA. He married Ann Eliza (b. ca. 1818) 1 Aug 1837. Her father is Jacob Sheets.

17. "Uncle Henry's first wife was his [Jake's] sister"—This was Anna Sheets, b. 1807 and d. Apr 1835. Henry and Anna were married 6 Jan 1825.

18. A juriscopist is a legal recorder of some kind (OED). "Copist" is an obsolete form of "copyist." Officials in Ecclesiastical Courts were so designated. There is something sexual here in JCH's comment.

19. The quotation is from "Death and Doctor Hornbrook," by Robert Burns. "Saw and whittles" are saw and knife. "Sal-marinum of the seas" is common salt. "Farina" is a fine meal or powder. "Aqua fortis" is nitric acid.

20. "John Barleycorn"—see note 3 to chapter 2.

21. The lines quoted are from "Kingry's Mill," by Indiana poet James Whitcomb Riley, who specialized in dialect poems. "Worter" as used here is dialect for "water." "Flume" refers to the wooden trough conveying liquid. "Slosh" is to splash a liquid. "Reel" refers to a cylinder that turns on its axis. "Flossier'n satin cloth" (flossier than satin cloth) refers to the surface of the liquid.

22. For the definition of fulling mill, see note 4 to chapter 1.

23. "Linsey-woolsey" is "originally, a textile material, woven from a mixture of wool and flax," "now, a dress material of coarse inferior wool, woven upon a cotton warp." It also refers to a garment of this material (OED).

24. Burdock is a coarse weedy plant common on waste ground, bearing prickly flowerheads called burs, and large leaves like those of the dock.

25. The quotation is from Sarah Doudney's poem "The Lesson of the Water Mill."

26. Thompson Craig (1809–82) married Catherine (Katy) Hartzell (George, George Henry, Conrad Hartzell), b. 1 May 1809 and d. 16 Dec 1882, Berlin Twp, Portage Co, OH. Her brother, Uncle Abe, is Abraham Hartzell, b. 1807 and d. either 27 Jan 1884 or 20 Jul 1884.

27. The river is personified as a woman. Its wildness helps to explain why it was made into a reservoir and dam in the 1940s to control flooding in Youngstown, OH. The reservoir eliminated about two-thirds of the farming community, including about one-third of the cemetery, resulting in the relocation of some graves.

28. John Diver, b. 2 Feb 1781 and d. 14 Apr 1864, married Christine Hartzell (George, George Henry, Conrad Hartzell), b. 29 Dec 1793 in Northampton Co, PA, and d. 12 Feb 1857.

Chapter 5

1. The quotation is adapted from Robert Burns's "Tam O'Shanter." "Blellums" are blobs, idle characters (*OED*).

2. JCH reveals envy of his older brother, Josiah, Wilbur's father. JCH again is the butt of the humor here.

3. Hebrews 12:6.

4. Sticking plaster is an adhesive bandage or dressing spread with a curative or protective substance. "Aunt Jemina" is the brand name.

5. To guy is to ridicule.

6. A leek is an onionlike biennial garden herb of the lily family.

7. A crowfoot is one of numerous plants having leaves with cleft lobes, especially the buttercup.

8. A plover is a shore bird similar to the sandpiper.

9. The quotation is from James Whitcomb Riley, "The Days Gone By."

10. Johnny-jump-ups are any of several kinds of wild or cultivated pansies or violets.

11. The quotations are from the hymn "There Is a Land of Sweet Delight," based on the poem "The Prospect of Heaven Makes Death Easy," by Isaac Watts; it has been set to a variety of tunes.

12. "A real Melba" is a reference to Nellie Melba, the stage name of Australian operatic soprano Helen Mitchell (1861–1931).

13. A chippy is a chirping sparrow.

14. The quotation is adapted from "To a Mountain Daisy," by Robert Burns; the original reads:

> The bonie lark, companion meet,
> Bending thee 'mang the dewy weet,
> Wi' spreckl'd breast!
> When upward-springing, blythe, to greet
> The purpling east.

15. "Burning lake" is perhaps an allusion to Hell from Dante's *Divine Comedy*.

16. "One gallus button to hinder"—that is, only one suspender button prevents JCH from removing his trousers and going swimming.

17. Snoodling, derived from *snood,* is netting suckers with a hair net or line with several hooks attached to it (*OED*).

18. A hoyden is a noisy, rude, or boisterous girl or woman.

19. The second sentence of the quotation is adapted from the refrain of Alfred Lord Tennyson's poem "The Brook": "For men may come and men may go, / But I go on forever."

20. "Uncle Nick Eckis, your grandmother's brother" is Nicholas Eckes, Mary Eckes Hartzell's brother. An ashery is a place for the manufacture of potash or pearl ash.

21. General Jubal Anderson Early (1816–94) was in the Shenandoah Valley in 1864 to divert Federal forces from Lee's army. The Confederate general was finally defeated by Sheridan at Cedar Creek, VA, in 1865. See *The Civil War Almanac*, exec. ed. John S. Bowman (New York: W. H. Smith, 1983), 330; *The Civil War Battlefield Guide*, ed. Francis H. Kennedy (Boston: Houghton Miflin, 1990), 250.

22. The quotation is from "Maud Muller," by John Greenleaf Whittier.

23. "Old Uncle George . . . your Great-grandfather's brother" is George Hartzell, b. 12 Mar 1768 and d. 14 Jul 1852. His brother is John Hartzell.

24. Isaiah 35:10.

25. George Hartzell is George Henry Hartzell (Conrad Hartzell), and his wife is Christina Nowlan Hartzell.

26. The children named are John (d. 5 Aug 1846); Joseph (d. 27 Jun 1830); William (William Henry, d. 1 Dec 1867); George (d. 14 Jul 1852); Abram (Abraham, d. 2 Feb 1864); Christina (d. 8 Apr 1853).

27. The quotation, slightly altered, is from the poem "Mortality," by the Scotsman William Knox (1789–1825); it was among Abraham Lincoln's favorite poems.

28. Alonzo Strong, b. 27 Nov 1805, Durham, Middleton Co, CT, and d. 2 Mar 1891, North Benton, Mahoning Co, OH, married Christina Lazarus (Christine Hartzell, George Henry, Conrad Hartzell), b. 8 Apr 1807 and d. 25 Mar 1843. Abraham Hartzell is Christina Hartzell's brother.

Chapter 6

1. A well-sweep is a long pole or timber pivoted on a tall post and used to raise and lower a bucket in a well.

2. "Our old Ivanhoe" is a reference to the hero of Sir Walter Scott's novel *Ivanhoe*.

3. "Duck Foot" is George Hartzell (William Henry, George Henry, Conrad Hartzell), b. 13 May 1811 and d. betw. 3 Apr 1881 and 1882. "Uncle Billy" is William Henry Hartzell, b. 16 Aug 1778 and d. 1 Dec 1867.

4. Tansy is bitters.

5. "Old Johnny Craig" is John Craig (Thompson Craig/Catherine Hartzell, George, George Henry, Conrad Hartzell), b. Oct 1843 and d. 8 Feb 1920.

6. The quoted lines are the final verse of the hymn "How Blest the Righteous When He Dies," text by Anna Barbauld (1743–1825). The hymn was frequently sung at funeral services, and the last verse is frequently quoted in obituaries from this period.

7. "Into green pastures" and "beside still waters" are phrases from Psalm 23.

8. John Christian Sheets, third son of Jacob Sheets and Elizabeth Hartzell, was b. 1828 and d. 22 Mar 1913 in Manchester, Dickinson Co, KS.

9. "Uncle John" is John McGowan (Adam McGowan), b. Nov 1806 and d. 18 Feb 1863.

10. JCH notes that the Golden Rule and sharing prevailed when he was a boy. The only duty of a justice of the peace was to make property deeds. Crime was almost nonexistent.

11. Sancho Panza is the credulous and amusing squire in Cervantes' romance, *Don Quixote de la Mancha* (1605–15). When Don Quixote refuses to pay the innkeeper, Sancho is tossed in a blanket as payment for his master's debt.

12. William Shakespeare's famous lines about the quality of mercy are quoted from *The Merchant of Venice*, act 4, scene 1.

13. The quotation is based on biblical passages that include Proverbs 31:12 and 2 Corinthians 7:2.

Chapter 7

1. "Rob and Rosey" are Frederick and Mary's youngest children: James Robert Hartzell, b. 22 Jan 1852 Portage Co, OH, and d. Jan 1934 in Minneapolis, Hennepin Co, MN; and Rosella Hartzell, b. 5 Apr 1855 in Portage Co, OH, and d. 17 Jan 1928 in Cleveland, Cuyahoga Co, OH.

2. A sally port is a large gate in a military fort permitting large numbers of troops to make a sortie.

3. "Uncle Peter" was Justice of the Peace Peter Hartzell, b. 8 Aug 1792 in Northampton Co, PA, and d. 26 Mar 1862 in Portage Co, OH. He married Rachel McGowan 19 Dec 1820 in Portage Co, OH. She was b. 23 Aug 1792 and d. 11 Sep 1886 in Portage Co, OH. John Hartzell, b. 26 Oct 1793 in Northampton/Lehigh Co, PA, and d. 1 Sep 1873 in Portage Co, OH, married Margaret Parshall 28 Jan 1841. She was b. 18 Aug 1816 and d. 22 Jan 1912 in Portage Co, OH.

4. This refers to the Old Testament story of Joseph and his coat of many colors. Chapters 42–43 of Genesis deal with the sons of Jacob journeying into Egypt after corn.

5. Hoarhound (or horehound) is a perennial, Old World herb containing a bitter, medicinal juice. Pennyroyal is an herbaceous plant used medically and yielding a pungent aromatic minty oil.

6. Once again JCH is the object of the humor of this passage. It is also a tribute to Aunt Mary's bravery. William Henry Hartzell (Uncle Billy) married Mary Hummell ca. 1805. She was b. Jun 1784 and d. 5 May 1849 in Portage Co, OH.

7. "Weel done cuttie sark"—The quotation is from Robert Burns's "Tam O'Shanter"; a cuttie sark or cutty sark is a Scots short garment, worn in the poem by the witch Nannie.

8. "Your Aunt Lucy" is Lucy A. Hartzell (Frederick, John, George Henry, Conrad Hartzell), b. 2 Jul 1840 and d. 12 Mar 1922, probably in Canton, Stark Co, OH. Lucy is JCH's sister, the fourth child of Frederick and Mary Ickes Hartzell.

9. Cossacks are members of various tribes of Slavic warriors living chiefly in southeast Russia; they often served as border guards. Napoleon began his disastrous Moscow campaign in June 1812.

10. "Walker's old dictionary" is a nineteenth-century word definition dictionary used in rural schools.

11. "Campbellites" was the (sometimes derogatory) name given to the members of the Disciples of Christ Church, cofounded by Alexander Campbell (1788–1866), a U.S. religious leader born in Ireland, and his father, Thomas (1763–1854), who emigrated to the United States in 1807.

12. James A. Garfield (1831–81) is the future twentieth president of the United States.

13. "Captain J. E. MacGowan" is Colonel John Encil MacGowan (Samuel Mc-Gowan/Susan Hartzell, John, George Henry, Conrad Hartzell), b. 30 Sep 1830 and d. 12 Apr 1903 in Chattanooga, TN, where he was editor of the *Chattanooga Times*.

14. The events listed here played roles in the final decision to go to war. "Tawney decision"—Tawney is a misspelling of Chief Justice of the U.S. Supreme Court Roger Taney (pronounced "Tawney"), who in 1857 issued the majority decision that Dred Scott was still a slave. Scott (1795–1858) had been taken as a slave from Missouri to Illinois and Wisconsin, where slavery was prohibited. Returning to Missouri, Scott sued for his liberty, based on residence in free territory. Taney held that Scott was not a U.S. citizen and thus could not sue in a federal court. The decision nullified the Missouri Compromise of 1820, which forbade slavery in Wisconsin, because it deprived persons of their property (i.e., their slaves) without the due process of law. In effect, Taney's decision made slavery legal in all territories.

"Missouri Compromise"—In 1820, Congress passed an act by which Maine was admitted as a free state, Missouri as a slave state; slavery was to be barred from the territory north of the line 36°30' acquired in the Louisiana Purchase. This was the first of many efforts to settle differences between the North and the South and to keep the number of free and slave states equal. The Kansas-Nebraska Act of 1854 repealed the Missouri Compromise.

"Lecompton constitution"—In December 1857, a proslavery constitution for Kansas was passed by the territorial legislature of Lecompton, Kansas. From January to April 1858 Kansans rejected this proslavery constitution, even though President Buchanan asked Congress to admit Kansas under this constitution. Eventually Kansans were allowed another popular vote on the issue, resulting in ratification of an antislavery constitution in October 1859. (Bowman, *Civil War Almanac*, 38–39.)

"Kansas war"—In 1854–55, proslavery and antislavery settlers in the territory of Kansas staked claims and fought each other. In March 1855, elections for a territorial legislature were held with several thousand proslavery Missourians crossing into Kansas to vote. Thus, a proslavery legislature was elected. In October/November 1855, antislavery, free-soil Kansans held their own convention in Topeka and adopted a constitution that banned slavery. Virtual civil war now existed, with frequent armed clashes between the two factions, eventually leading to John Brown's attack at Pottawotomie Creek in May 1856. (ibid., 37–38.)

These events, as well as arguments put forward by defenders of slavery such as George Fitzbugh of Virginia and Senator John C. Calhoun of South Carolina, led to a conviction in the North that the South—and soon the entire country—would be ruled by a ruthless "Slave Power" conspiracy led by Southern slaveholding planters and political leaders determined to convert the whole nation into masters and slaves. Thus, many Northern citizens felt their rights and liberties as freemen were imperiled (Kenneth M. Stamp, ed., *The Causes of the Civil War* [Englewood Cliffs, NJ: Prentice Hall, 1959], 1). As Russel B. Nye, in *Fettered Freedom* ([East Lansing: Michigan State University Press, 1949], 223–31 and 248–49), concludes, "By 1858 a significantly large segment of the population in the North and West was of the opinion that unless the Slave Power was defeated by the abolition of slavery, the nation could no longer exist as a free republic. . . . As the fear of 'black Republicanism' was used by the pro-slavery element in the South to unify opinion, so the threat of the Slave Power became an important factor in consolidating antislavery sentiment in the North." John Rankin asserted that Slave Power already controlled the government, having overthrown the rights of free states and made citizens slaves. The antagonistic principles of slave and free institutions "cannot exist long together—one or the other must fall" (Stamp, *Causes*, 3).

15. The literary societies fostered patriotism and awareness of constitutional issues and trained fine debaters, resulting in future soldiers who were educated beyond their formal schooling. JCH's younger brother Jesse, who served in the 12th Ohio Cavalry, observed in his unpublished "Some Autobiographical Writings by . . . Jesse Hartzell" that a Southern doctor, "a fine old gentleman of the old school," allowed him to peruse his large, private library—"the largest . . . I saw in the South." The doctor, curious about the literary habits of Yankee soldiers, "seemed very much astonished" when Jesse informed him that "most of them had read Scott, Dickens, Hugo, Don Quixote, and all the standard American Historians, such as Prescott and Bancroft."

16. "Your Aunt Lide" is JCH's wife, Louise Ann Lowrie Thompson. JCH refers to letters written by her brothers.

17. "Tommy" is Thomas E. Hartzell, b. 25 Dec 1842 and d. 24 Sep 1844.

18. This is a tribute to the hard-working, honest old cattle drivers before the railroads came. JCH prefers the ways of the past to the present industrial development in eastern Ohio.

19. George Lazarus (Christina, George Henry, Conrad Hartzell), b. 2 Jan 1809 and d. 8 Feb 1897, married Jane Craig 10 Nov 1837. Jane was b. 16 Dec 1811 and d. 6 Apr 1885.

20. Solomon Hartzell (William Henry, George Henry, Conrad Hartzell) was b. 13 Aug 1813 and d. 2 Nov 1897.

21. Henry Hartzell (John, George Henry, Conrad Hartzell) was b. 10 May 1811 and d. 6 Aug 1895.

22. Dorothea Kleinhans, the daughter of George Frederick Kleinhans and Elizabeth Oberly, married John Hartzell (George Henry, Conrad Hartzell) ca. 1792 in Northampton Co, PA. She was b. 21 Apr 1770 and d. 21 Nov 1848.

23. "Ossawattomie John Brown" (1800–1859) was a leader of the radical abolitionist movement who led the attack at Harpers Ferry, where he was captured, tried for treason, and hanged. He epitomized the Southerners' fear of the North's intentions to destroy slavery.

24. "Blue mass"—Blue cohash, a perennial herb of the Eastern United States used medicinally.

25. "Oliver always wanted more"—This is an allusion to Charles Dickens's novel *Oliver Twist*, in which the foundling Oliver commits the unspeakable crime of asking for more gruel during a meal in the workhouse.

Chapter 8

1. "Our old Dutch ancestors" refers to German and Swiss immigrants who came largely to Pennsylvania during the seventeenth and eighteenth centuries, often at the invitation of William Penn.

2. Pennsylvania Dutch ancestors called rising or yeast "sots" and the container a "sots crock." Every household had a sots crock, which was essential in bread making.

3. Stump apple pie is a Pennsylvania Dutch apple pie recipe. The word "stump" perhaps pertains to the thickness of the pie.

4. "Kirby Smith" is Major General (later Lieutenant General) Edmond Kirby Smith, the Confederate commander in eastern Tennessee in 1862.

5. Colonel Albert S. Hall commanded the 105th OVI in 1862. He was promoted to brevet brigadier general 8 Oct 1862, and d. 10 Jul 1863 at Murfreesboro, TN (Tourgée, *Story of a Thousand*, appendix, xi).

6. Second Lieutenant James H. Bard of the 105th OVI, Company C, was promoted to first lieutenant 17 Jan 1863 (ibid., xv, xxx).

7. Indian turnip is also known as Jack in the Pulpit. Its acrid root causes a fire in the mouth that can be put out only by holding apple butter in one's mouth for an hour.

8. "New England primer"—This famous early textbook was used for teaching the alphabet and reading, using woodcuts illustrating simple verses based on Bible stories. First printed in Boston sometime between 1686 and 1690 by Benjamin Harris, *The New England Primer* was reprinted many times, and countless copies were sold through the nineteenth century. *The New England Primer* contained an alphabet with illustrations and verse, hymns, prayers, rules for behavior, and pious stories of martyrs such as John Rogers. The 1749 edition included the children's prayer "Now I Lay Me Down to Sleep" (*Benét's Reader's Encyclopedia*, 3rd ed. [New York: Harper & Row, 1987]).

9. Ephraim Hubbard, b. 1792 and d. 8 Jul 1876, married Mary McGowan, who was b. 2 Oct 1794 and d. 13 Oct 1839. Her father was Adam McGowan.

10. Once again JCH is the butt of humor in this story of a school trial held when several boys disobeyed director Ephraim Hubbard's Rule Eight, which forbade skating at noon when school was in session. Jim Hartzell (Henry, John, George Henry, Conrad Hartzell) was b. 19 Aug 1838 and d. 4 Aug 1925. Jim and JCH had frequent contacts during the war. "Cals" is Caleb Lazarus (Peter Lazarus,

Christina Hartzell, George Henry, Conrad Hartzell), b. 1838 and d. 7 Feb 1865 in the Civil War. "Mart" is Martin Lazarus (Peter Lazarus, Christina Hartzell, George Henry, Conrad Hartzell), b. 1840 and d. 17 Sep 1862 in the Civil War.

11. Sam McGowan (Adam McGowan) was b. 12 Aug 1796 and d. 28 Jul 1860. He married Susan Hartzell 4 Jan 1821. She was b. 3 Jul 1797 and d. 11 Nov 1864. Adam McGowan was b. 10 May 1772 and d. 26 Jan 1858. He married Elizabeth Miller, who was b. 8 Jun 1772 and d. 8 Mar 1846. John McGowan (Adam McGowan) was b. 28 Nov 1806.

12. "Walker Place" probably refers to Dr. Samuel Walker, who married Rebecca McGowan (Adam McGowan), b. 11 Oct 1808, who married again to a Curtis and moved to Kansas. Dr. Walker died 27 Apr 1850 and is buried in Hartzell cemetery.

13. "Uncle Billy" is William Henry Hartzell (George Henry, Conrad Hartzell), b. 16 Aug 1778 and d. 1 Dec 1867.

14. "Crowing and crape"—Boasting and humiliation (the crape of mourning) went hand in hand.

15. *The Western Calculator; or, A New and Compendious System of Practical Arithmetic*, by Joseph Stockton (1779–1832), was first published in Pittsburgh in 1818.

16. "Kirkham's" is the popular nineteenth-century grammar textbook used in the school, *English Grammar in Familiar Lectures*, by Samuel Kirkham. Abraham Lincoln used the same text to teach himself grammar in 1830, at the age of twenty-one ("Abraham Lincoln," edited by Ida Tarbell, *McClure's Magazine* 6, no. 2 [January 1896]: 120). Somewhat ironic is the fact that JCH's writing skills are quite good and not a "mystery," as he claims here.

17. A kerchy is a curtsy.

18. "We roused the Romans" is possibly a reference to the popular recitation piece, "Horatius," from *Lays of Ancient Rome* (1842), by Thomas Babington Macaulay (1800–1859). "The boy stood on the burning deck" is the first line of "Casabianca" (1829), by Felicia Hemans, long popular for school recitations. "Oh! were you ne'er a school-boy, / And did you never train, / And feel that swelling of the heart / You ne'er can feel again?" is the opening of a poem widely disseminated in JCH's youth through *McGuffey's Eclectic Second Reader*, by William H. McGuffey. In the 1848 edition (*McGuffey's Newly Revised Eclectic Second Reader: Containing Progressive Lessons in Reading and Spelling*, published in Cincinnati by Winthrop B. Smith), the poem, titled "Young Soldiers," appears on pages 98–99. It is perhaps worth noting that the same poem is quoted in other contemporary sources, including a letter of May 18, 1864, by a fellow Ohio recruit, Private Henry S. Chapin (Company F, 144th OVI), originally published in the *Perrysburg Journal*, June 1, 1864, and available in a transcription on the Bowling Green State University Center for Archival Collections website (http://www .bgsu.edu/colleges/library/cac/transcripts/mms1585c.html).

19. Sulphur, red precipitate, and fine-tooth combs were used to control lice and the itch they caused. Red precipitate is red mercuric oxide used as a local antibacterial agent (*Dorland's Illustrated Medical Dictionary*, 24th ed. [Philadelphia: W. B. Sanders, 1965], 900, 1211).

20. "Gad and ferule"—A gad is a goad or pointed stick for driving cattle. A ferule is a rod, cane, or flat piece of wood (such as a ruler) used for punishing children, especially by striking them on the hand.

21. "Bunker Hill and Valley Forge"—Bunker Hill was the first major battle of the American Revolution on June 17, 1775. Valley Forge was a village in southeastern Pennsylvania that served as General Washington's army winter quarters in 1777–78 amid much suffering and hardship. "La Fayette" is the Marquis de Lafayette, a French statesman who served (1777–81) the American cause during the Revolutionary War as a major general in Washington's army. "The Swamp Fox" is Francis Marion (1732?–95), an American Revolutionary soldier who earned the name Swamp Fox because of his skill in using Indian tactics in retreating to swamps and forests after quick and effective raids on British forces. "Paul Jones" is John Paul Jones (1747–92), the famous American naval officer during the Revolutionary War. "Constitution and Guerriere"—The USS *Constitution*, popularly known as "Old Ironsides," was an American 44-gun frigate famous for its exploits in the War of 1812, including the capture of the frigate HMS *Guerrière* on August 19, 1812. JCH asserts here that schools teaching events such as this helped instill patriotism in their students.

22. Egg pudding is a Pennsylvania Dutch breakfast dish similar to the German griddle cake "durch und unter" and the Austrian "Kaiserschmarren."

23. "Sim"—This is possibly a typographical error for Jim. It could also refer to Simeon F. Hartzell (Abraham, George Henry, Conrad Hartzell), b. 30 Sep 1820, and d. 22 Aug 1897. Another possibility is Simon Hartzell (Henry, John, George Henry, Conrad Hartzell), b. 31 Dec 1827; and d. 21 Jun 1917. Since Jim Hartzell is a contemporary of JCH's, Simeon Hartzell, eighteen years older, fits the context of this passage better.

24. "Aunt Lucy" is Lucy A. Hartzell, who is JCH's sister.

25. "Dave Hartzell's" refers to David Hartzell (Jacob, George Henry, Conrad Hartzell), b. 20 Oct 1807, d. 2 Jul 1881, and married Elizabeth Linton 30 May 1833.

26. "Your Uncle Bob" is James Robert Hartzell (Frederick, John, George Henry, Conrad Hartzell), JCH's brother and ninth child of Frederick and Mary Ickes Hartzell. He was b. 22 Jan 1852 and d. Jan 1934 in Minneapolis, Hennepin Co, MN. Uncle Bob was named after James Robertson, a frequent visitor in the Frederick Hartzell home.

27. James Robertson's theology was that of John Calvin (1509–64), a French Protestant reformer. Calvin's doctrine had a great influence, especially among the Puritans of England, Scotland, and America. His pessimistic doctrine of the total depravity of men led to a repressive attitude toward pleasure.

28. John Wesley (1703–91), English evangelist and theologian, is best known as the founder of Methodism.

29. Alexander Campbell (1788–1866), a U.S. religious leader born in Ireland, cofounded the Disciples of Christ in 1830 with his father, Thomas (1763–1854), a Presbyterian minister who emigrated to the United States in 1807. The Disciples of Christ are often referred to as Campbellites.

30. "Howling Methodies" refers to the vocal quality of Methodist worship as well as its methodical nature. "Kamalites" is a corruption of "Campbellites." The

adjective "watherey," apparently a dialect form of "watery/wathery," probably refers to the Disciples' usual practice of baptism by immersion.

31. "Death and Doctor Hornbrook"—See chapter 4, note 19. JCH here accounts for his fondness for the works of Robert Burns, which he quotes frequently in these memoirs.

32. The Cleveland and Pittsburgh Railroad, chartered in 1836, opened from Cleveland to Hudson, OH, in 1851.

33. The Underground Railroad station on Frederick Hartzell's farm was part of an organized secret system for transporting slaves to freedom in Canada before the Civil War. The system was supported by Northern abolitionists, many of whom were Quakers. Samuel McGowan maintained another station in the system in his new residence in Orland, IN.

34. This account of a "Manual Labor School in Athens County . . . open to both white and black" may be unique in that there may be no other memoir by a white student attending an integrated school in the North before the Civil War. Because of homesickness, JCH's experience was not a good one.

35. "Your Aunt Lide" is Louise Ann Lowrie Thompson, who married JCH 16 Aug 1865.

36. JCH recalls that Josiah's "head was just about as vacant" as his own, despite his elder brother's superior education. This passage again shows JCH's sibling rivalry.

37. "Sometime . . . in the spring of the next year" would be the spring of 1856. "Your Father, Mother, John MacGowan and Aunt Melvina came"—Josiah Hartzell married Mary K. Johnson (b. 28 Oct 1833 in Stark Co, OH, and d. 16 Aug 1911 in Canton, Stark Co, OH) 21 Feb 1856. John MacGowan is John Encil MacGowan, b. 30 Sep 1830 and d. 12 Apr 1903. He married Maria Melvina Johnson 30 Oct 1855. This is Aunt Melvina, b. ca. 1835 and d. 2 Dec 1896.

38. "Uncle Jonas Hartzell" is Jonas Hartzell (John, George Henry, Conrad Hartzell), b. 19 Oct 1803 in Northampton/Lehigh Co, PA, and d. Aug 1884 in Davenport, Scott Co, IA. Jonas was a Campbellite preacher.

39. The chime is the edge or rim of a cask.

Chapter 9

1. The first railroad bridge across the Mississippi River was completed April 22, 1856. It was a five-span wooden bridge that connected Rock Island, IL, to Davenport, IA.

2. The sidewheeler *Effie Afton* ran into a pier of the Rock Island Railroad Bridge over the Mississippi River on the night of May 6, 1856. Two years later, Abraham Lincoln was retained by the Rock Island Railroad Company to defend it against the steamboat owner's charges that the bridge was a public nuisance. The jury decision was split, but the case was a decisive turning point in Lincoln's career.

3. Trot lines are lines with fish hooks attached at intervals.

4. JCH is correct in stating that Billy's army affiliation was with the 65th OVI.

5. Wilbur was b. 22 Nov 1856 in Davenport, Scott Co, IA.

6. "Hartzell Shafer" is Hartzell John Schaeffer (Mary, John, George Henry, Conrad Hartzell), b. 20 Oct 1832 and d. betw. 1907 and 1922. He married Mary Ellen Taylor 20 Oct 1857 in Mahoning Co, OH.

7. "Uncle John, his oldest brother" is John Hartzell (John, George Henry, Conrad Hartzell), b. 26 Oct 1792 in Northampton/Lehigh Co, PA, and d. 1 Sep 1873.

8. "Riving great trees to flinders" means splitting trees into splinters or small fragments.

9. The number of Hartzell/MacGowan first cousins fighting in the Civil War for the North is truly remarkable. JCH's list is incomplete. Actually, at least eighteen first cousins fought in the war. Samuel McGowan had four sons in the war. John Encil MacGowan (1830–1903) enlisted as a private in 1860 and mustered out a colonel in 1865 (brevetted Brigadier General). Richard Eli McGowan (1835–99) was a captain and quartermaster. Jonas Hartzell McGowan (1837–1909) later served in the U.S. House of Representatives. In addition, George McGowan served for one year. John McGowan had two sons who served in the war—Irenus and Melitus (25 Feb 1841–7 Feb 1936). Both were captured at Chickamauga. Irenus was a second lieutenant and Melitus an orderly sergeant. Of the Hartzells, there were Adam Hartzell (Jacob, John, George Henry, Conrad Hartzell), b. Mar 1831, and his brothers Seth, b. 22 Jul 1834 and a member of the 2nd Iowa Cavalry unit, and Joshua, b. Feb 1845 and d. ca. 1910 in San Bernardino Co, CA; Jim Hartzell (Henry, John, George Henry Hartzell), b. 19 Aug 1838 and d. 4 Aug 1925, who attained the rank of first lieutenant; Jess Hartzell, JCH's brother, b. 21 Jan 1845 and d. 7 Feb 1937, who was a member of the 12th Ohio Cavalry and wrote a brief memoir of his experience; and the author of this memoir, JCH, who served in the 105th OVI as captain and commander of company H. Additionally there were four Lazarus first cousins who served in the war—William Lazarus (Joseph Lazarus, Christina Hartzell, George Henry Hartzell), b. 1836 and d. 1865 in the Civil War; Orrin Lazarus (Sarah Hartzell/Joseph Lazarus, John Hartzell, George Henry Hartzell), b. 1844 and d. before 1890 in Soldiers and Sailors Home; Caleb Lazarus (Peter Lazarus, Christina Hartzell, George Henry, Conrad Hartzell), b. 1838 and d. 7 Feb 1863 in the war; and Caleb's brother Martin, b. 1840 and d. 17 Sep 1862 in the war. There were also first cousins William Craig (Catherine Hartzell/Thomas Craig, George, George Henry, Conrad Hartzell), b. 1841 in Berlin Twp, Trumbull/Mahoning Co, OH, and d. 1863 in the war, and Levi Strong (Christina Lazarus/Alonzo Strong, Christina Hartzell, George Henry Hartzell), b. 1835 and d. Aug 1864 in Andersonville Prison, GA.

10. JCH believes that the worth and dignity of the individual—one of the hallmarks of the nineteenth century in the United States of America—had greatly diminished by the turn of the century and that America was now dominated by the machine.

11. It was a common practice, especially in mideastern states, to elect company officers.

12. "Kirby Smith" is Major General Edmund Kirby Smith, a prominent Confederate general, in command of East Tennessee and later the Trans-Mississippi Department (which became known as Kirby Smithdom) (Bowman, *Civil War Almanac*, 379).

13. "Generals Morgan, Baird" are Brigadier General George W. Morgan, Seventh Division commander in the Fourteenth Corps, and General Absolom Baird, who was also division commander in the Fourteenth. Morgan guarded the "Cumberland Gap" in 1861–62 (Gerald I. Prokopowicz, *All for the Regiment: The Army of the Ohio, 1861–1862* [Chapel Hill: University of North Carolina Press, 2001], 95, 118, 137, 141).

14. General Braxton Bragg was a leading, but frequently indecisive, general for the South, who antagonized his fellow Confederate leaders. He commanded the Army of Tennessee through 1863 and the Chattanooga siege (Bowman, *Civil War Almanac*, 315–16).

15. "Colonel" is Colonel Albert Hall, commander of the 105th Ohio regiment (Prokopowicz, *All for the Regiment*, 179).

16. Henry Clay (1777–1852) was an American statesman from Kentucky. He served in the House of Representatives (Speaker 1811–20, 1823–25) and the U.S. Senate (1831–42, 1849–52). He was secretary of state under President John Quincy Adams. He was an unsuccessful presidential candidate in 1824, 1832, and 1844. Devoted to preserving the Union, he was largely responsible for the passage of the Compromise of 1850.

17. "Formed in line of battle"—Gerald Prokopowicz notes that "the training of the Army of the Ohio consisted almost exclusively of close order drill, performed by individual regiments. Little training took place at higher organizational levels. By emphasizing the perfection of small-unit drill, [General Don Carlos] Buell improved the efficiency of individual regiments, but did nothing to encourage soldiers to see themselves as members of any larger entity" (*All for the Regiment*, 46–47). Four to eight hours of drill daily prepared men to fight. Close order drill, repeated endlessly, taught the required battle movements so thoroughly that soldiers obeyed commands automatically, even when instincts of self-preservation otherwise would cause them to seek safety (47–48). "The most common formation," Prokopowicz observes, "used for dress parade as well as in combat, was the 'line of battle,' two ranks deep" (49). It allowed every soldier to fire his weapon simultaneously, resulting in maximum firepower. Regiments could quickly form into several battle columns: by companies (one company wide and twenty ranks deep); by divisions (two companies wide, ten ranks deep), or, for road marches, by route (four men abreast and up to two hundred ranks). "Much time was spent . . . learning to deploy rapidly from column into line and back again" (49).

18. A thill is one of a pair of shafts of a vehicle; between which a draft animal would be harnessed to pull it.

19. "General Terrell" is Brigadier General William R. Terrill, who was killed 8 Oct 1862 in the Battle of Perryville.

20. Robert Wilson, captain of Company H, 105th OVI, a veteran of the Mexican War, d. 8 Oct 1862 at Perryville. JCH assumed command of the company.

21. "Frank Mansfield" is Ira Franklin Mansfield, b. 27 Jun 1842 in Poland, Geauga Co, OH. He served three terms in the Pennsylvania state senate.

22. Brigadier General Jefferson C. Davis is best known for shooting and killing General William Nelson in the lobby of the Galt House Hotel in response to Nelson's slapping Davis. Davis had demanded that Nelson apologize for some past in-

sult, but he refused. Most supported Davis and felt Nelson deserved his fate. Davis was never brought to trial. JCH, during the battle of Chickamauga, disobeyed Davis's order to attack a Confederate brigade, choosing to protect his wagon train instead.

23. "Butternuts" is a term for Confederates, so named from their use of the oily nut of the American tree of the walnut family for dyeing their uniforms.

24. "General Starkweather" is Colonel John C. Starkweather. An inexperienced regiment, the 21st Wisconsin, was placed in the cornfield that JCH mentions here. See Prokopowicz's account of these actions, *All for the Regiment*, 176–77.

25. "Brigadier-General Correll" is probably Brigadier General William R. Terrill, commander of the Thirty-third Brigade, which included the 105th OVI. Terrill previously was captain of Company H, 5th Artillery, before General Buell promoted him to brigadier general (ibid., 37).

26. "The Colonel" is Albert S. Hall of the 105th OVI.

27. "Our Captain" is Robert Wilson. "The First Lieutenant" is William H. Clark (Tourgée, *Story of a Thousand*, appendix, xxiv). Second Lieutenant Hartzell, with neither training nor experience, was made commander of Company H, 105th OVI, but without promotion in rank. (He was promoted to first lieutenant 13 Jan 1863 and to captain 8 Sep 1864.)

28. Captain Byron W. Canfield of Company E, 105th OVI, was wounded 8 Oct 1862 at Perryville (ibid., xxxvii).

29. General Don Carlos Buell, commander of the Army of the Ohio until removed after Perryville in 1862, was a solid general who was arguably a victim of politically motivated officials (Bowman, *Civil War Almanac*, 318–19).

30. "Colonel Stratten" is Henry G. (Gran) Stratton, commander of Company C of the 19th OVI at this time and wounded at Stones River.

31. General William Starkie Rosecrans (known as "Old Rosey") was given command of the Army of the Cumberland in October 1862. He became involved in a quarrel with his superiors in Washington over whether he was pursuing Bragg aggressively enough. When his forces were decisively defeated by Bragg at Chickamauga in September 1863, Rosecrans was relieved of his command. Later historians came to regard Rosecrans as one of the better strategists on either side (Bowman, *Civil War Almanac*, 371).

32. Lieutenant Colonel William R. Tolles of the 105th OVI had been promoted from captain of Company B, 41st OVI.

33. JCH's dislike of "critter companies" (cavalry) from either side was quite typical of infantrymen. Consequently his company practiced forming hollow squares, "in which movement we became very efficient," in order to "guard against surprise and resist cavalry." Company H became proficient at tactics and drill through hard practice.

34. "Country pumpkin roller"—This may be for "country bumpkin," a term for an awkward, clumsy yokel. A "roller" is possibly a roly-poly, pudgy person.

35. "Contentments of outlying troops" means the quartering of troops.

36. Sibley tents, invented by Henry Hopkins Sibley (*The Civil War*, ed. Robert Paul Jordan [New York: National Geographic Society, 1969], 80–81), were conical

tents, thirteen feet high and eighteen feet in diameter, which proved to be superior to the older and much more crowded bell and wedge tents and resulted in a dramatic decrease in sickness (Prokopowicz, *All for the Regiment*, 86–87). Each company received three to five Sibley tents in 1862. Men slept "spoon" fashion in these tents. They would roll over in unison when someone yelled "Spoon!" (Jordan, *Civil War*, 87).

37. "Seven-league boots"—In Arthurian legend, seven-league boots (invented by the wizard Merlin) allowed the wearer to stride seven leagues (about twenty-one miles) in a single step.

38. "Route step" is "with four men abreast and as many as two hundred ranks" (Prokopowicz, *All for the Regiment*, 49).

39. Ambrose C. Mason (1840–64), promoted from first lieutenant to captain of Company C, 105th OVI, 14 Mar 1863, d. 27 Aug 1864 at East Point, GA (Tourgée, *Story of a Thousand*, 300).

40. "Month of December"—The year is 1862.

Chapter 10

1. In the Fifth Division, under Brigadier General Joseph J. Reynolds, Colonel Albert S. Hall of the 105th OVI replaced Brigadier General William Terrill, killed at Perryville October 8, 1862, as commander of the First (late Thirty-third) Brigade, which included the 80th and 123rd Illinois and the 101st Indiana in addition to the 105th Ohio. For information on Terrill's military career, see note 25 to chapter 9.

2. Stones River, the site of the battle near Murfreesboro, TN, is often referred to in contemporary accounts as Stone River. The battle between the Confederate Army of Tennessee, led by General Braxton Bragg, and the Union Army of the Cumberland, under Major General William S. Rosecrans, occurred December 31, 1862–January 2, 1863.

3. See note 2 to this chapter; the battle at Stones River actually lasted three days.

4. For information on Colonel Gran Stratton, see note 30 to chapter 9.

5. Captain James McCleery was commander of Company A, 41st OVI. "Major Wolcott" cannot be positively identified from the roster of the 41st OVI, though he is possibly Lieutenant Harlan P. Wolcott, Company K, 41st OVI.

6. "Captain Erwin" cannot be identified from the roster of the 19th OVI, reproduced at http://www.mahoningvalleycwrt.com/Regiments/19th.asp.

7. In this, JCH is at least partially mistaken. Captain James McCleery survived the war, attaining the rank of brevet brigadier general, and later served as a congressman from Louisiana.

8. Colonel James P. Brownlow commanded the 1st East Tennessee Cavalry, one company of which acted as guides for the 105th OVI.

9. JCH's memory is faulty on this point: Captain Samuel J. Harris commanded the 19th Indiana Light Artillery Battery, not the 10th.

10. A shindy is a skirmish.

11. Lieutenant Daniel B. Stambaugh of Company A, 105th OVI, was promoted to captain 24 Mar 1864 (Tourgée, *Story of a Thousand*, app., xxix).

12. JCH quotes Robert Burns's poem "To a Mouse."

13. The following paragraphs describe the action that took place at Vaught's Hill, near Milton, March 20, 1863.

14. A parrot (properly Parrott) is a field artillery piece, named after its designer Robert Parker Parrott (1804–77). His first rifled cannon design, a 10-pounder (2.9-inch calibre), was turned out in 1860. He also developed the 20-pounder (3.67-inch calibre) and 30-pounder (4.2-inch calibre) versions, among other models.

15. Lieutenant William P. Stackhouse ("Stack") of the 19th Indiana Light Artillery Battery commanded a field artillery piece, or Parrott, during the battle of Milton (Vaught's Hill).

16. Grape is cast iron cannonballs.

17. Captain Ambrose C. Mason was from Company C, 105th OVI (see note 39 to chapter 9); there was in fact no "Company R." JCH calls Mason "the rascal" because he laughs "shamefully" at JCH as he dodges bullets while Mason has "his back to a big rock."

18. "Uncle Dan" is Captain Daniel B. Stambaugh, commander of Company A.

19. "Gillies at Bannockburn"—Gillies are guides for sportsmen or male attendants of a Scottish Highland chief. Bannockburn, in central Scotland, is the site of the defeat (1314) of the English by the Scots led by Robert the Bruce.

20. John Hunt Morgan led the Confederate cavalry unit that became famous as "Morgan's Raiders." Beginning in 1862, Morgan led a series of harassing raids in Kentucky, Mississippi, Tennessee, Indiana, and Ohio, culminating in the December 1862 raid at Hartsville, TN, where they captured 1,700 federals. Then in June 1863 he led 2,000 men on a 1,100-mile jaunt into Ohio where Morgan was finally captured and imprisoned. Escaping four months later, he continued raids in Kentucky and Tennessee, and while making a raid at Greenville, TN, in September 1864, was killed by Union troops (Bowman, *Civil War Almanac*, 360–61). For an account of Morgan's Raiders, see JCH's first cousin John Encil MacGowan's "Morgan's Indiana and Ohio Raid," in *Annals of the War Written by Leading Participants, North and South* (Dayton, OH, 1988), 750–69.

21. This line is from Joel Chandler Harris's *Uncle Remus, His Songs and His Sayings* (1880), a famous book of folk tales. Uncle Remus, an old black servant, tells a young white boy stories based on traditional tales of his race. Many of the characters are animals given human qualities, especially speech. These fables Harris himself heard as a boy are excellent examples of dialect (as quoted in this passage by JCH) and regional writing.

22. JCH has telescoped some events in this paragraph. Colonel Albert S. Hall died of disease 10 Jul 1863, at Murfreesboro, TN. JCH was promoted from second lieutenant to first lieutenant 13 Jan 1893. William R. Tuttle was promoted from first lieutenant of Company E to captain of Company H 8 Oct 1862, after Captain Robert Wilson's death at Perryville, and was detailed as assistant provost marshal to General Sherman's staff (Tourgée, *Story of a Thousand*, app., xxxii).

23. Ira Mansfield was promoted from first sergeant to second lieutenant 12 Feb 1863 (ibid.).

24. William R. Tolles, captain of Company B, 41st OVI, was promoted to lieutenant colonel, 105th OVI, 9 Aug 1862; then to colonel, 19 Jul 1863 (ibid., xi).

25. James E. Murdock, a famous nineteenth-century public speaker, was a guest of General Philip H. Sheridan after the loss of Murdock's son at Missionary Ridge. His reading of the third chapter of John impressed JCH.

26. General James A. Garfield, future president of the United States, and John Encil MacGowan, JCH's first cousin, son of Samuel McGowan, visited JCH in camp while he was still in hospital.

27. Jerry Whetstone was the tallest soldier in the 105th OVI. Tourgée, in a picture caption in *The Story of a Thousand* (8), gives Whetstone's height as six feet seven inches and claims that he is the tallest man in the Army of the Cumberland.

28. Champing is a vigorous chewing or biting movement by animals with jaws and teeth as in champing at the bit, showing impatience.

29. The Grand Review was held May 23–24, 1865, in Washington, D.C., before the White House reviewing stand, to honor the victorious defenders of the North. The Army of the Potomac veterans marched on May 23. William T. Sherman's army marched along the same route the next day, their more casual array in sharp contrast to the polished Army of the Potomac (*Civil War*, 307–9; Bowman, *Civil War Almanac*, 268). JCH was able to rejoin his comrades of Company H during the Grand Review.

30. General John Fulton Reynolds (1820–63) was at this time commanding the First Corps, Army of the Potomac.

31. "Whetstone and Silver"—Whetstone is Jeremiah Whetstone, Company H, and Silver is either Private Allen Silver or Corporal Jason W. Silver, both of Company H.

32. "Our Major" is (depending on the date) either George T. Perkins, promoted to lieutenant colonel 10 Jul 1863, or Charles G. Edwards, promoted to major to replace him (Tourgée, *Story of a Thousand*, app., xi).

33. "Sharp" here refers to a sharpshooter. Colonel Hiram Berdan commanded the 1st Regiment of U.S. Sharpshooters, better known as Berdan's Sharpshooters. Selected marksmen, riflemen with great accuracy, were armed with the 52-caliber Sharps rifles, many with telescopic sights.

34. The campaign against the Confederate position at Tullahoma, TN, opened June 24, 1863. According to Tourgée's account, the 105th OVI entered Tullahoma July 1 without firing a shot (*Story of a Thousand*, 204).

35. "Pappy Thomas," General George H. Thomas, distinguished himself during the Battle of Chickamauga as the "Rock of Chickamauga" and thereafter assumed command of the Army of Tennessee.

36. Words are missing from the text here. The context suggests that the probable missing words are "candle holder."

37. The Bessemer process makes steel from pig iron in a blast furnace. The process is named after English engineer Sir Henry Bessemer (1818–98).

38. General John B. Turchin was brigade commander in JCH's division. Turchin's discipline was rather lax compared to Colonel Edward King's in the 105th OVI. Turchin allowed his troops to freely take of the spoils of the land.

39. These insects were probably lice.

40. "Jiggers" is a variant spelling of "chiggers," six-legged larval mites that suck blood and cause intense irritation and infection.

Chapter 11

1. Minnies are minié balls, rifle bullets used in muzzle-loading firearms.

2. "That's our Harris" probably refers to Captain Samuel J. Harris, commander of the 19th Indiana Light Artillery Battery.

3. The victories at Gettysburg and Vicksburg, July 3 and July 4, 1863, respectively, boosted the morale of the Northern troops.

4. The two quotations are from the popular song "Home Again" (see note 3 to chapter 4) and "When Johnny Comes Marching Home," a Civil War song written by Patrick Sarsfield Gilmore, an Irish immigrant and band leader from Boston whose band enlisted in the Union army. Sheet music for the song was first published by Henry Tolman and Company of Boston in 1863 under the pseudonym Louis Lambert.

5. Parrotts and Rodmans are examples of artillery that accompanied the field army. The most productive siege gun was the thirty-pounder Parrott, used by Union troops—4.2-inch bore firing a twenty-nine-pound projectile 2,200 yards and capable of great destructive power. JCH errs in calling the Parrotts smoothbores; they were rifled, which resulted in greater range and accuracy. Rodmans were of greater caliber, up to twenty inches, and the heaviest of the mobile guns. They were named after Thomas Jefferson Rodman (1815–71), who devised a special method of casting that strengthened the gun barrel. The most effective light artillery weapon used by the Union was the smoothbore twelve-pounder "Napoleon" model of 1857 (Bowman, *Civil War Almanac*, 294–96). An identical six-pound howitzer was also popular. Crews for these artillery weapons ranged from five to seven members. For a detailed discussion see "Weapons of the Civil War," ibid., 279–98.

6. Tourgée records that the 105th OVI began its march from Shell Mound over the Sand mountains on September 4 and was in position on Lookout Mountain September 8, when Bragg evacuated Chattanooga. Tourgée bitterly reviles Rosecrans for ordering the Army of the Cumberland to pursue an attack against the protests of General George H. Thomas (*Story of a Thousand*, 207–17).

7. A scap is evidently a hive; the word occurs in other nineteenth-century sources, but not in modern dictionaries.

8. "My friend Stambaugh" is Captain Dan Stambaugh, commander of Company A, 105th OVI. JCH refers to him as "Uncle Dan" several times.

9. Regimental bands played a key role on both sides during the Civil War. Not only did these bands boost morale, entertain, and provided the cadences for close order drill as regiments marched into battle. At the outset of war, each Union brigade was authorized a twenty-four-piece band; each regiment a sixteen-piece band. General Sherman especially loved bands and expected them to play under fire on numerous occasions. In return, he rewarded them with the best of instruments and fancy uniforms. For a discussion of regimental bands and their role in the Civil War, see William Rosengren, "Regimental Bands in the Civil War," *Journal of American & Comparative Cultures* 24.2 (2001): 191–205. In this incident described by JCH, the regimental band assisted the movement of heavy artillery over rugged terrain. Alice MacGowan, in her novel *Sword in the Mountains*,

borrowed this scene to describe Seacrest's wagon train descending a mountain (261–63).

10. JCH here describes the difficulty of putting into words feelings and emotions of great complexity and depth. The stakes were high for the Union. If the Union were to lose control of the eastern theater of the war, it could very well be the turning point leading to potential Confederate victory.

11. This passage was also borrowed by Alice MacGowan and incorporated into *Sword in the Mountains*, 339–40.

12. Colonel Charles E. Manderson is the commander of the 19th OVI. Lt. Colonel James M. Nash, Colonel Gran Stratton and the others listed also served on Manderson's staff. Stratton replaced Manderson as commander later.

13. The Man of Destiny is Napoleon Bonaparte (1769–1821), Emperor of France (1809–15), who was born in Corsica and had an outstanding military career.

14. The reference is to Lew Wallace's popular novel, *Ben-Hur: The Tale of the Christ* (1880). The novel's main character, Jewish Judah Ben-Hur, is converted to Christianity. The climactic scene of the book is a chariot race with his betrayer, Messala, whose Roman backers cheer him on with calls of "Jove with us!" Wallace (1837–1905) served in the Union army, rising to the rank of major general.

15. Union officers Major General Gordon Granger and Brigadier General James Steedman played a major role in protecting Snodgrass Hill during the Battle of Chickamauga (*Civil War Battlefield Guide*, 154).

16. JCH lists the Confederate commanders at the Battle of Chickamauga (September 18–20, 1863): Lt. General James Longstreet, Major General Joseph B. Kershaw, Colonel Daniel Chevilette Govan, Major General Simon B. Buckner, Brigadier General Edward C. Walthall, Major General John B. Hood, Major General Thomas C. Hindman, and Brigadier General William B. Bate; Colonel Colquitt is either Peyton H. Colquitt of Brigadier General States R. Gist's brigade or John W. Colquitt of General Lucius E. Polk's brigade.

17. Next JCH lists Union commanders during the Battle of Chickamauga: Major General George H. Thomas ("The Rock of Chickamauga"); Brigadier General Absolom Baird; Brigadier General Horatio Van Cleve, division commander; Brigadier General Thomas J. Wood; Colonel Ferdinand VanDerveer; Major General John Basil Turchin; Major General Thomas L. Crittenden, commander of the First Corps; Brigadier General John Brannan, division commander; Major General Joseph J. (Joe) Reynolds, JCH's division commander; and Colonel Edward A. King, commander of the Second Brigade.

18. In this paragraph, JCH gives his readers another perspective—that of 1896, when Chickamauga has become a national park (through the efforts of former general Ferdinand VanDerveer) and there are monuments pointing out significant battle sites.

19. This story of JCH's confrontation with General Jeff C. Davis is difficult to verify, since no official report was ever filed for Colonel King's brigade because of his death.

20. Such compliments ("who were certainly fine fellows") as paid to the Confederates by JCH might be considered disloyal, but were a common phenomenon during the Civil War, when truces were frequently held, materials such as tobacco,

trinkets, and food were exchanged, and opposing regimental bands contested with their music. William Rosengren attempts to explain this as behavior of a "prismatic" society soon to shift to an "urban/industrial" society: a prismatic society is much more individualistic while urban society is socialistic in emphasis ("Regimental Bands," 191–205). Thus, JCH could appreciate Confederates while otherwise condemning their racial and disunionist beliefs.

21. "World's Fair" is the World's Columbian Exposition of 1893, which was held in Chicago, IL.

22. Longstreet and Kershaw are two of the major Confederate commanders in the Battle of Chickamauga; see note 16 to this chapter.

23. "Fort Negly" apparently does not refer to the well-known Fort Negley at Nashville. After Union forces captured Nashville in 1862, they heavily fortified the city. The largest fort, to the south of the city, was Fort Negley, named for U.S. General James Scott Negley, provost marshal and commander of Federal forces in Nashville. Under the direction of army engineer Captain James S. Morton, the Union army and a force of mostly black laborers completed construction December 7, 1862.

24. Note that here JCH gives slavery as "the cause of this war," but elsewhere he indicates that the preservation of the Union was the major cause of the war. For Henry Clay (1777–1852), see note 16 to chapter 9.

Chapter 12

1. "Gray stragglers" are again probably lice.

2. JCH refers to the practice of exchanges between Union and Confederate pickets, when they "are good and friendly." Reading Charleston, Richmond, or New Orleans papers would give Union soldiers a Confederate viewpoint on the war.

3. The visitors include Captain William Wallace, Company I; Captain Ambrose Mason, Company C; and First Lieutenant Albion W. Tourgée, Company G. Judge Albion Tourgée was not only the author of an account of the 105th OVI, *The Story of a Thousand,* but also a popular novelist; his best-known novel was *A Fool's Errand.* Captain E. Abbott Spaulding, commander of Company E, 105th OVI, d. 26 Sep 1863 at Chattanooga.

4. The grand reserve, as the basic unit, is regimental in size. JCH describes here in detail the military tactics employed via close order drill by the Union in the event of an attack.

5. Charlie Fowler, surgeon for the 105th OVI, was taken prisoner to Libby, but did survive the war.

6. JCH treats Willie, JCH's nephew Wilbur, as Dick Cobb's companion in this dramatic context. In response to a request from Wilbur to complete the story of Dick Cobb, JCH provided an addendum to his manuscript in the form of a letter to his nephew dated April 22, 1898; it is printed at the end of the memoirs.

7. The women are probably volunteers from either the Christian Commission or the Sanitary Commission. Both were aid societies that cared for the wounded and provided food at railroad station drop-offs. When in war zones, they often put

themselves in harm's way. The organizations were quite competitive rather than cooperative, according to JCH.

8. For "Fort Negly," see note 23 to chapter 11.

9. A strong skirmish line was another military tactic used by both sides. Gerald Prokopowicz observes that some regiments supplemented close order drill training with skirmish (open order) drill consisting of skirmish lines with soldiers singly or in small groups spaced several yards apart, usually placed some distance in advance of the main body of the regiment. Since skirmishers operated outside the control of regimental commanders, they learned to respond to bugle or drum commands. The importance of skirmishers became clear by late 1862 and the tactic was used increasingly thereafter (Prokopowicz, *All for the Regiment*, 50).

10. Captain Marshall W. Wright was quartermaster of the 105th OVI.

11. "General VanderVeer" is Colonel Ferdinand VanDerveer, commander of the Second Brigade.

12. The 9th OVI was the first all-German unit in the Union army. Its commander was Colonel Robert Latimer McCook, who was later replaced by Colonel Gustav Kämmerling. (JCH's spelling of their names is inaccurate.)

13. "Our cracker line"—During this siege the Union supply line has been cut off. Rumors have it that Lincoln (Father Abraham) is sending help. JCH is keenly aware of the high stakes involved. Defeat at Chattanooga will be a disaster for the North.

14. "Uncle Fred" is JCH's father, Frederick Hartzell.

15. JCH's comments on endowed professors, lawyers, and politicians are particularly bitter here, perhaps the hardest-hitting comments in the autobiography.

16. Major Charles G. Edwards is a staff officer of the 105th; see note 32 to chapter 10.

17. "My old toad sticker"—This refers to JCH's old sabre.

18. "Old Colonel Hammerling" and "Colonel Kammarling," probably refer to the same person, Colonel Gustav Kämmerling, a commander of the 9th Ohio. Josephine Hartzell, when typing copies, was working with a handwritten manuscript, which probably accounts for some of these errors, but JCH's spelling is no doubt erratic, as he was writing mainly from memory.

20. Kinnikinnick tobacco is a mixture of dried leaves, bark, and sometimes tobacco smoked by Indians and pioneers, especially in the Ohio Valley. The leaf commonly used was from the redosier dogwood, noted for its bright-colored yellow or red bark. Native Americans called redosier dogwood kinnikinnick.

21. Colonel John T. Wilder commanded the brigade charged with chasing down Morgan's cavalry in the winter of 1862/63. Because he had only regular infantry, he sought and, in February 1863, obtained permission to mount his infantry units, which became known as the Lightning Brigade.

22. "Crittenden of the first corps" is Major General Thomas L. Crittenden, actually commander of the Twenty-first Corps during the Battle of Chickamauga.

23. "Bush-whackers" are Confederate guerrillas, so named for making their way through dense woods by cutting at undergrowth and branches.

24. Colonel Emerson Opdycke was succeeded as commander of the 125th OVI by Lieutenant Colonel Joseph Bruff.

25. "Old Joe Hooker" was Major General Joseph Hooker (1814–79), commander of the Army of the Potomac. A graduate of West Point, he was defeated by rivalries among Union generals more often than by enemy forces (Bowman, *Civil War Almanac*, 345).

26. "Pat juba" is a dance of Southern plantation blacks accompanied by complex, rhythmic hand clapping and slapping of knees and thighs.

27. The year of jubilee is to be the year in which all slaves are set free.

28. President Lincoln had been advocating that black volunteers should be organized into regiments under the command of white officers. JCH's cousins John Encil MacGowan and Eli McGowan would soon be assigned to the 1st U.S. Colored Troops.

29. Variations on this bit of doggerel show up in other Civil War memoirs, as well as in diverse sources such as autograph albums. For example, James A. Wright, a sergeant in Company F of the 1st Minnesota, records in his memoirs (edited by Steven J. Keillor as *No More Gallant a Deed* [St. Paul: Minnesota Historical Society Press, 2001]) another version he heard sung by minstrels in camp.

30. James Hartzell (Henry, John, George Henry, Conrad Hartzell) is JCH's first cousin, b. 19 Aug 1838 and d. 4 Aug 1925.

31. Colonel William R. Creighton and Lieutenant Colonel Orrin J. Crane are from the 7th OVI.

32. "General Garry" is Major General John W. Geary, commander of the Second Division, Twentieth Corps.

33. "Knap's battery" is Independent Battery E, Pennsylvania Light Artillery.

34. Captain Robert Wilson, commander of Company H before JCH, was killed October 8, 1862, at Perryville.

Chapter 13

1. "Mission Ridge" is a common variant of what is known today as "Missionary Ridge." The battle of Missionary Ridge was fought November 25, 1863.

2. "Flags and guidons" were battle flags that, according to Gerald Prokopowicz, were among the "few visual landmarks available during the battle" (*All for the Regiment*, 106). Most regiments carried two, a national flag and a regimental flag, which was usually a modification of the unit's state flag with the regiment's name prominently incorporated. These banners were large and colorful in order to be visible during the smoke of battle. Banners served the practical purpose of identifying the regiment and locating the center of its line. Thus, the flags helped orient the regimental formations and guide the soldiers' movements during battle. Moreover, the flags helped give the soldiers courage during battle, as the phrase "rally 'round the flag" suggests. Flags and guidons, then, played a tactical as well as a patriotic role, and the "loss of a flag in battle was a calamity that often signaled the end of a regiment as a coherent body of men" (105–6). Union national and regimental colors epitomized the honor and pride of the regiment and during battle became the focal point for hostile fire. An added feature of the regimental colors was the embroidering of past battle achievements.

During the Battle of Perryville, Prokopowicz relates, the 105th Ohio and 123rd Illinois were inexperienced in close order drill tactics and lacked the unity these drills gave. Furthermore, the luckless 105th Ohio did not have its own regimental flag. Curiously, the 105th carried the flag of the 101st Indiana, which was placed in its custody when the latter regiment was being disciplined. The 105th Ohio kept the Indiana colors encased throughout the battle. This circumstance added to the lack of cohesiveness in the 105th during Perryville (*All for the Regiment*, 174–75).

By the time of Missionary Ridge, the 105th Ohio still did not have its own regimental flag. Based on the Ohio Historical Society collection, no regimental flag survives.

3. Sergeant John Geddes of Company C apparently escaped uninjured from Missionary Ridge (Tourgée, *Story of a Thousand*, app.).

4. Abatis are defensive obstacles formed by felled trees with sharpened branches facing the enemy.

5. William Wallace was captain of Company I, 105th OVI.

6. Spencer rifles were the first repeating rifles to be widely used in the Civil War; they were issued to Union troops beginning early in 1863 and gave the North a definite advantage in weaponry. At the outbreak of the Civil War, most muskets were flintlock and percussion guns essentially unchanged since the Revolutionary War, although these smoothbores soon were replaced with rifled barrels. The mechanical revolution in firearms was the development of breech-loading weapons. The Springfield Model 1842 smoothbore and the British Enfield Pattern 1853 were bought in large numbers by the U.S. Army. The Sharp rifle, patented in 1848, was favored by sharpshooters. After breech loading, the next technological development was the repeating weapon, the best known of which was the 52-caliber Spencer of 1860. The other famous repeater was the Henry .44 rimfire; it was thought to be less rugged than the Spencer and so relatively few were used. It was the forerunner of the famous Winchester (Bowman, *Civil War Almanac*, 287–89].

7. JCH here describes the psychological state he calls "the exultation or ecstasy of battle" and soldiers' behavior when in this state. This is the state of mind and body that Henry Fleming, the protagonist of Stephen Crane's *The Red Badge of Courage*, experiences after suffering his earlier agony and humiliation.

8. Major Charles G. Edwards, Lieutenant Colonel George T. Perkins, and Colonel William R. Tolles were promoted to their respective positions July 10, 1863.

9. General Ulysses S. Grant had been given overall command of the western campaign October 23, 1863. In this description of the charge up the hill, JCH ironically understates a heroic action.

10. Alice MacGowan incorporated this scene, in which JCH wakes up when the fire gets too close and discovers a dead Confederate soldier whose feet are on fire, in her novel *Sword in the Mountains*.

11. Colonel William R. Creighton and Lieutenant Colonel Orrin J. Crane of the 7th OVI d. 27 Nov 1863 at the battle of Ringgold, GA.

12. A mudsill is a supporting sill of a structure, often resting on earth, and by extension a person of the lowest social level.

13. "Gimp" is dialect for spirit, vigor, or ambition.

14. At the outset of the war, the tenets of Charles Darwin's theory of evolution by natural selection were not widely known. By the time of JCH's writing, 1896–98, the concepts of *Origin of Species* (1859)—variation, natural selection, survival of the fittest—were well known and had become part of popular culture.

15. Since the core of the U.S. Army had signed up in 1861 for a three-year term, 1864 became a climactic year in which the army was in danger of collapse: almost half of the volunteer regiments and artillery batteries were about to cease to exist. Without the veterans, the war could not be won. As the three-year enlistment period came to an end, all reason and logic would lead one to believe that most soldiers would resign, given their miserable experiences, but in fact 136,000 three-year veterans reenlisted, for a variety of reasons. JCH speculates that the thirty-day furlough and the four-hundred-dollar bounty helped, but that pride in the regiment was also significant.

16. The quotations are from Julia Ward Howe's text to "The Battle Hymn of the Republic."

17. According to JCH, the pride and cohesion in regiments is reflected in the way they go through the manual of arms. These are "evangelists," and the religious images underscore the sense of mission in these veteran regiments.

18. In 1864, almost all regiments were below the full complement of soldiers, officers, field staff—quartermasters, surgeons, etc.

19. It would appear that JCH's initial assignment to report to Colonel Sidney Burbank, mustering officer at Camp Jackson near Columbus, was more a matter of the luck of rotation than a deliberate choice by General Thomas, though undoubedly Thomas had veto power. Thereafter, JCH's continued assignment to deliver recruits and bounties to all theaters of the war was based on the performance of his duties.

20. "Get another bar": be promoted to captain, which occurred September 15, 1864.

21. JCH lists commanders of the companies of the 105th OVI: Captain Alfred G. Wilcox, Co. F; Captain Andrew D. Braden, Co. B; Captain Daniel B. Stambaugh, Co. A; Captain William Wallace, Co. I; Captain William S. Crowell, Co. G; and Henry H. Cummings, Co. D.

22. "Mostly colts and remingtons revolvers"—There was a great variety of pistols and revolvers used during the war, but Colts and Remingtons were the most common. Samuel Colt, with a well-drawn patent, had a virtual monopoly on revolvers with mechanically rotated cylinders. No sooner had Colt's patent expired than Smith & Wesson obtained a patent giving them a monopoly for breechloading cartridge-firing revolvers until 1869 (though these weapons saw relatively little combat use). Percussion pistols of the type Colt developed, 44-caliber, continued to be the dominant weapon used because of their reliability. The next most popular revolver used was the Remington, .44 Army, with over 125,000 models bought by the Union. Other models were the .42 Starr, North and Savage .36, and the LeMat revolver, popular with the Confederates (Bowman, *Civil War Almanac*, 381–86).

23. After Abraham Lincoln issued the March 3, 1863, Enrollment Act of Conscription, resentment of the act boiled over into a violent riot in New York

beginning July 12, the day after the first drawing of draftees' names. A mob of more than fifty thousand, mostly Irish working men, destroyed the New York draft office and set fire to the building. Over the next four days, the violence increasingly was directed at blacks, who were attacked and killed at random. General looting of businesses also created widespread destruction. Federal troops were called in to quell the mob, leaving more than one thousand dead and wounded and "ending what history will note as one of the darkest home front episodes of the war and the worst race riot in American history" (ibid., 162). Other less serious draft riots broke out in Boston and other towns in the East and Ohio.

24. Before going to see his family, JCH first wanted to visit his girlfriend, Louise Ann Lowrie Thompson, who was b. Aug 1842 and d. 03 Oct 1914. They married 16 Aug 1865.

25. "Calion" is probably Galion, OH.

26. "There was a balm in Gilead" is a Biblical reference to Jeremiah 8:22. Gilead is an important source of spice and medicinal herbs.

27. "Rosy, Bob, and Isa"—All are JCH's siblings and Frederick and Mary's children. Rosy is Rosella Hartzell, b. 15 Apr 1855 and d. 17 Jan 1928 in Cleveland, Cuyahoga Co, OH. Bob is James Robert Hartzell, b. 22 Jan 1852 and d. Jan 1934 in Minneapolis, Hennepin Co, MN. Isa is Isaiah Hartzell, b. Nov 1848 and d. 8 Mar 1913 in Smith Twp., Mahoning Co, OH.

28. "Your Uncle Jess" is Jesse Miller Hartzell, b. 21 Jan 1845 and d. 7 Feb 1937 in Smith Twp, Mahoning Co, OH. The sixth child of Frederick and Mary Hartzell, he served in the 12th Ohio Cavalry, Company B, from September 1863 to discharge at Columbus, OH, 14 Nov 1865. Jess wrote an account of his service, "Some Autobiographical Writings by Jesse Hartzell," which is preserved in the same typescript as JCH's memoirs.

29. The draft act was designed to attract new recruits but contained a serious loophole: it allowed a draftee to avoid service by paying a $300 fee or, even better, by hiring a substitute to take his place. Enterprising brokers or traders went into business and collected substitutes for up to $1,000 apiece (and JCH cites higher prices as high as $2,000 by the end of the war). As a group, substitutes made less than ideal soldiers.

Chapter 14

1. This passage in German is translated as follows:

> "Dark clouds I see hanging
> Between me and our times"

JCH sees the Civil War as "the tragedies of a gigantic war for national existence."

2. The secretary of war is Edwin McMasters Stanton (1814–69).

3. The quotation, slightly altered, is from James Shirley (1596–1666); his poem "Death the Leveler" in *The Contest of Ajax and Ulysses* contains the lines "The glories of our blood and state / Are shadows, not substantial things."

4. Large cash bounties, up to $1,000, were offered to enlistees (see note 29 to chapter 13). Consequently, large numbers of men enlisted for the money and de-

serted as quickly as possible, then relocated and enlisted under a different name, collected another bounty, and deserted again. Many repeated this process several times and were known as "bounty men." The procedure followed in Ohio, as described by JCH, was designed to prevent this abuse.

5. "A mob of human-carrion crows" followed JCH's command and consisted of all kind of human scum, including bounty hunters.

6. The haversack, of course, contained a large amount of bounty money.

7. "The decalogue" refers to the Latin and Greek forms of the Ten Commandments.

8. "Boots and saddles" (a corruption of the original French, "boute-selle," the command to saddle horses) is the bugle call for the cavalry to mount.

9. The quotation is again from Robert Burns's "Tam O'Shanter."

10. Captain William Clarke Quantrill (also spelled Quantrell; 1837–65) and Captain Champ Ferguson of the Confederate independent cavalry are among the best-known Confederate guerrilla chiefs. (Champ, an unusual first name, may have been the source of Champ Seacrest, the name Alice McGowan gave to the Union hero of her novel *The Sword in the Mountains*.) The guerrillas, also called bushwhackers, caused widespread destruction and proved difficult to capture. Quantrill's notorious raid on Lawrence, KS, on August 21, 1863, killed at least 150 people. Among his men were Cole Younger and Frank James, who became outlaws after the war. On May 10, 1865, Quantrill was wounded by Federal troops in Kentucky. He died twenty days later.

11. "Uncle Billy" was a nickname given to Union General William Tecumseh Sherman, considered "one of the most successful military heroes by the North, but the South would always consider him the arch-enemy because of his famous march to Atlanta and the sea" (Bowman, *Civil War Almanac*, 376). In March 1864 he was made commander of the military division of Mississippi.

"Pappy Thomas" was the nickname given to Major General George Henry Thomas, a meticulous tactician who came to be regarded as one of the most effective Union commanders. During the siege of Chattanooga, "The Rock of Chickamauga," when Grant told him to hold on, replied, "We will hold the town till we starve." Thomas's Army of the Cumberland provided half of the forces in Sherman's march to Atlanta. Thomas also defeated the Confederates outside Nashville in December 1864 (ibid., 385–86).

Major General Oliver O. Howard, Fourth Corps commander, was one of Sherman's generals, commanding the Army of Tennessee during the Atlanta campaign. After the war, President Johnson appointed Howard to head the Bureau of Refugees, Freedmen, and Abandoned Lands. The Freedmen's Bureau oversaw the care of Southern refugees in the postwar period, including helping newly freed blacks adjust to their freedom.

Major General John Alexander Logan, commander of the Fifteenth Corps in the campaign against Atlanta, was briefly named to lead the Army of Tennessee in July 1864. After the war, he helped organize the Union veterans into the Grand Army of the Republic, serving three times as president. His "most enduring contribution" was his work in establishing Memorial Day, first observed May 30, 1868 (Bowman, *Civil War Almanac*, 354–55).

Major General James B. McPherson, commander of the Army of Tennessee, participated in the Atlanta campaign, but was killed July 22.

12. Johnson's Island in Sandusky Bay was the site of a Union prison for Confederate officers.

13. Frank Lebby Stanton (1857–1927), a popular poet and journalist, published a daily column from 1889 to 1927 in the *Atlanta Constitution*.

14. Case shot is an artillery projectile consisting of a number of balls or metal fragments enclosed in a case. Double case caused "Old Mary" to kick out of her breeching. The breech is part of the firearm at the rear of the bore. "Out of her trunnions" is out of the pins or pivots—two opposite gudgeons on which a cannon is swivelled. "Old Betsy" had her cascabel knob (a projection behind the breech of a muzzle-loading cannon) knocked off, so she is going to be called "Bobtailed Betsy."

15. Bob Heller was a popular magician.

16. "Artemus Ward" was the pen name of Charles Farrar Browne (1834–67), a popular American humorist, newspaperman, editor, and lecturer, who wrote in a Yankee dialect of his adventures with his traveling museum of war figures. He befriended Mark Twain and exerted an important influence on Twain's work.

17. "An old roller" refers to an unstable military transport for carrying soldiers and military supplies.

18. Didoes are antics, pranks, and mischievous events by the sea or ocean.

19. The *Monadnock* was a double-turret monitor (a heavily armored warship named after the first ship of its type) with sixteen guns, in service for the Union from 1864 to 1874.

20. A lighter is a large, usually flat-bottomed barge used especially in unloading or loading ships.

21. JCH admits here that some of his accounts of the actions of Company H, 105th OVI, have been called into question. His reply to these charges of lying is brief and ironical—that Captain Dan Stambaugh himself is guilty of gross exaggeration.

22. A mere is a lake or pool.

23. By "mailed prayer," the poet apparently means prayer protected by armor made of metal links or plates.

24. Huns were nomadic Mongolians who gained control of much of eastern and central Europe under Attila. Hence, Huns are wantonly destructive vandals, and Timrod suggests here that Union soldiers are Huns.

25. "Carolina," by Henry Timrod (1828–67), is typical of his pro-South poetry with its call for action. Timrod, a member of the Charleston school of Southern writers, is known for his emotional poems written in classical styles. During the war he was given the title Laureate of the Confederacy (*Benét's Readers's Encyclopedia*).

26. Major General Francis P. Blair Jr. commanded the Seventeenth Corps during Sherman's campaigns of 1864–65, including the march to the sea.

27. James Hartzell (Henry, John, George Henry Hartzell) was a first cousin to JCH.

28. Brigadier General Erastus B. Tyler (1822–91) commanded the First Brigade, Third Division, Fifth Corps at Antietam. He continued to lead the brigade

at Fredericksburg, where he was wounded, and Chancellorsville. The brigade included horse guards and other second line troops.

29. Major General Henry W. Slocum (1827–94) was given command of the Twelfth Corps after Antietam and later commanded the Twentieth Corps and the Army of Georgia on Sherman's final march to the sea.

30. Seth Hartzell (Jacob, John, George Henry, Conrad Hartzell) is a first cousin of JCH. Champ Seacrest, hero of Alice MacGowan's *Sword in the Mountains*, is probably modeled after Seth Hartzell. He is the basis of Texan characters in other novels and short stories by Grace MacGowan Cooke and Alice MacGowan.

31. The poem quoted slightly inaccurately here, "Parting" by Coventry Patmore (1823–96), begins:

> If thou dost bid thy friend farewell,
> But for one night though that farewell may be,
> Press thou his hand in thine.
> How canst thou tell how far from thee
> Fate or caprice may lead his steps ere that to-morrow comes?

32. General Thomas Jonathan Jackson (1824–63) or "Stonewall Jackson," next to Robert E. Lee the most famous Confederate general, lost his life at the midpoint of the war when accidently shot by a Confederate soldier.

33. "My Colonel" is Lt. Colonel George Perkins.

34. "The Father of Waters" is the Mississippi River.

35. "Old Kenesaw" is a misspelling of Kennesaw Mountain, elevation 1,809 feet.

36. Abatis and chevaux-de-frise are defense constructions. An abatis is a defense obstacle formed by felled trees with sharpened branches facing the enemy. The chevaux-de-frise is a defense consisting of timber or iron barrels covered with projecting spikes and often strung with barbed wire.

37. A prolonge is a rope having a hook on one end and a toggle at the other end, used for various purposes, such as here to pull a boat stuck in mud.

38. Here and elsewhere (e.g., chapter 12) JCH speaks of the practice of truces during which both sides exchanged articles and "gossiped." The irony of fraternizing and engaging in the work of killing "with the same good-will" is brought out here.

39. To hone is to yearn for something.

40. From this paragraph on, JCH wanders from subject to subject, often writing of events prior to his assignment of delivering troops to various battle zones. In this least organized chapter, Harzell covers a miscellany of topics, mostly concerning the everyday life of the common soldier.

41. As Gerald Prokopowicz stresses, the training for company soldiers never went beyond "small-unit close order drill" (*All for the Regiment*, 184). JCH adds that the "soldier's duty and place is with his own regiment, and as soon as he gets into any other brigade, or corps he is a stranger." Prokopowicz argues that a regiment might prove "amazingly resilient . . . but incapable of following up any of its limited battlefield successes" (188). It was inherent in the army's social structure—

a decentralized group of military communities with no organization beyond the regiment (188–89). The infantry regiment, then, as Prokopowicz demonstrates, became the basic unit of command and maneuver and for most soldiers "the source of their identity" (28). JCH's autobiography would appear to verify these observations—soldiers were unable to identify their loyalty beyond the company and regiment.

42. JCH describes here an exception to the regiment or fundamental unit. Perhaps as the war proceeded, better coordination among regiments was possible, for JCH describes seeing a brigade or division moving into battle, unfolding "like a huge fan," advancing "in line of battle"; it was a "glorious" sight.

43. Copperheads were Northerners sympathetic to the South, mostly Democrats outspoken in their opposition to the Lincoln administration. They were especially strong in Illinois, Indiana, and Ohio, where Clement L. Vallandigham was their leader.

44. For the Christian Commission and the Sanitary Commission, see note 7 to chapter 12.

45. The Confederate concentration camp at Andersonville, GA, was the most infamous prison for Union soldiers during the Civil War. In February, 1864, Federal soldiers arrived at an unfinished prison compound called Camp Sumter. Because of the large number of prisoners, the sixteen-acre log stockade proved inadequate and conditions deteriorated until disease and death resulting from poor sanitation, overcrowding, exposure, and poor diet became devastating (Bowman, *Civil War Almanac*, 185). Captain Henry Wirz, former commander of the prison at Andersonville, was hanged after being found guilty of cruelty to Union prisoners. Several of JCH's relatives were incarcerated at Andersonville. Irenus and Miletus McGowan, sons of John McGowan, were captured at Chickamauga and sent to Andersonville. Captain Alonzo Strong was also imprisoned here.

46. The first three lines of this unidentified poetry quotation also appear in school souvenir cards from Pennsylvania and Kansas contemporary with JCH's memoirs (1896–98).

47. This is JCH's interpretation of events after Mission Ridge. This may be true of the 105th Ohio, but a questionable statement concerning Sherman's army.

48. JCH quotes lines from the first verse of "The Old Oaken Bucket" (1818) by Samuel Woodworth.

49. These lines echo words from Lincoln's "Gettysburg Address."

50. Throughout JCH's account of the war, he has tried to emphasize the life of the common volunteer infantryman—"he stood a sentinel faithful to his trust."

51. JCH gives here examples of Confederate breakthroughs during the war: General Braxton Bragg and General Kirby Smith and their campaigns in Kentucky and Tennessee in 1862; General Robert E. Lee and his campaigns at Gettysburg in 1863; John Hunt Morgan's Ohio raid in 1863; and General John B. Hood's Franklin and Nashville campaigns in 1864 when Sherman began his march to the sea.

52. JCH lists the commanders he served under: General William Nelson; General James S. Jackson, Commander of the Tenth Division and First Brigade commander, killed at Perryville; General Don Carlos Buell, Commander of the

Fourteenth Corps; General William Rosecrans (Rosey), Commander of the Fourteenth Corps; Colonel Albert S. Hall, brigade commander, who died of disease at Murfreesboro; Colonel Edward A. King, killed at Chickamauga; General J. J. Reynolds, division commander; General George H. Thomas, corps commander; Colonel Ferdinand VanDerveer, brigade commander; at different times under General Philip Henry Sheridan, General Baird, and General Jefferson C. Davis, with General Ulysses S. Grant or General William Tecumsah Sherman as chief commander. Along with other commanders of higher rank, JCH fails to list Colonel George Perkins, regimental commander.

Works Cited

Alliance (Ohio) Review. Obituary of John Calvin Hartzell, April 27, 1918.

Ayre, Josiah. *The Civil War Diary of Private Josiah Ayre.* Transcribed by James Glauser. [1975?] Held by Cleveland Public Library.

Bentley, Christopher. *The Double Life of Stephen Crane.* New York: Alfred A. Knopf, 1992.

Bierce, Ambrose. *Ambrose Bierce's Civil War.* Ed. William McCann. Chicago: Gateway Editions, 1956.

Bowman, John S., ed. *The Civil War Almanac.* New York: W. H. Smith, 1983.

Chowder, Ken. "A Writer Who Lived the Adventures He Portrayed." *Smithsonian* 25 (January 1995).

Dyer, Frederick H. *A Compendium of the War of the Rebellion.* Vol. 2. Dayton, OH: Morningside, 1979.

Fradenburgh, J. N. *In Memoriam: Henry Harrison Cumings, Charlotte Cumings.* Oil City, PA: Derrick Publishing, 1913.

Jordan, Robert Paul. *The Civil War.* New York: National Geographic Society, 1969.

Kennedy, Francis H., ed. *The Civil War Battlefield Guide.* Boston: Houghton Miflin, 1990.

MacGowan, Alice. *The Sword in the Mountains.* New York: Grosset & Dunlap, 1910.

Madden, David. "The Civil War as a Model for the Scope of Popular Culture." *Journal of American and Comparative Culture* 23 (Spring 2000).

Morse, Bliss. *The Civil War Diaries and Letters of Bliss Morse.* Ed. Loren J. Morse. Wagoner, OK: Heritage Printing, 1985.

Nye, Russel B. *Fettered Freedom: Civil Liberties and the Slavery Controversy, 1830–1860.* East Lansing: Michigan State College Press, 1949.

Prokopowicz, Gerald I. *All for the Regiment: The Army of the Ohio, 1861–1862.* Chapel Hill: University of North Carolina Press, 2001.

Rosengren, William. "Regimental Bands in the Civil War." *Journal of American and Comparative Cultures* 24, no. 2 (2001).

Stamp, Kenneth M., ed. *The Causes of the Civil War.* Englewood Cliffs, NJ: Prentice Hall, 1959.

Switzer, Charles I. "The MacGowan Sisters: Early-Twentieth-Century Popular Writers." *Journal of Popular Culture* 34 (Summer 2000).

Tourgée, Albion W. "A Civil War Diary of Albion W. Tourgée." Ed. Dean H. Keller. *Ohio History* 74, no. 2 (1965).

———. *The Story of a Thousand: Being a History of the Service of the 105th Ohio Volunteer Infantry.* Buffalo, NY: S. McGerald, 1896.

Index

flags, 204n8, 225–26n2; colors, 149, 191; guidons, 149, 225n2; national, xxvi, 8, 94, 128, 156, 225n2; regimental, xxvi–xxvii, 126, 149–50, 225–26n2; signal, 137, 147

flax, 6–7, 23, 41, 202nn6, 10 (chap. 1), 203n8

food, on Hartzell farm, 3, 11, 12–13, 17, 23, 25, 30–32, 51, 73, 78, 204n5, 213n22

food, Union army, 94, 102, 109, 115, 116, 117–19, 122, 124, 132, 137, 141–44, 146, 147, 155–56, 157, 158, 189, 204n8; foraging for, 94, 107, 108; pilfering of, 117–18, 122; rations, 94, 102, 107, 117, 128, 143, 146, 156, 157, 158, 160, 174; trading for, 122, 156

Forney (neighbor), 13

fortifications, 128, 132, 135–36, 137, 140, 150, 155, 156, 173, 188. See also Negly/Negley, Fort; Pickering, Fort; Wood, Fort

Fort Wayne and Chicago Railroad, 64, 143

14th Corps, 114, 142, 159; corps badge, 185, 186

Fowler, Charlie, 112, 114, 115, 131, 134, 146, 191

Foy, Sam, 41

Frame, Lieutenant, 168

Frankfort, KY, 92

fulling mill, 2, 37, 67, 201n4

furs. See trapping

Galion, OH, 163, 229n25

Gallatin, TN, 103

Galt House (Louisville, KY), 93, 195, 216n22

gambling, 144–45

Garfield, James A., 63, 114, 209n12, 220n26

Geary, John W., 147, 153–54, 225n32

Geddes, John, 150, 226n3

Georgetown, OH, 89

Georgia, 34

Gettysburg, battle of, 121, 128, 129, 221n3

gigging fish, 19–21, 45, 203n1

Girard, OH, 104

Glasgow, TN, 103, 104, 106

Govan, Daniel Chevilette, 127, 222n16

grain cradle, 204n6. See also wheat

Grand Army of the Republic (GAR), xxi

grand review, of 105th OVI, 93

Grand Review, Washington, DC, xvi, 115, 193, 220n29

Granger, Gordon, 126, 222n15

Grant, Jesse, 34, 205n15

Grant, Ulysses S., xii, 35, 127, 153, 159, 177, 178, 195, 205n15, 226n9; Grant's army, 179

Grant, William (cousin), 86–88

grapevine telegraph, 162–63

graybacks. See lice

Great Rebellion (War of the Rebellion). See Civil War

Green River, KY, 99–100

grindstone, 5, 6, 25

guerrillas, Confederate, 108, 162, 173, 185, 186, 187, 229n10. See also bushwhackers

guidon, xxvi, 149, 225n2

guns, 10–12, 87, 138, 180, 187, 227n22; pistols, 91. See also artillery; musket; rifles

Hall, Albert S., 73, 91, 94, 95, 98, 100, 106, 108, 112, 113, 195, 211n5, 216n15, 218n1, 219n22

Harper's Weekly, 139

Harris, Joel Chandler, 219n21

Harris, Samuel J., 108, 120, 218n9, 221n2

Hartzell family (relationship to John Calvin Hartzell is given if known):

Hartzell, Abraham (Old Abram; great-uncle), 1, 49, 201n3, 207n26

Hartzell, Abraham (Young Abe), 1, 10–12, 18, 48, 49, 80–81, 201n3, 203n14, 205n26

Hartzell, Adam (first cousin), 89, 215n9

Hartzell, Bertha O. (daughter), xxi, 199n1

Hartzell, Bob. See Hartzell, James Robert

Hartzell, Catharine B. Sullivan (wife of Henry Hartzell), 201n3

Hartzell, Catherine (cousin), 200n3, 205n26

Hartzell, Charles (nephew), xx, 200n2

Hartzell, Christina Nowlan (great-grandmother), 49, 75, 207n25

Hartzell, Christina (great-aunt), 49, 200n3, 207n26

Hartzell, Christine (cousin), 206n28

Hartzell, Conrad (great-great-grandfather), 199n1

Hartzell, David (cousin), 1, 79, 200n3, 213n25

Hartzell, Dora Virginia (niece), 200n2

Hartzell, Dorothy Kleinhans (grandmother), 2–3, 12, 199–200n2, 202n5 (chap. 1)

Hartzell, Elizabeth (aunt), 34, 204n14, 208n8

sick call, 190
signal stations, 137, 147
singing schools, 62
Skiles, John W., 164–65, 167
skirmish line, xxv–xxvi, 108, 116, 136, 188, 224n9
slavery, xvii, xviii, xxiii, 81, 90, 129, 187, 209n14
slaves, 94, 183; following Union army, 180
Slocum, Henry W., 185, 186, 231n29
smallpox, 181
Smart, Jane. See Hartzell, Jane Smart
Smart, John, 68
Smith, Kirby, 73, 91, 92, 195, 211n4, 215n12
Smith, Preston, 127
Smith, Ruth Rebecca, 199n1
Smith's Ferry, PA, 64
Snider, Jerry, 6
Snider, John, 6
Snodgrass Hill, 125, 127, 128
snoodling fish, 45, 206n17
soap making, 57–58
songs, 55, 77, 146, 225n29
sots, 72, 211n2
South Carolina, 183
Spaulding, E. Abbott, 133, 223n3
spelling bees, 63
Spencer rifles, 151, 226n6
Spokane Falls, WA, 75
spring, on Hartzell farm, 2, 14, 26, 32, 71–72; spring house, 73; spring race, 14–15, 26, 51, 71
Springfield rifles, 138, 226n6
Stackhouse, William P., 111, 112
stagecoach, 64, 83
Stambaugh, Daniel B., 108, 111, 122, 145, 218n11, 219n18, 221n8; account of Missionary Ridge, 182–83, 230n21
Stanton, Edwin M., xiii, 166, 176, 228n2
Stanton, Frank Lebby, 178–79, 230n13
Stark County Republican, 88
Starkweather, John C., 96, 217n24
"Star-Spangled Banner," 204n8
steamboats, 68, 82; armed, on Mississippi, 187; owners of, 85, 214n2
Steedman (Steadman), James, 127, 128, 222n15
Steel, Caleb, 61
Steubenville, OH, land office, 67–68
Steven's Gap, 122–23
Stevenson, TN, 142, 147
Stewart, Ambrose P., 128
still, still-house, 2, 14, 34–35, 202n9

Stones River, battle of, 106, 107, 218nn2–3
strategy. See military strategy
Stratton, Gran, 75, 99, 107, 125, 211n10, 217n30, 222n12
Stringer's Ridge, 142
Strong, Alonzo, 49, 207n28
Strong, Levi (first cousin), 215n9
substitutes, 165, 167, 193, 228n29. See also draft, military; bounty jumping
sugar camp, 16–18, 32, 43, 44
Sullivan, Catharine B. See Hartzell, Catharine B. Sullivan
swamp angel (Parrott), 131, 141. See also artillery
Sword in the Mountains, The (A. Mac-Gowan), xvi–xvii, xxv, 221–22n9; 222n11, 226n10, 229n10, 231n30

Taft, Dr., 97
tallow making, 23
Tannehill, William, 139
tanning, 69
tansy (bitters), 53
Taney decision, 64, 209n14
Taylor, Camp, xi
Taylor, George, 38, 48, 51, 66
Taylor, Hiram, 51
Taylor, Morris, 138–39
temperance, 28, 35–36
Tennessee River, 103–4, 118, 120, 121
Tennyson, Alfred Lord, 207n19
tents, Sibley, 101, 217–18n36
Terrill, William R., 93, 97, 106, 216n19, 217n25, 218n1
35th OVI, 137
32nd OVI, 184
33rd Brigade, 94
Thomas, George H., xii, 116, 127, 128, 153, 159, 160, 161, 176, 195, 222n17, 229n11
Thompson, John and Mary Wilkinson, xxi
Thompson, Louise Ann Lowrie. See Hartzell, Louise Ann Lowrie Thompson
Thompson, Rebecca, 82
threshing, 4, 5, 31, 32
timbering, 60, 86; during siege of Chattanooga, 139; in South, 184
Timrod, Henry, 184, 230n25
Todd barracks (Columbus), 165, 166, 167
Toledo, OH, xx, 82, 83–84
Tolles, William R., 100, 113, 151–52, 217n32, 219n24, 226n8

Wolcott, James, 107, 218n5
Wolf Track/Trap Run, 38, 54
wolves, 34, 86–87
women's societies, 135, 192–93, 223–24n7
Wood, Fort, 137, 156–57
Wood, Thomas J., 127, 222n17
Woodworth, Samuel, 232n48
wool, 27–28, 37, 67, 68

World's Fair, 128
Wright, Florence, 199n1
Wright, Marshall W., 136, 224n10

yeast, 72–73
Youngstown, OH, 90, 104, 206n27

Zollikoffer barracks (Nashville), 175

www.ingramcontent.com/pod-product-compliance
Lightning Source LLC
Chambersburg PA
CBHW021821090426
42811CB00028B/1938